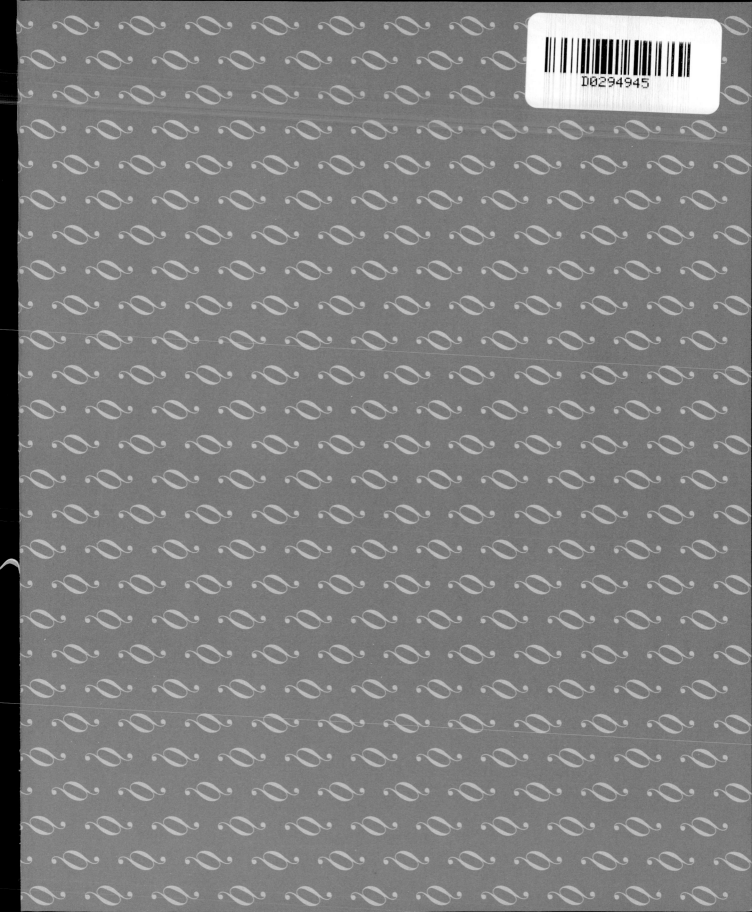

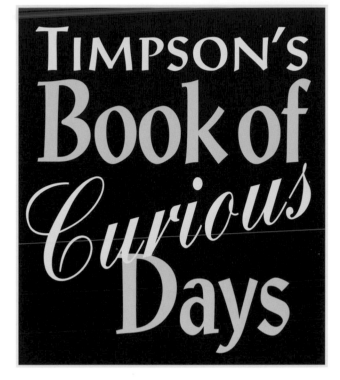

A YEAR OF
ENGLISH ODDITIES

John Timpson

JARROLD
PUBLISHING

Timpson's Book of Curious Days:
A Year of English Oddities

Designed and produced by
Jarrold Publishing, Whitefriars, Norwich NR3 1TR

Author:	John Timpson
Researcher:	Mari Roberts
Editors:	Mari Roberts, Donald Greig
Designers:	Visual Image, Brian Skinner, Reina Ruis
Photographers:	Dennis Avon, John Brooks,
	Neil Jinkerson, Charles Nicholas,
	Andrew Perkins

ISBN 0-7117-0861-4

Printed by Jarrold Book Printing 1/96

Contents

❧ *FOREWORD* 4

❧ *JANUARY* 7

❧ *FEBRUARY* 27

❧ *MARCH* 45

❧ *APRIL* 65

❧ *MAY* 83

❧ *JUNE* 103

❧ *JULY* 121

❧ *AUGUST* 141

❧ *SEPTEMBER* 161

❧ *OCTOBER* 179

❧ *NOVEMBER* 199

❧ *DECEMBER* 217

❧ *INDEX* 237

❧ *BIBLIOGRAPHY* 240

❧ *ACKNOWLEDGMENTS* 240

Foreword

It was a Victorian gentleman called Chambers, so far as I am concerned, who started it all. *Chambers' Book of Days* was published in the eighteen-sixties, two weighty volumes running to some five hundred pages apiece, packed with small print.

Each day went on and on – not just the events that had occurred on that date, but the thoughts of Mr Chambers on almost anything connected with them, plus quite a few which had no connection at all; they just seemed to occur to him while he was writing. It was, I suppose, a sort of "commonplace book" – with dates.

Timpson's Book of Days is more, I hope, an "uncommonplace book". It concentrates on one particular happening on each day of the year which is in some way odd, or unexpected, or distinctly unlikely. If a well-known event is recorded, it must have some little-known aspect. If it is an anniversary of some famous person, it is not what he or she is famous for that features, but the more obscure stories associated with them.

There are lesser-known happenings too, which have had some unexpected impact on history. Not least, there are quirky customs attached to particular dates which have somehow survived through the centuries, not the universal festivals we are all familiar with, but local traditions only found in particular areas.

The *Book of Days*, in fact, is a personally picked potpourri, and I hope you will never quite know what the next day will bring. In a random week in February, for instance, you can visit a hill that moved in Herefordshire, and Mary, Queen of Scots' staircase in a Northamptonshire hotel. You can hear the first BBC "pips", and how Carlyle reacted when he found a maid had burnt his first manuscript of the History of the French Revolution.

You can celebrate the opening of the first woman's public lavatory, discover why Samuel Plimsoll had plimsolls named after him as well as the Plimsoll Line – and sing "God Save the King" seventeen times on a German railway station, waiting for Edward VII to struggle into his trousers . . .

There are days of great disasters (no, the band did not play "Nearer my God to Thee" as the *Titanic* went down) and great heroism (can we learn from Edith Cavell – "I realize that patriotism is not enough"?). But mostly they are days which I hope will make you blink a little, or marvel a little, or smile a little.

Enjoy your day . . .

John Timpson

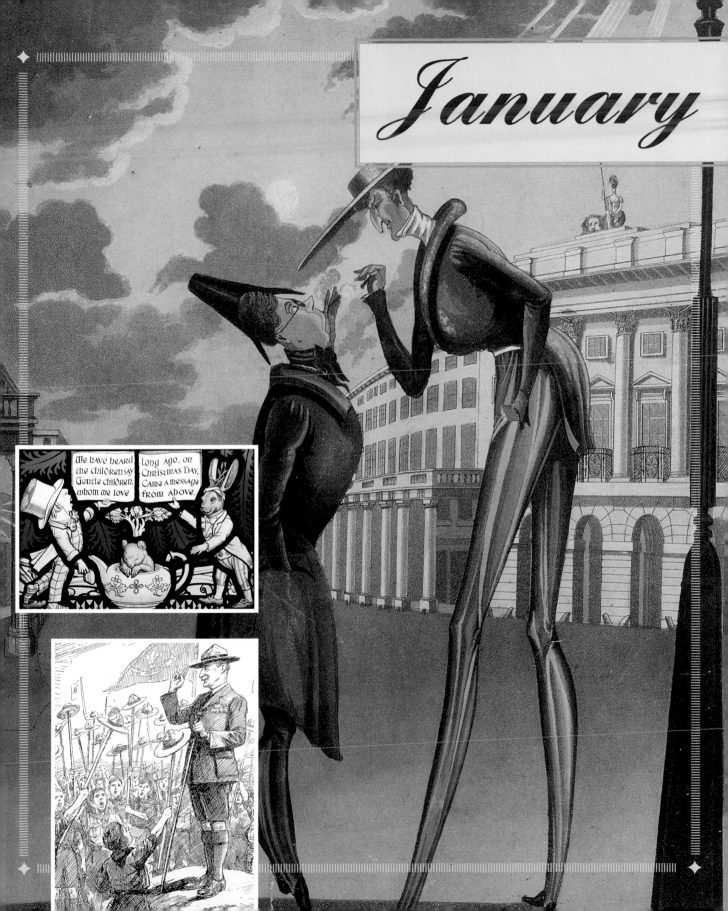

January

What also remained, however, was the impact he made on his customers when hiring out horses. He would not allow them to choose their own mount, he had to select it himself. "This or none," he would tell them – and "Hobson's choice" went into the phrasebooks. Not even Lady Thatcher's "TINA" – "There Is No Alternative" – has superseded it. Nearly four centuries later, "Hobson's choice" is still, well, Hobson's choice . . .

JANUARY 1ST
Thomas Hobson, the Cambridge carrier who left us with no alternative to Hobson's Choice

1st

Lady Thatcher's "TINA" – Seventeenth-century Style

Thomas Hobson, who died on this day in 1631, deserves to occupy two modest niches in history – one for being the first to launch a horse-for-hire business, forerunner of the car-rental system, and the other for introducing a new saying into the English language.

Instead of niches, he got an epitaph from John Milton, who may have written it as a bit of light relief from *Paradise Lost*. It makes no reference to these achievements, but concentrates on making puns about his main day-job. Thomas was a carrier licensed by Cambridge University to deliver packages and people between Cambridge and London, and Milton has a joke about the waggon he drove – "strange to think his *wain* was his *increase*" (ho-ho) – and ends with the crisp couplet:

"His letters are delivered, all are gone;
Only remains this superscripti-on."

2nd

The Hubberholme Parliament – Westminster was Never Like This

Throughout the year a candle burns on the bar of the George Inn at Hubberholme, a remote little Wharfedale village which J.B. Priestley called "one of the smallest and pleasantest places in the world"; his ashes are buried in the churchyard. The candle is a reminder of the annual candle auction which takes place on this date if New Year's Day falls on a Sunday, otherwise on the next Monday following.

Until 1965 the inn belonged to the church, and the 16-acre field behind it still does, held in trust for the poor of the parish. Each year the tenancy of the "Poor Pasture" is auctioned by the Vicar at the George, in what is known as the Hubberholme Parliament. He and his churchwardens, the "Lords", meet the outgoing tenant in one bar while the prospective bidders, the "Commons", assemble in the other. Then, in a ceremony which is almost like a reversal of the Queen's

JANUARY 2ND
The candle which burns for one night of the year at the George Inn – a reminder of the Hubberholme Parliament

Speech at Westminster, the Lords join the Commons, the candle is lit, and the auction begins. Whoever makes the last bid before the candle expires has the Poor Pasture for the next twelve months.

This can last for hours, of course, depending on the candle, and the beer flows throughout. Even a canny Yorkshireman can get carried away in such a situation, and I wonder if the bidding sometimes reaches heights as dizzy as the bidders – but it's all in a good cause.

3rd
J A N U A R Y

〜

The Earl died, Cairo blacked out, even the Dog expired

The Curse of Tutankhamun, the young Egyptian king whose tomb remained undisturbed for nearly four thousand years, is said to date from this day in 1923. Howard Carter had been excavating in the Valley of the Kings for years, but this was his greatest discovery, the magnificent sarcophagus of Tutankhamun surrounded by all the objects that had been buried with it to help the king on his final journey.

It was not such good news, however, for his patron, the fifth Earl of Caernarvon. According to Sir Arthur Conan Doyle, a devoted spiritualist who claimed to have a direct line to Ancient Egypt, this desecration of the king's tomb was highly unpopular with Tutankhamun's

priests, and he was not at all surprised when Lord Caernarvon died in Cairo soon after the discovery. Back in England the earl's dog expired on the same day, and for good measure the whole of Cairo was blacked out by a power failure.

The cause of Caernarvon's death, Conan Doyle maintained, was not just pneumonia after infection from a mosquito bite, as the naive doctors believed, but was brought about by the Curse of Tutankhamum. So inevitably all eyes turned to Howard Carter, who had actually entered the tomb. After a while they gave up looking, because it was another sixteen years before he died. But if the spirit of Conan Doyle was still around by then, I bet it was muttering, "I told you so."

JANUARY 3RD
The discovery of Tutankhamun was a triumph for Howard Carter, but bad news for Lord Caernarvon – and his dog

4th
J A N U A R Y

"Ladies and Gentlemen, is there a Monarch in the House?"

This was the day when Charles I made the final mistake that sparked off the Civil War. It was the only occasion that a monarch has burst into the Chamber of the House of Commons – and the Commons never forgave him.

Charles's earlier mistake was to levy an old Saxon tax called Ship Money, which was originally used to defend the coast from invaders; Charles wanted it to defend himself. A Buckinghamshire MP called John Hampden – who just happened to have a brother-in-law called Oliver Cromwell – was ordered to pay twenty shillings; he refused to do so.

"Would twenty shillings have ruined Mr Hampden's fortune?" asked Edmund Burke later. "No, but the payment of twenty shillings on the principle it was demanded could have made him a slave." Instead, he and four other MPs drew up a "Grand Remonstrance", listing all their complaints against Charles. They pushed it through Parliament, circulated it widely, and sent a complimentary copy to the King.

It was the last straw. On this day in 1641 Charles took a band of soldiers to the Commons and stormed into the Chamber, demanding that Hampden and his friends should be handed over – but they had already escaped by another door. The only sound in the Chamber, one gathers, was the gnashing of the royal teeth.

The seething sovereign made an excuse, as they say, and left – but the damage was done. Soon afterwards, the Civil War began. Hampden died on the battlefield, Charles in due course died on the block.

JANUARY 4TH
A memorial to John Hampden, the MP whose opposition to Charles I provoked the King's "invasions" of the House of Commons – and led to the Civil War

5th
J A N U A R Y

Ash to Ashes on Twelfth Night – twelve Days late

When the calendar was changed a couple of centuries ago, and Christmas was moved from January to December, it caused a glorious mix-up between the traditional pre-Christmas celebrations and those which marked the end of the Christmas season.

Wassailing, for instance, the feasting and drinking which started in pagan times to celebrate the winter solstice, was enthusiastically extended to fill up the gap between the old Christmas Eve and the new. And lighting the ashen faggot, traditionally carried out on Christmas Eve, was postponed until the new Twelfth Night. To add to the confusion, Twelfth Night was celebrated on January 5th, the night before Twelfth Day.

JANUARY 5TH
Celebrating the "burning of the faggot" at the King William, Curry Rivel, on Twelfth Night

This meant the faggot-burning rather lost its point, because the idea was originally to keep the ash glowing as long as possible over Christmas. However, for many years there was a combination of wassailing and ash-burning on this day, and in some rural areas it still happens.

At Curry Rivel in Somerset, for instance, the faggot is carried round the village this evening, with many a toast en route, then taken to the King William Inn and burnt, while the festivities continue. By the time the ash is reduced to ashes, I imagine no one is too bothered whether they are celebrating Old Christmas Eve or New Twelfth Night . . .

6th
JANUARY

JANUARY 6TH
"Running the Hood" at Haxey, a reminder of how Lady de Mowbray lost hers, and had it retrieved by locals

This Sway for the Haxey Hood

"Running the Hood" on this day in Haxey, North Lincolnshire, is one of those traditions which started as a quaint piece of English folklore and developed into an annual excuse for letting off steam. One bewildered

spectator described it as "something straight out of Michael Bentine's *Square World*"; another called it "a curious kind of Rugby" – though I doubt that either the Rugby Union or the Rugby League would appreciate the comparison. One hundred and fifty years ago a visitor considered it was "a disgrace to our country", but he was of course a Victorian.

It all started in the thirteenth century. Lady de Mowbray was riding to church when her hood blew off, and a group of passing labourers retrieved it for her. She was so impressed by their courtesy that she gave a piece of land, still called the Hoodland, which provides the income for the annual celebration of this event.

It involves twelve players called Boggans, a King Boggan who carries a wand made from thirteen willow branches, a Fool who declaims a quite baffling explanation of what it is all about while paper is burnt behind him – a touch of pagan ritual about those two – and the Hood itself, a leather one which is fought for in a contest called the Sway. It only ends when the Hood finds, as it were, its Sway into one of Haxey's three pubs – along with most of the village.

I'm not entirely sure Lady de Mowbray would approve.

7th
JANUARY

Going for a Spin on St Distaff's Day

This is when they used to celebrate St Distaff's Day, but St Distaff was a stick, not a saint. In medieval times today marked the end of the Christmas break, when women went back to their spinning – especially the single ones, the "spinsters" – using a spindle and a stick called a distaff. The men, on the other hand, took an extra day's holiday, and their idea of celebrating St Distaff was to set fire to the flax which the women were spinning. It was then the custom for the women to dowse them with water while they were putting out the flames. It was all reckoned to be rather jolly:

"If the maids a-spinning go,
Burn the flax and fire the tow.
Bring in pails of water then,
Let the maids bewash the men.
Give St Distaff all the right;
Then bid Christmas sport goodnight.
And next morning every one
To his own vocation."

The spinning, the flax-burning and the dowsing have long since gone, but the name of today's "saint" survives. The female side of a family is still called the distaff side.

Away-days for Top People

When William Hawtrey built his grand Elizabethan mansion in the Chilterns, a few miles from Princes Risborough, he may have had princes in mind for his guests rather than prime ministers, but four centuries later it became an up-market country cottage where weary premiers can spend a rejuvenating weekend. David Lloyd George was the first to move into Chequers, on this day in 1921.

The house was presented to the nation by Sir Arthur Lee, who later became – understandably – Lord Lee. He and his American-born wife had lived there for

J A N U A R Y 8 T H
Chequers was given
to the nation as a
country cottage for
weary prime
ministers; Lloyd
George was the first
to use it

several years while they restored it to its former glory.

Since then it has functioned as a useful tourist centre for top people. Hundreds of distinguished guests from all over the world have come to know the delights of the Chilterns, and the actual tenants of Chequers have often returned to the area in their retirement.

Clement Attlee settled at nearby Prestwood, Harold Wilson wrote his memoirs in a farmhouse near Great Missenden, and Ramsay Macdonald's daughter Isabel became landlady of the village pub at Speen, only five miles from where Dad entertained the leading statesmen of the day. It would be nice to think that, as Britain's first Labour prime minister, he sometimes took them down there for a drink.

9th
JANUARY

Who comes here?
The Loony with the Lamp?

Sir Humphry Davy is rightly credited for inventing the Davy miners' lamp, but he never actually tried it out in a mine himself. The real hero is an obscure rector of Jarrow, the Rev. John Hodgson, who agreed to test the lamp in Hebburn Pit, on this day in 1816.

He lit the flame and took it into a mine renowned for firedamp, the lethal explosive gas. But no one had warned the miners he was coming, which seems a little naughty; they could have been the victims of a major disaster if Davy's theory had proved unsound. As it was, the first miner to see the apparently naked flame approaching through the darkness had the fright of his life. He yelled a desperate warning.

"No regard was paid to his cries," wrote a local historian, "which then became wild, mingled with imprecations against the comrade (for such he took Hodgson to be) who was tempting death in so rash and certain a way . . . Oaths turned into prayers, until there stood before him, slightly exulting in his success, a grave and thoughtful man, a man whom he knew well and respected, holding up in his sight, with a gentle smile, the triumph of science, the future safeguard of the pitman." Hodgson admitted later he should have explained his actions straight away. I hope at least he stood the poor chap a stiff drink.

Davy himself, incidentally, never patented the lamp. He did not wish to make money, he said, from saving miners' lives.

10th
JANUARY

In for a Penny –
Now it's 26p

The man who invented the adhesive postage stamp and the front-door letter-box, Rowland Hill, achieved his greatest success on this day in 1840, when his third brainchild, the Penny Post, was introduced – the delivery of letters anywhere in the UK for a penny.

Hill was an obscure civil servant when he got the idea of letters being paid for by the sender instead of the recipient. Each letter had to be handed personally to the addressee, who then had to find the money, and an enormous amount of time was

JANUARY 9TH
When the Davy miners' lamp had its first test, nobody warned the miners – but luckily it worked

wasted on doorsteps. By providing stamps to stick on the letters, and slits to put them through the door, all that time could be saved.

He worked out that the Post Office could introduce a penny post under this system and still show a profit. At first nobody would accept this, particularly peers and MPs, who were allowed free postage, not only on their Parliamentary mail, but for their private letters, their businesses and their friends. All that would stop. The Postmaster General, Lord Lichfield, was quite appalled: "Of all the wild and visionary schemes which I have ever heard of or read of, it is the most extravagant."

But Hill had public opinion behind him, and he was given a top post in the Treasury to introduce penny postage. It was an immediate success; the number of letters doubled in the first year. In 1995 he was paid the ultimate tribute: the Queen's head shared a postage stamp with a portrait of Rowland Hill. Pity about the (then) 25p . . .

JANUARY 10TH
When the man who introduced the Penny Post eventually appeared on a stamp it was the Twenty-Five New Pennies post

complicated than it is today.

Instead of one company running the lottery, the Government virtually auctioned the tickets to lottery offices, which had to bid more than the face value of the tickets. That gave the government its profit, since the total value of the prizes was the same as the total face value of the tickets. Then the lottery offices sold on the tickets to the public at a higher figure still, to make a profit themselves. It was an early example of the famed "free market".

Competition was understandably keen. One lottery office found a lady called Mrs Goodluck and paid her fifty pounds a year to use her name as a partner, just to impress the punters.

National lotteries continued, on and off, until 1826, when it was felt that, as one virtuous Victorian wrote, "the inducement to gambling held out by lotteries was a great moral evil, helping to impoverish many, and diverting attention from the more legitimate industrial modes of moneymaking."

Ho hum. . .

11th
JANUARY

"Ho there, Varlet; whither the jackpot?"

There is nothing new about a National Lottery. The first draw for a lottery in England began on this day in 1569, outside the west door of St Paul's Cathedral. Instead of lasting just a frenzied fifty-odd seconds, it is said to have continued day and night until May 6th. That seems a little excessive, but the whole system was much more

12th
JANUARY

The Greeks had a (Quicker) Word for it

Most people think of Isaac Pitman, who died on this day in 1897, as the pioneer of shorthand, but in fact the idea of writing in symbols started with the Egyptians, and systems of "condensed" writing were used by the Greeks and Romans. All the speeches of Cicero, for instance, were noted down and recorded for posterity as he spoke.

Then in 1588 a Yorkshire clergyman called Timothy Bright published a pamphlet called *An Arte of Shorte, Swifte and Secrete*

Writing by Character – and you can't get a much clearer (or Brighter) definition of shorthand than that. Since then over two hundred systems have come and gone; one of them, invented by Thomas Shelton, was used by Pepys in his diaries. Pitman's was the first which really caught on, and his success was partly due to his other invention, the correspondence course.

In January 1840 Pitman took advantage of the newly introduced penny post to offer shorthand lessons by letter, in return for a shilling and a stamped addressed envelope.

JANUARY 12TH
Isaac Pitman's home at Wotton-under-Edge, Gloucestershire, where he invented his shorthand system in his spare time from being a schoolteacher

The response was so great that he had to recruit a team of volunteers to check the pupils' work.

His system of phonetic shorthand still had plenty of competition, but by the turn of the century he was first in the field – and I duly acquired my certificate in Pitman's shorthand to get my first job as a cub reporter, the only male in a class of trainee secretaries. Those journalists who prefer a tape-recorder to Isaac Pitman don't know what they've missed . . .

13th
JANUARY

"Give us back our Eleven Days!"

Until 1752 this was New Year's Day in Britain. Most other countries altered their calendars nearly two hundred years earlier, when Pope Gregory decreed that, as the old Julian calendar was based on 365 and a quarter days in a year, eleven days had to be lost to straighten things out. But – to nobody's great surprise – Britain preferred to remain out of step with its neighbours, which no doubt caused enormous confusion in the international trading world. In modern times, being just an hour different under British Summer Time has caused problems enough; being eleven days adrift must have wrought havoc.

When the Government decided to fall into line and lose eleven days in 1752, they announced that September 2nd would be immediately followed by September 14th. There was, of course, a public outcry. Many people believed they were losing, not only eleven days of their lives, but more importantly, eleven days' pay.

"Give us back our eleven days!" was the cry – except among convicts.

The protests died out, but the problems remained. Should ancient customs be observed on their traditional days, or according to the New Style calendar? If you were born between September 2nd and 14th in the old calendar, when should you celebrate your birthday in 1752? And would the seasons recognize the change – would all those thorn bushes said to bloom on Christmas Day bloom on January 5th instead?

But at least for compilers of the 1752 Book of Days there was good news; they only had to fill 354 . . .

They rowed past Binsey, which has what is called a "treacle well" in the churchyard. To keep the girls amused he told them a story about a dormouse who knew three little girls living at the bottom of a treacle well.

The children were enthralled, so they all landed and sat in the shade of a hayrick while he developed the story further. It became the Mad Hatter's Tea Party. "Alice" was named after one of his three young listeners, Alice Liddell.

The hayrick has gone but the well is still in the churchyard. If you want to start at the beginning of the story, the famous rabbit-hole was in the Liddells' garden at the Deanery – but do ask first.

JANUARY 14TH
The Mad Hatter's Tea Party in Lewis Carroll's memorial window at Daresbury, Cheshire

14th
JANUARY

The Treacle Well that grew into a Tea Party

The first handwritten version of *Alice in Wonderland*, under its original title "Alice's Adventures Underground", had illustrations by the author and an elegantly decorated dedication. Charles Lutwidge Dodgson, better known as Lewis Carroll, who died on this day in 1898, intended his book as "A Christmas Gift to a Dear Child in Memory of a Summer Day".

The first edition can only be seen by arrangement in the British Museum, but anyone can visit the place which he is probably referring to on that summer day. One day in 1862, in his spare time from teaching mathematics at Oxford University, Dodgson went rowing on the Thames with his friend Robinson Duckworth (his real name, not a *nom de plume*) and the three young daughters of his colleague Henry Liddell, Dean of Christ Church.

15th
JANUARY

The First Woman Doctor – and the First Madam Mayor

On this day in 1870 Britain's first woman doctor, Elizabeth Garrett Anderson, passed

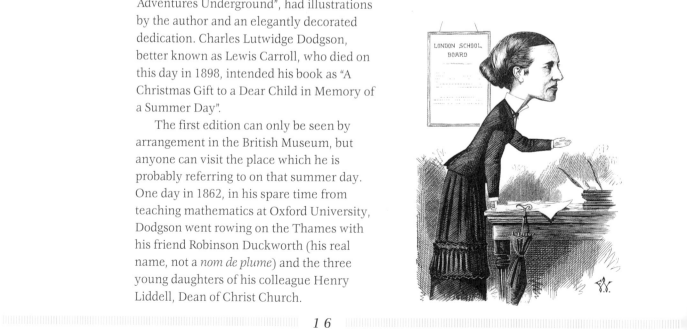

the final examination of the Medical Faculty of the Sorbonne and became a fully qualified MD. It was the final victory in a ten-year battle against the medical hierarchy, the Royal College of Surgeons, the examining boards, and not least her fellow students, who successfully petitioned against her admission to lectures, on the grounds she was making them a subject of ridicule. They were certainly embarrassed, but only because she was so much brighter than they were.

She qualified after finding out that the charter of the Society of Apothecaries made it illegal for them to exclude her. As soon as she was allowed to practise she founded a dispensary for women and children in what were then the slums of Marylebone. It developed into the hospital named after her.

Mrs Garrett Anderson made another little piece of history in a quite different field. In 1908 she was elected Mayor of Aldeburgh in Suffolk, the first woman in Britain to hold such an office. She was elected on King Edward VII's birthday, and her first mayoral duty was to send him a telegram of congratulation. It would have been interesting to see the old chap's face when he realized it was signed by a woman.

16th
JANUARY

"Out to the Ramparts they hurried"

Sir John Moore's retreat to the Spanish seaport of Corunna during the Napoleonic Wars was the nineteenth-century equivalent of Dunkirk. The number of British troops involved was less than a tenth – 25,000 compared with 300,000 – but as in 1940 they were all the army we had.

The idea had been to drive the French out of Spain, but Napoleon poured in reinforcements, the Spanish army collapsed, and Moore found himself outnumbered and outgunned, three hundred miles from the coast and separated from it by the Cantabrian mountains.

JANUARY 16TH
The death of Sir John Moore at Corunna – the 19th-century equivalent of Dunkirk

JANUARY 15TH
Elizabeth Garrett Anderson was the first woman in Britain to qualify as a doctor – in spite of the doctors

It was a nightmare retreat, in bitterly cold weather along snowbound roads, with very little food. Unlike Dunkirk, discipline broke down, villages were plundered, men drank themselves senseless on the local wine. It was not a chapter in British military history to be proud of – until the final page.

Ships were waiting at Corunna, but the French were too close behind, so Moore rallied his men and drew them up to face a full-scale attack by twice their number. On January 16th, 1809, in the Battle of Corunna, they drove the French back in confusion.

The army sailed away safely the same night, except for Sir John Moore himself. He was fatally wounded by a cannon-ball at the moment of victory. As his main force embarked, a small detachment carried him on to the defence lines – "out to the ramparts they hurried" – and buried him there, wrapped in his military cloak. Years later, a monument was erected on his grave.

them with mulled cider, made to his own secret recipe. Thus fortified, they adjourn to the neighbouring orchard, where a bonfire is lit and wassailing songs are sung, followed by three cheers for the apple trees.

Shotguns are fired to frighten off the bad spirits (which in apple trees take the form of grubs) and slices of toast soaked in cider are hung in the branches to attract alcoholic robins, in the hope that they will feed on any grubs that remain.

Having ensured a plentiful and grub-free harvest, the wassailers return to the bar to finish off the mulled cider – with perhaps a closing chorus of "Wassails in the Sunset".

JANUARY 17TH
Frightening away the bad spirits, an essential feature of "wassailing the apples" at Carhampton in Somerset

17th
J A N U A R Y

As they say in the Apple Orchards: "Hallo, Wassailer!"

Among the apple orchards of the West Country there was the ceremony on Twelfth Night of wassailing the apples, drinking a salutation to the apple trees to ensure a good crop later in the year. That was before the calendar was changed, and Twelfth Night was no longer celebrated on January 17th, but the Butcher's Arms at Carhampton claims to be the only inn in Somerset which still maintains this tradition, and observes it on its original date.

So tonight the participants assemble in the bar, to be greeted by the landlord – "Hallo, wassailer", perhaps? – who plies

18th
J A N U A R Y

A Treasury of Words from the Good Doctor

The English physician who compiled the first and definitive *Thesaurus of English Words and Phrases* was born on this day in 1779 – and he has bedevilled me for the last fifty years. The Thesaurus – does it rhyme with brontosaurus or pessaries? I used to wonder – has sets of alternative words with roughly the same meaning, and somewhere among them must be just the one you want; but as I once observed in an anarchic little volume called *The Anti-Booklist* (co-edited by one Brian Redhead): "To step into the good

JANUARY 18TH
Dr Peter Mark Roget, compiler of the famous Thesaurus – or treasury, bank, almonry, safe, strongbox, coffer, hanaper, porte-monnaie . . .

doctor's pages in search of a word is like plunging into a marsh in search of a will-o'-the-wisp."

For instance, try looking up "thesaurus". "Treasury," it says. Well, that's a possibility – but read on.

"Bank," it says. "Exchequer, almonry, safe, strongbox, coffer, hanaper, porte-monnaie." No thanks. So let's try the other headings the index suggests: List, Book, Words and Store.

Under List it gives "directory, gazetteer, dictionary, glossary, compendium . . ." Very nearly, but then it goes berserk: ". . . scroll, manifest, bill of lading, menu . . ."

Many times over the years I have wandered through this etymological orchard, reaching for words which were always just out of reach. I know, "etymological" is not quite the right word. How about "lexicological, phonological, logoleptic, glossographic . . ."

I rather wish that Dr Peter Mark Roget had stuck to medicine.

First World War.

When the war ended he also became a source of great debate in the village. Did he qualify to have his name on Wellingham's war memorial, along with the local men who had died in France – including, alas, the rector, who followed them out there and was killed just before the Armistice?

The anti-Pile lobby argued that he had not been killed on active service. Never mind that, said the Pile supporters, he had been killed by enemy action. It must have been a Norfolk Solomon who found the solution. Frederick Pile's name does appear on the memorial outside Wellingham church – but while the others are in alphabetical order, his comes last. So at least he shares in the annual tribute on Poppy Day, even though he's at the bottom of the pile.

19th
JANUARY

The Pile at the Bottom of the Pile

A new kind of warfare was introduced on this date in 1915: a German airship dropped the first bombs on Britain which killed civilians. The Zeppelin and its successors had two main targets, Great Yarmouth and King's Lynn, but for no obvious reason they dropped a few bombs in between. One of them fell on the remote little Norfolk village of Wellingham, where Frederick Pile was out for a stroll, and in this singularly unmilitary rural backwater, Mr Pile became perhaps the unluckiest and unlikeliest casualty of the

20th
JANUARY

Spouse-spotting, Courtesy of St Agnes

This is St Agnes' Eve, the traditional night for girls to discover, by all manner of bizarre methods, who their future husband will be. The procedures range from sowing barley grains under an apple tree to eating salted herring before bedtime. The future spouse will appear during the night, holding a rake in the case of the barley grains, ready for an early harvest, or in the salted-herring version carrying a welcome glass of water.

The most authentic routine dates back to

1696, when a knowledgeable Mr Aubrey advised the eager maiden to take a row of pins, pull them out one after the other, and stick the final one in her sleeve before going to sleep, at the same time reciting a paternoster. Her love would appear in a dream.

Or – from a later source – she could knot her left garter round her right stocking and recite the lines:

"I knit this knot, this knot I knit,
To know the thing I know not yet.
That I may see
The man that shall my husband be."

John Keats incorporated the idea in his own spouse-spotting recipe, in the lengthy (and rather sexy) poem "The Eve of St Agnes":

"Supperless to bed they must retire
And couch supine their beauties, lily white;
Nor look behind, nor sideways, but require
Of Heaven with upward eyes for all that
they desire."

And my word, in the rest of the poem, they get it.

Getting the Needle – the Hard Way

Cleopatra's Needle, which has little to do with Cleopatra and is certainly no needle, was towed up the Thames on this day in 1878, after a nightmare sea voyage from Alexandria in which six men died.

It had got to Alexandria in the first place because Caesar Augustus wanted to put it in front of the palace where Cleopatra died; that was the tenuous Cleo connection. But it was originally erected in Heliopolis some 1500 years before.

When Britain defeated Napoleon in Egypt in 1798, some enthusiastic trophy-hunters decided to bring it back home. They got as far as knocking it down, but it weighed nearly two hundred tons, and nobody could shift it. Some years after that it was offered to George IV as a Coronation gift, but he

*J A N U A R Y **21**S T*
Cleopatra's Needle,
encased in its metal
"needle-box", sets off
from Alexandria on
its precarious voyage
to London

wisely turned it down. Then the land on which it lay was bought by a property developer who threatened to smash it up if it wasn't shifted, so private funds were raised to bring it to England.

Encased in a metal cylinder, it was towed into the Bay of Biscay, where a violent storm started it yawing wildly. The captain of the tug cut it adrift – with eight men still clinging to its superstructure. He launched a lifeboat to save them, but it foundered. A passing steamer towed the Needle to port, and the eight men on it were saved, but the crew of six in the lifeboat were lost.

The Needle still stands on the Embankment in London. On it, in addition to the original hieroglyphics, there is a plaque in memory of the men who died getting it there. I hope someone thought it was worth it.

22nd

St Vincent, it's your Day – and your Round!

If there is a guardian angel who watches over drunks – and how else do they tumble downstairs without even a bruise? – then it must be St Vincent, whose day it is today. The connection, however, is entirely spurious, based on a misunderstanding going back to the sixteenth century.

Indeed, Vincent deserves a better reputation than being the patron saint of drunkards. He suffered the most appalling tortures before he died – the rack, the gridiron, the scourge – and was left lying in a cell strewn with sharp shards of broken pottery. But it was not the manner of his death, but the time of year it happened, which led to the confusion.

Just as St Swithun's day is linked with rainfall, St Vincent's Day is linked with sunshine. If the sun shines today, it should be a dry year – which benefits the vines. So St Vincent, not unreasonably, is patron saint of vintners. But why drunks?

In Victorian times a Guernsey man came across a sixteenth-century verse in old provincial French, which translated: "If the sun shines clear and well on St Vincent's Day, we shall have more wine than water." Fair enough: it meant there would be a good wine harvest. But it could also mean – and this is the way the Victorians took it – that if the sun shines, "we shall *drink* more wine than water"; in other words, St Vincent says it's all right to get sloshed.

The drunks had found their patron saint.

23rd

The Spirit from Spion Kop

On this day in 1900 the British forces in South Africa attacked the Boer positions at Spion Kop. In the advance column was a young officer called Captain George

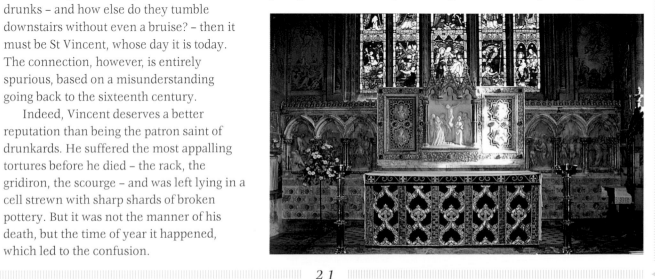

JANUARY 23RD
The altar in Ryde church, Isle of Wight, where a ghostly soldier appeared after the battle of Spion Kop

Raynham. The battle that followed has been called perhaps the bloodiest and certainly the most futile engagement of the whole South African War. Captain Raynham was reported missing, and was never seen again – except for one strange appearance in All Saints' Church, Ryde, on the Isle of Wight.

The Raynham family had been associated with the church since it was built, thirty years before. Soon after the Battle of Spion Kop, George's sister Amelia, a noted opera singer of her day, visited the church with a woman friend for a little quiet meditation. They were alone in it when the door opened and they heard footsteps walk past them to the altar – heavy steps like army boots. It was broad daylight, but they saw nothing.

Then they heard the footsteps again, and this time they saw a uniformed figure, with head bowed, facing the altar. The figure turned and came towards Amelia, arms outstretched, and she recognized her brother, his face covered in blood from a gaping wound. He came close, then disappeared.

Nobody has seen Captain George Raynham again. But if you happen to be in All Saints' Church on your own, on the anniversary of Spion Kop . . .

camps before the start of the Boer War, he had no idea it would be adapted for training boys. It was only when he came home from South Africa that he found it was being widely read by schoolmasters, youth leaders, and in particular the officers of the Boys' Brigade.

Although Baden-Powell has gone down in history as the founder of the Boy Scouts, a lot of the credit should go to the lesser-known William Smith, who launched the Boys' Brigade nearly twenty years before the hero of Mafeking appeared on the scene. It was he who urged "B-P" to re-write his book and call it *Scouting for Boys*, and it was he who found the site on Brownsea Island in Poole Harbour for the first Scout camp in 1907.

It was an enormous success. Informal Scout groups were formed all over the country, too many to be absorbed by the existing youth organizations. So B-P, who had thought scouting might just be an extra activity for the Boys' Brigade, found himself at the YMCA Hall in Birkenhead, Chief Scout of what became the largest international voluntary organization in the world.

JANUARY 24TH
"B-P" got all the cheers, but William Smith should get some credit too

24th

B-P was a Good Scout, but don't forget W.S.

In the unromantic surroundings of the YMCA Hall in Birkenhead, on this day in 1908, the Boy Scout movement was officially launched – rather to the astonishment of a certain Lieutenant-General Sir Robert Baden-Powell. When he wrote a book called *Aids to Scouting* for use in military training

25th

The Real Star of "The Star of Africa"

"The Star of Africa", the magnificent diamond which adorns the Royal Sceptre in the Crown Jewels, was discovered in a South African mine on this day in 1905. It was the largest uncut diamond in the world, weighing over three thousand carats, about one pound six ounces.

The finder was a Captain M.E. Wells. One wonders what a captain was doing down a diamond mine, but happily he was a gentleman as well as an officer, or the diamond might never have got as far as the Royal Sceptre. Before it was given its more glamorous name it was known simply as the Cullinan Diamond, named after the equally gentlemanly owner of the mine, who passed it on to the South African Government. They in turn presented it to Edward VII.

But the real star of the Star of Africa story is a diamond-cutter called Isaac Asscher. These days a cutter can use computers and high-speed saws, but Isaac had little more than a hammer and chisel. He was given the responsibility of cutting the biggest, most valuable and most famous diamond in the world.

He studied it for nine months, then picked up his tools, took a deep breath and struck the vital blow. He saw what he had done – and fainted.

When he came round, there was a smile on his face; he'd got it right.

26th
JANUARY

Was he Foolhardy against the Mahdi?

It was one of the great dramatic moments in British military history. On this day in 1885, General Gordon, after being besieged in Khartoum for ten months, walked nobly on to the steps of his residence to face the spears of the Sudanese rebels. The British public were bowled over by his courageous death, and furious that the Government had apparently let him down.

There is no doubt about his courage, but unfortunately his death was largely his own fault. He was sent to the Sudan with orders to bring out the Egyptian garrisons which were being attacked by the rebels, led by the fanatical Mahdi. (His palace still stands, and I always think of the splendid lawn outside it as the Mahdi Grass.)

Instead of leading them to safety, Gordon decided to stay and smash the rebellion himself, just as he had done in China, which earned him the title of "Chinese" Gordon. Perhaps he fancied being "Sudanese" Gordon instead. When he found himself trapped in Khartoum, the Government may well have muttered "Serves you right", but in due course they sent a force to relieve him. Various difficulties arose on the way, and it entered Khartoum just two days too late.

But at least Gordon shed the "Chinese"

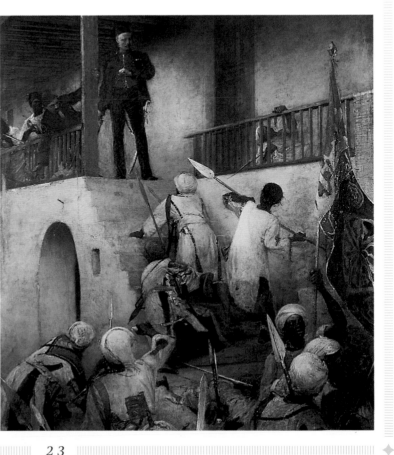

JANUARY 26TH General Gordon's final courageous confrontation in Khartoum. But should he still have been there?

nickname. He went down in history as Gordon of Khartoum – not for a famous victory, but for a gallant but unnecessary defeat.

27th
JANUARY

It started with a Biscuit Tin, a Bicycle Lamp – and Brains

The television era opened on this day in 1926 when a penniless inventor, who had been toiling away for years in the traditional garret, gave the first public demonstration of a television transmission to a group of forty scientists. He went on to develop colour television, achieve the first transatlantic TV transmission, and invent "noctovision", using invisible infra-red rays to see in the dark.

John Logie Baird started his experiments in an attic in Hastings, using the washstand as a workbench, a biscuit tin to hold the projector, and bicycle lamp glasses for lenses. The whole contraption was held together with string and sealing wax. It was the typical equipment of a "mad inventor" –

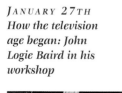

JANUARY 27TH
How the television age began: John Logie Baird in his workshop

but in this case, it actually worked. He relayed the image of a Maltese cross a few feet, and on the strength of that he moved to another garret, this time in Frith Street, Soho. In October 1925 he paid an office boy half-a-crown to stand in front of his makeshift camera, went into the next room, and saw the boy's image on the screen. From then on, it was downhill all the way . . .

28th
JANUARY

Lightening our Darkness – by Gas

On this night in 1809 the lamp-posts in Pall Mall were switched on, and Europe had its first gas-lit street. Britain was ahead of the field – but only because of a German.

Successful experiments with gaslight had been carried out some years before by William Murdock, down in Cornwall; his house in Redruth was the first in the country to be lit by it in 1792. But nobody thought of using gaslight in the streets until a Herr Winser started promoting the idea in London.

Most people thought he was dotty. The illustrious Sir Walter Scott wrote that a madman was proposing to light London with – yes, smoke! Even the forward-looking Sir Humphry Davy, inventor of the Davy miners' lamp, could not equate gas with light. But Winser persisted, and Pall Mall was the result.

The public was still confused about gas. There was a popular belief that the pipes carrying it were as hot as the lamps. When one adventurous shopkeeper installed gas lamps in his shop, a customer was so impressed she wanted to buy them and take them home – still alight – to put in her drawing room.

Westminster Bridge was lit by gas in 1812 and other cities followed. Gasworks sprang up all over Britain, and investors made fortunes. Then along came electricity.

The first electric street lamps in London were lit on the Victoria Embankment in 1878. This time it wasn't a German who did it, but nor was it an Englishman It was the Société Générale d'Electricité de Paris.

29th
JANUARY

The Bronze Guns have been used up – but the VCs continue

Queen Victoria decided to institute, on this day in 1856, a new award for conspicuous valour in the presence of the enemy – and made the radical condition that it should be awarded regardless of rank. The Victoria Cross is still the premier award, taking precedence over all other decorations.

It was the Crimean War that prompted the idea, and the medals were made from bronze cannon captured at Sebastopol until the supply ran out in 1942. The design remains unchanged, a Maltese cross with the royal crown surmounted by a lion, and the simple inscription "For Valour".

The award was made retrospective, and the first VC was won in 1854 by Mate (later Rear-Admiral) Charles David Lucas of HMS *Hecla*, who threw a live shell overboard just before it exploded. At the first investiture in Hyde Park in 1857 there were sixty-one VCs in the line-up, drawn as the Queen had desired from all ranks: twenty-five officers, fifteen NCOs and twenty-one privates and ordinary seamen.

The medal is still awarded evenhandedly, but some schools do better than others. Captain H.H. Jones, hero of the Falklands, was the thirty-sixth Old Etonian VC.

30th
JANUARY

The Statue that paid Dividends in Fake Cutlery

Charles I awoke between five and six on this chilly morning in 1649, drew back the bed-curtain and called to his attendant: "I will get up. I have a great work to do this day."

He put on an extra shirt so that he would not shiver and give the impression of fear as he stepped on to the scaffold in Whitehall. He had prepared a speech, but the crowd was too far away to hear, so he spoke briefly to those around him; they say that his last word before the axe fell was "Remember".

And his admirers still do. On this day each year they place a wreath on his statue at the head of Whitehall by Trafalgar Square, which was commissioned long before his death by the Earl of Portland. It was the Earl who died first, before the statue was finished, and it was stored in a church crypt until

someone could decide what to do with it.

The "someone" turned out to be Oliver Cromwell. He sold it to a dealer called Revett, on condition it was broken up for scrap. Instead, the shrewd Mr Revett buried the statue in his garden and for the next decade did a brisk business with Royalist supporters in bronze knives and forks, all allegedly made from it. When the monarchy was restored he dug it up and sold it back to Charles II, who erected it in London. Mr Revett, I imagine, then left the country – before all those fake knives and forks landed between his shoulder-blades.

JANUARY 30TH
The Civil War Society
on parade – with
youthful supporter –
to honour the
anniversary of
Charles I's execution
in Whitehall

not in London but in Derby, where his campaign came to an end. His officers, thinking all was lost, insisted he returned to Scotland, though in fact King George was already packing his bags. The King rapidly unpacked them when he heard the news, while the retreating Scots were defeated at Culloden.

The campaign to erect the statue was nearly as ill-fated as the '45. After the cost of £100,000 was approved by Derby Council, Labour gained power and cancelled it. That looked like the end, until the millionaire owner of Derby County Football Club stepped in and footed the bill.

The statue was erected in December 1995. It depicts, not an ageing exile, but a handsome young Scot mounted on a charger. Bonnie Prince Charlie is bonny again, and a Derby winner at last.

31st
JANUARY

Charles III, a Derby Winner at Last (Charles the Who?)

On this day in 1788, one day after the anniversary of the execution of Charles I, Charles III died in exile. Charles the Who? You may think the title a little premature. But not according to Bonnie Prince Charlie's supporters. When he fled back to the Continent after the ill-fated '45 Rebellion, he still maintained he was Charles III, rightful king of England. George II, who actually occupied the throne, was not too bothered and left him to it.

Unlike his great-grandfather, whose statue at Charing Cross was sculpted before his death, "Charles III" had to wait for two-and-a-half centuries after his attempt on the throne to be put, as it were, on a pedestal. It was

JANUARY 31ST
Bonnie Prince
Charlie rides again
in Derby, where his
campaign ended

WESTONS

THE WONDER (LANDSLIP A.D. 1575)
SLIP TAVERN

February

1st

*A Man's Home is his Castle –
unless it's the Tower*

The wife of a Norfolk barrister gave birth on this day in 1552 to a son who had a

*FEBRUARY 1ST
Sir Edward Coke, the
Attorney-General
who seemed to lose
every round at
Raleigh's trial, but
still won the verdict*

spectacular legal career prosecuting some notable defendants, but whose lasting memorial is a simple sentence which became a basic tenet of the law: "A man's home," he ruled, "is his castle."

Sir Edward Coke (pronounced as in a kitchen, not in the coal merchant's) became Speaker, Solicitor-General and Attorney-General. Historians praise his legal acumen and his courage in opposing James I and Charles I when they tried to set aside the law, but his courtroom style was hardly in the Kavanagh QC class. His vituperative attacks would have staggered any fair-minded juror.

At one trial he told the defendant: "Thou hast a Spanish heart, and thyself art a spider of Hell" – which is not how we normally picture Sir Walter Raleigh. "You are the absolutest traitor that ever was."

Raleigh replied coolly: "Your phrases will not prove it, Mr Attorney."

"Thou viper!" blasted Coke.

Sir Walter was gently reproving. "It becometh not a man of quality and virtue to call me so. But I take comfort in it, it is all you can do."

But of course it wasn't. Raleigh won every round, but Sir Edward won the verdict, and had him sent to the Tower for execution. His blunderbuss style must have been fascinating to watch; if he went for Raleigh like that, imagine what he might have said to Guy Fawkes. What a television series it would make: *Coke's Tours de Force?*

2nd

*Rock-a-bye Baby – up
on the Altar*

This is Candlemas Day, the Feast of the Purification of Mary after the "uncleanliness" of birth, and the presentation of the infant Jesus – the "Light of the World", hence the candles – in the Temple. At the Church of St Mary of the Purification at Blidworth in Nottinghamshire, in what used to be Sherwood Forest (Will Scarlett is said to be buried in the churchyard), this is remembered in the Rocking Ceremony, which dates back to medieval times.

On the Sunday nearest to February 2nd there is first the baptism of whichever male child was born in Blidworth closest to Christmas Day. In a separate ceremony the

*FEBRUARY 2ND
Not a novel idea for a
flower festival – this
is the Rocking
Ceremony at
Blidworth in
Nottinghamshire on
Candlemas Day*

baby is blessed, presented to the Holy Table, and rocked in a hundred-year-old cradle bedecked with flowers.

In earlier times, when Blidworth was a small village, the baby was then carried through the streets in the cradle "amid much rejoicing", but as it has now grown into a town of nearly eleven thousand people, that part of the proceedings has been dropped. In fact the whole ceremony fell into disuse for some years, but it was revived – without the procession – in the 1920s. There is a Register of Rockings on the wall in the Baptistry.

3rd
FEBRUARY

As the Mayor said: "Guare wheg ya guare teg!"

Feast Monday at St Ives has just about everything – a mayoral procession, a rugby match, a meet of the local Hunt, a coffee morning and a concert; everything, in fact, except a Feast. Instead there is Hurling the Silver Ball, a custom so old that nobody knows when or why it started, but it always takes place on the Monday nearest to February 3rd, when the Parish Church was dedicated.

The silver ball is actually a wooden one, about the size of a tennis ball and covered in a thin layer of silver which was originally obtained – quite illegally, I imagine – by melting down silver coins collected around the village. These days it is just silver leaf.

It was originally used in a game on the sands between two teams, one composed of men called Thomas, William or John, who played everyone else. "Toms, Wills and Jans, take off all's on the san's." The idea was to throw the ball into the opponents' goal, a net on a pole.

Over the years the game deteriorated into a romp through the streets but in 1972 the Mayor put it back on a more formal basis. The ball is blessed at the Holy Well at Porthmeor, then the Mayor carries it in procession to the parish church and throws it into the crowd, with the Cornish cry: "Guare

wheg ya guare teg" – "Fair play is good play". It is passed from hand to hand around the town, and whoever has it at noon should, if diligent about the exhortation, bring it back to the mayor.

FEBRUARY 3RD The silver ball is handed back to the Mayor of St Ives by a young protégé of the ancient custom

4th
FEBRUARY

The Flaming Nightmare of the Sage of Chelsea

"The Sage of Chelsea" died on this day in 1881, and a statue was erected in his memory only a short distance from the house where he lived for nearly fifty years.

Thomas Carlyle wrote a number of massive door-stopper volumes in a style called Carlylese – "ragged, broken, often jerky and abrupt, often jaw-twisting in its phraseology", as one commentator described it. It hardly sounds a recipe for a bestseller, and indeed he had great difficulty getting his early works published, but he finished up as one of the most revered writers of his age. The Sage, it would seem, knew his onions.

It is his self-control, however, which impresses me most. His first major work, after he moved to Chelsea, was a monumental history of the French Revolution. It took him a year to complete the first volume, and he lent the manuscript to a literary friend, John Stuart Mill, to get his opinion.

Then came the nightmare that haunts all writers. Mill left the manuscript in his library, and an over-zealous servant girl gathered it up as rubbish and put it on the fire.

This is where Carlyle showed his self-control. No raging, no despair, not even a slap on the wrist for the girl. He just spent the next year writing it all again. But his bottled-up feelings may have exploded when he reached the final sentence of the third and final volume: "You have not had for a hundred years any book that comes more direct and flaming from the heart of a living man."

I like "flaming"...

FEBRUARY 4TH
The Sage of Chelsea, Thomas Carlyle, still looked as composed as this, even when the maid burned his manuscript

5th
FEBRUARY

No, it wasn't Arthur Askey who gave us the Pip

Whenever I hear the "pips" on the BBC I visualize the scene in an early Arthur Askey film, in which he marches into Broadcasting

House, passes through innumerable security checks, dons a white coat and white gloves, and enters a heavily guarded cubicle with a clock on the wall and a large knob on the desk. When the clock reaches five seconds to the hour, with a magnificent flourish the little man extends a white-gloved finger and presses the knob six times . . .

It doesn't happen quite like that. The real star of the story is a long-forgotten horologist, Frank Hope-Jones, who was not only an expert on electric clocks but also happened to be chairman of the Wireless Society of London. In a talk on the BBC about time measurement, he concluded by counting down the last five seconds to 10 p.m., and suggested that this kind of signal should be broadcast regularly, to help listeners set their clocks and watches more accurately.

The BBC, being what it is, took nearly a year to make up its mind, but on this day in 1924 it broadcast the first "pips". They ended, not on the hour but on the half-hour. At 9.30 p.m. the Greenwich Time Signal was born.

Greenwich was involved because the two chronometers which triggered the signal were at the Royal Observatory; it was sent to the control room by telephone line, and the actual "pips" were broadcast automatically. So the services of Arthur Askey were not required – but he may well have inspired the weekly ceremony of starting the draw for the Lottery.

*FEBRUARY 5TH
The Royal
Observatory, home of
the Greenwich Time
Signal and the
famous "pips"*

6th
FEBRUARY
❧

*FEBRUARY 6TH
From soaring
fountains to sunken
ha-has – they were
all within the
capability of
Capability Brown.
The garden at
Blenheim was one of
his creations*

He didn't Raise a Laugh – he Sank it

The man who caused the first ha-ha died on this day in 1783. He was not a music-hall comedian but a landscaper of aristocratic estates – a sort of up-market gardener. And he did not achieve the ha-ha by raising a laugh but by lowering the ground level; it is of course a ditch that acts as a sunken fence, so as not to interrupt the view.

Lancelot Brown is better known as Capability Brown, because he always flattered his rich clients by telling them their land had great "capabilities". He followed the example of his mentor, William Kent, who ended the tradition of laying out gardens geometrically, rather like outdoor rooms connected by "corridors" of bushes and trees, and instead created broad lawns, winding paths, small coppices and big vistas – the "natural" look.

The idea caught on, and Lancelot was commissioned to landscape some of the largest back gardens in the country. His biggest job was at Blenheim Palace, where he had 2500 acres to play with. He dammed a river to make an ornamental lake, spanned by a 400-foot bridge, and laid out the trees and paths to match, so it is said, the actual Battle of Blenheim.

He achieved royal recognition when he was put in charge of the gardens at Hampton Court, a daunting task for most gardeners, but for Lancelot Brown well within his capability.

7th
FEBRUARY
❧

At Much Marcle it was the Hill that made the First Move

The peaceful little Herefordshire village of Much Marcle achieved considerable notoriety in 1995 as the original home of Frederick West, who committed suicide in prison after admitting the murder of several young girls. But long before he and his wife appalled the nation with their activities at 25 Cromwell Road, an event occurred at Much Marcle which created almost as great a

sensation, in quite a different way. On this day at six o'clock in the evening, Marcle Hill started moving. "It roused itself with a roar, and by seven next morning had moved forty yards."

It was still moving three days later, leaving a trail of destruction in its wake. In those three days some twenty-six acres of hill moved a distance of four hundred yards. Two roads were moved well away from their original routes, cattle and sheep were killed, trees and bushes were uprooted, and little Kinnaston Chapel completely disappeared under the hill. Nearly three centuries later the chapel bell was re-discovered when it was dug up by a plough.

No convincing explanation has ever been found, scientific or supernatural. But it seemed to give the locals an understandable thirst, and in the nineteenth century it was a Marcle man who set up the first cider factory – the village is conveniently surrounded by apple orchards.

8th
FEBRUARY

The End of Mary, Queen of Scots – or was it?

Mary, Queen of Scots, after spending many years of imprisonment at Fotheringhay Castle in Northamptonshire, was beheaded in the Great Hall on this day in 1587, on the orders of her cousin, Queen Elizabeth. Nothing remains standing of the Great Hall or the castle; Mary's son, James I, had the whole place demolished. It is said that the thistles which now grow on the castle

mound were planted by her to remind her of home – or more romantically, they grew where her tears fell.

Bits and pieces of the castle were used by local builders, and sections of the staircase down which she walked to her execution are said to be still in existence – in two different places. One is the privately owned Manor House at Warmington, the other is Oundle's Talbot Hotel.

Experts suggest that neither staircase dates back that far. On the other hand, the Talbot was rebuilt in 1626, which was not too long after the castle was demolished; the staircase, or part of it, might have been installed at that time.

Certainly the story goes that Mary's ghost came too, and can sometimes be seen descending the stairs on this day, the anniversary of her death. If it does, it is in for a pleasant surprise. Instead of leading down to the execution block, the stairs lead to the lounge bar . . .

9th
FEBRUARY

God Save the King. And Save Him. And Save Him . . .

The National Anthem has obscure origins. The English Hymnal merely says source unknown. Some have attributed it to a seventeenth-century organist at Antwerp Cathedral, Dr John Bull, perhaps because his name seems so appropriate. Others say it originated in Paris in 1686, when a Mme de Brinon sang a French version which comes pretty close to ours:

Grand Dieu sauvez le Roi,
Grand Dieu vengez le Roi,
Vive le Roi . . .

But it first came into its own in England in 1745, during the Jacobite Rebellion, when it was sung for the first time at Drury Lane by a patriotic audience in the presence of George II.

However, it was on this day in 1909 that "God Save the King" had its finest hour – and it nearly was a whole hour. King Edward VII was on a state visit to Germany, and a military band was awaiting him on the platform at Rathenau station, Brandenburg. As the royal train pulled in, they struck up the National Anthem.

Inside the train, however, the King was having great difficulty getting his considerable girth into the uniform of a German field-marshal. Rather than leave an embarrassing pause, the band played the anthem again. And again. And again . . .

By the time he had managed to do up the final button and emerge from the train, the exhausted bandsmen were embarking on "God Save the King" for the seventeenth time. They earned the gratitude of the organizers – and a place in the *Guinness Book of Records*.

10th
FEBRUARY

The Line that links Shipping and Shoes

Samuel Plimsoll MP, one of the very few people whose name has been immortalized in two totally different fields – merchant shipping and lawn tennis – was born on this day in 1824. The Plimsoll Line marks the maximum load for a British merchant ship in salt water; the level of the water must not rise above it. Plimsolls were the first lightweight canvas shoes to be introduced in this country for playing croquet and tennis.

Mr Plimsoll worked hard to achieve the first of these distinctions. He led a six-year campaign against the dangerous overloading of cargo ships, culminating in the Merchant Shipping (Plimsoll) Act of 1876. The sporting connection is rather more tenuous; in fact Mr Plimsoll had nothing to do with it personally at all.

It so happened that in the year his Act was passed, the New Liverpool Rubber Company produced their new croquet shoes with canvas uppers and rubber soles, and some shrewd marketing man spotted that the line round the shoe where the upper joined the sole was rather like the Plimsoll Line round the hull of a ship. They have been known as plimsolls ever since – in Britain, that is. The Americans, who had probably never heard of Mr Plimsoll, preferred to call them "sneakers".

Happily the word never caught on here.

FEBRUARY 10TH Samuel Plimsoll may look a little gloomy, but he did not know his name would live on, at sea and on the sports field

11th
FEBRUARY

The First Chance to Spend a Penny – for Fourpence

The first women's public lavatory was opened in Bedford Street, off the Strand, on this day in 1852 – to the immense relief, one would have thought, of the local female population. A men's lavatory had been opened down the road in Fleet Street nine days before, perhaps with the bibulous gentlemen of the Press in mind.

Alas, both projects were a total disaster. By the end of February just fifty-eight gents had used the gents', and only twenty-four ladies had been in the ladies'. The whole idea was dropped.

The problem could not have been lack of publicity. Fifty thousand handbills were distributed and advertisements were placed in *The Times*. Nor could it have been lack of demand – the public's internal organs must have functioned just as inconveniently in those days as they do now.

The main reason was the cost. Although the lavatories were public, they were owned privately, and their object was not just altruistic – they had to make a profit. The charge was tuppence for using the WC, and tuppence more to wash your hands. Multiply fourpence into present-day values, and it is not surprising there were so few takers.

The public had to wait three years before the City of London provided the first municipal lavatory outside the Royal Exchange. The charge was only a penny – and we have been "spending a penny" ever since.

12th
FEBRUARY

He sent them a Rocket – it saved their Lives

The first time a mortar-fired lifeline was used to save a person from shipwreck was on this day in 1808, off the coast of Norfolk. It was invented by George William Manby, a Norfolkman who went to school with Nelson, but instead of turning his talents to taking lives at sea, devoted himself to saving them. He was prompted to do so when he watched helplessly from the beach at Great Yarmouth as a ship foundered offshore with the loss of two hundred lives.

Manby lived in the Norfolk village of Hilgay, where his father was Lord of the Manor, and it is said he test-fired his life-saving apparatus from the tower of Hilgay Church. Certainly the mortar which he used is depicted on his tombstone in the churchyard.

It was first put to use at Gorleston, only a mile along the coast from that original shipwreck off Yarmouth. A plaque in the

FEBRUARY 12TH George Manby's invention was soon put to good use. This was one of the earliest rescues with his self-propelled lifeline

High Road records that the crew were saved by firing a rope over the stranded vessel, "a method now universally adopted and to which at least a thousand sailors of various nations owe their lives". The plaque was erected in 1845; many thousands more lives have been saved since.

Fleming continued his experiments, but it was not until a purified form was produced by two other scientists in 1940 that its real value was understood. Happily Fleming was still around in 1945 to share with them the Nobel Prize.

FEBRUARY 13TH
The discoverer of the marvel mould, Alexander Fleming – with admirers

13th

FEBRUARY

The Mould that Grew into a Marvel

On this day in 1929 a little-known professor of bacteriology read a paper to the Medical Research Club about a curious discovery he had made in his laboratory at St Mary's Hospital, Paddington, when he returned from holiday. He was annoyed to find that some culture plates of bacteria which he was growing for his experiments had developed an unpleasant-looking mould, like the mould on stale food. He noticed, however, that the mould had killed or at least stopped the growth of the bacteria around it. His laboratory assistant happened to have a sinus infection, and when some of the mould was applied, the infection improved.

The Medical Research Club listened to this in silence. When the time came for the usual questions, none was asked. Nobody realized, least of all the lecturer himself, that they had been hearing about one of the greatest medical discoveries of the age. The lecturer was Alexander Fleming, and the discovery was penicillin.

14th
FEBRUARY

"Galloping Horses" – and a Flying Heart

The Lynn Mart, the first major event in the showmen's year, starts on this Day at King's Lynn in Norfolk. Originally the town had two major fairs in July and August, but the dates clashed with similar events in nearby towns, and since the reign of Elizabeth, the Mart has been held in the Tuesday Market in February.

This was where witches were burned at the stake as an alternative form of entertainment. The carved outline of a heart, high up on one of the older buildings, is said to be where a witch's heart ended up after bursting from her body as the flames rose around her. It was taken as proof of her innocence – just a little too late.

FEBRUARY 14TH
Dignity on the dodg'ems: the Mayor of King's Lynn opens the annual Mart

When the showmen set up their rides for the Mart – a rather more cheerful occasion – many of them appreciate that this was where they started. In 1885 a young Lynn engineer called Frederick Savage, having already invented a mechanical winnowing machine, took out a patent for his "galloping horses". He was made Mayor, though probably because of the winnowing machine rather than the roundabout.

Even so, it is entirely appropriate that the Mayor of King's Lynn, in robes and regalia, always takes a ride on the "galloping horses" – or their modern rivals, the dodg'ems – to open the Mart.

And – oh yes. There is absolutely no connection with St Valentine.

15th
FEBRUARY

How many New Pence in Half a Crown, Sebastian?*

The old systems of pounds, shillings and pence finally gave place to decimal coinage on this day in 1971, and the British had to get used to the idea of having a hundred pence in the pound instead of two hundred and forty.

The politicians had tried to convert us before. A Conservative MP first proposed decimal coinage in 1816, and it came up again in Parliament four more times in the next forty years. On one of these occasions, in 1849, it came so close to materializing that some decimal florins were actually minted, but again the traditionalists won. It took another hundred years and the impetus of the Common Market to get the change through.

* Twelve and a half – we think.

Even then it was not easy, and various devices were used to educate the public about decimalization – not least a 12-year-old boy called Sebastian, who made regular appearances on the early-morning *Today* programme on Radio 4, answering questions from the public. The apparent boy-wonder was actually helped with the answers, and even then his advisers were not infallible, but it was an ingenious way of getting the message across. I like to think Sebastian learned quite a lot too.

16th
FEBRUARY

The Stadium that Concrete Bob built

The contract to build Wembley Stadium was signed on this day in 1922 by McAlpines, at a price of about £75,000. The stadium was completed in three hundred working days, and the first major event in it was the 1923 Cup Final. Most people remembered that day for the policeman on the white horse who cleared the spectators off the pitch, but

FEBRUARY 15TH "How many of these will I need for an iced lolly?" A young spender studies the new decimal coinage

the McAlpine family must remember it as marking one of the greatest triumphs of the firm's founder, Sir Robert McAlpine, universally known as Concrete Bob.

He was the first builder to use concrete for bridges and viaducts, back at the turn of the century, and when the government architects decided that Wembley Stadium should be built almost entirely of concrete, the job was not put out to tender – it went straight to McAlpines.

Those distinctive twin towers are made of concrete; so are the famous Wembley lions. The terraces are built of reinforced concrete beams, the outside wall has thirty-seven concrete arches, there are concrete fountains and concrete lamp-posts. Altogether they used over twenty-five thousand tons of the stuff – and Concrete Bob must have loved every mixer-ful.

17th
FEBRUARY

The Great Synod Debate: a Roman Tonsure or a Celtic Cut?

If St Finan of Lindisfarne, whose day this is, had won the debate at the Synod of Whitby in AD664, the English Church might well be run today in the Celtic style, with independent communities linked in a sort of federation, instead of the Roman system of dioceses and bishops. The monks might look different too; instead of the circular "crown of thorns" tonsure preferred by the Romans, they might still have the Celtic cut – the front half of the head shaven, the hair at the back growing long.

It all arose when the Pope started sending representatives such as St Augustine to Britain to tighten up the rather haphazard organization of the home-grown Celtic

FEBRUARY 16TH Wembley Stadium was one of the most famous creations of "Concrete Bob" McAlpine. The photo shows the pitch invasion which occurred during the first Cup Final played there in 1923

missionaries. The argument came to a head when the King of Northumbria, a Celtic convert, found that he was celebrating Easter on a different day from his Queen, who came from Rome-dominated Kent. As one historian put it: "While one was fasting for Lent, the other was feasting to celebrate the Resurrection."

The Synod of Whitby adopted the Roman system, and a disconsolate Finan was rowed back to Lindisfarne (by Finan's salts, perhaps?). But he was made a saint anyway.

18th
FEBRUARY

Yes, but where's the "Palace Beautiful"?

Pilgrim's Progress, the story of Christian and his helpfully named associates Mr Worldly Wiseman, Mr Feebleminded, Mr Valiant-for-Truth and the rest, was published on this day in 1678, and it became an immediate bestseller. It's thought a hundred thousand copies were sold during the lifetime of its author, John Bunyan, and since then it has been translated into nearly a hundred and fifty languages, from Eskimo to Tibetan.

Bunyan wrote the first part of it while spending six months in the town lock-up on Bedford Bridge, but he fitted the rest of it in during his preaching tours in the surrounding countryside, and one school of thought argues that he based one of the places in the book on the village of Stevington, three miles west of Bedford. It is the passage where Christian finds himself at "a place somewhat ascenting, and upon that place stood a cross, and a little below, in the bottom, a sepulchre".

A cross stands in the centre of Stevington, and "a little below, in the bottom"

– just down the lane which leads from the cross to the church – is Bunyan's "sepulchre", the holy well by the churchyard wall.

The Slough of Despond could be the boggy area around the well, but I have yet to identify any village called Morality. As for Bunyan's "Palace Beautiful", no one has ever suggested it's in Bedford . . .

FEBRUARY 18TH
The holy well at Stevington in Bedfordshire may have been the "sepulchre" in Bunyan's Pilgrim's Progress

FEBRUARY 19TH
David Garrick is best remembered as an actor, but he wrote the odd sea-shanty between shows

19th
FEBRUARY

"'Tis to Glory he Steered" – on the Stage, not the Sea

The man who wrote the words of "Heart of Oak" – "Come, cheer up my lads, 'tis to glory we steer" – was born on this day in 1717 at the Angel Inn, Lichfield, Staffordshire, where his Army officer father was on a recruiting campaign. Fortunately he never persuaded his son to join the colours. Instead, David Garrick decided to go on the stage, and became one of the great names of the English theatre.

As well as his famous Shakespearian performances, he introduced some novel ideas into stage production, like insisting on the supporting actors learning their lines properly and attending rehearsals. He banished the more privileged from their traditional seats alongside the stage, and devised lighting which ensured the actors were not only visible on the front apron. As for his acting technique, his fellow-actor James Quin observed: "If Garrick is right, then I and all the other actors are wrong."

Quin was right about that at least.

After playing a few bit-parts he made his debut in a major role as Richard III at a little playhouse called Goodman's Fields. The playbill announced, slightly inaccurately, that the king would be played by "A Gentleman who has never appeared on any stage". The "Gentleman" was an instant success, and Garrick enjoyed top billing, under his own name, for the rest of his career – and even found time to write the odd sea-shanty between shows. "We'll always be ready; steady, boys, steady . . ."

20th
FEBRUARY

They wore Red Feathers – but no Hooley-hooley Skirt

In the City of London on this day, a procession of boys and staff walks from the Sir John Cass School to the adjoining Church of St Botolph-Without-Aldgate. They wear the usual school uniform – plus a scarlet feather in their caps or lapels. It is their birthday gesture of homage to their founder, Sir John Cass, Master of two Livery Companies, City alderman, Sheriff of London, Member of Parliament for the City – and wielder of a bloodstained quill pen.

Sir John built the school in 1710, next to the church where he was baptized. He waited another eight years, however, before making the legal arrangements to ensure that its endowment continued after his death. As it turned out, he very nearly left it too late. He was actually completing his will when, according to school legend, he had a sudden fatal haemorrhage. He just managed to sign the vital document before he died; the quill pen he used was stained red by his blood.

Hence the scarlet feathers worn at his memorial service – not exact replicas, these are dyed turkey quills. But the hot mulled wine in which the staff and school managers drink his health afterwards is definitely the real thing.

21st
FEBRUARY

Two-and-a-quarter Miles an Hour into the History Books

George Stephenson is the name most associated with the birth of the steam locomotive, but he was still a young engineer looking after a pumping station in a Newcastle coalmine when, at the other end of the country, a Cornishman called Richard Trevithick built and successfully tested the first steam locomotive.

Trevithick may have got the idea from a fellow Cornishman, William Murdock, who was making models of steam carriages at Redruth in 1786, but it was Trevithick who first built a full-size version and tried

driving it up a steep hill near Camborne. "She went off like a little bird," he wrote afterwards.

His really revolutionary development, however, was to run a steam carriage on rails. He found a disused horse tramway at a colliery at Pen-y-darren in South Wales, and on this day in 1804 his steam locomotive hauled ten tons of iron and seventy passengers for a distance of nine miles. The ride lasted four hours, and the passengers, standing up crammed together in an open waggon, would probably have preferred to get out and walk, but they had shared in making railway history.

Trevithick's loco had no name that I know of, but he might have called it *The Blue Touchpaper*, because it eventually set off Stephenson's *Rocket*.

FEBRUARY 20TH
Be-feathered pupils of the Sir John Cass School in the City of London remember their founder's bloodstained quill pen

FEBRUARY 21ST
One of Richard Trevithick's early steam railways – a circular track in Euston Square, London which ran rings round George Stephenson at that stage, well ahead of the Rocket

FEBRUARY 22ND
Britain's first purpose-built cinema was at Colne in Lancashire; this could have been the queue for the first children's matinee . . .

22nd
F E B R U A R Y

Let's go to the Movies – at Colne?

The Lancashire market town of Colne does not come immediately to mind as a centre of the English film industry. In the gazetteers its only tenuous link with the movies is Wycoller Hall, just outside the town, on which Charlotte Brontë based Ferndean Manor in her novel – later a film – *Jane Eyre*, but even that is now a ruin. It was at Colne, however, that an enterprising showman called Joshua Duckworth opened Britain's first purpose-built cinema, the Central, on this day in 1907.

Each programme lasted two hours and Mr Duckworth liked to include a travelogue or some other educational film. "This I find gives dignity to the show." Surprisingly, knockabout comedy was a flop. "Breaking crockery, tumbling over furniture, or running against the banana cart fails to draw a smile, if not positive disapproval." In spite of that, breaking things and falling over things seem to have caught on (what happened to the banana cart, one wonders), and so did the Central.

It continued to function as a cinema until 1924, when it became a Spiritualist Chapel and the ephemeral images on the screen gave place to other manifestations. These

FEBRUARY 23RD
Catherine de Valois, the queen on whom Samuel Pepys bestowed his birthday kiss – over two hundred years after her death

days it is devoted to another form of non-human activity: it houses the robotics section of an engineering works.

23rd
F E B R U A R Y

In which Mr Pepys indulges himself with a Birthday Treat

Samuel Pepys, devoted diarist and incorrigible gossip, was born on this day in 1623, and on this, his birthday, he regularly gave thanks for his continued good health and fortune.

"This is now 28 years that I am born," he wrote in 1661, "and blessed be God, in a state

of full content, and a great hope to be a happy man in all respects." And the following year: "This day by God's mercy I am 29 years of age and in very good health, and like to live and get an estate. I think I may reckon myself as happy a man as any in the world, for which God be praised. So to prayers and to bed."

Apart from these self-congratulatory comments, Samuel's birthday entries were much like any other day's, but in 1669 he did take himself and his family to Westminster Abbey for a bizarre birthday treat. The skeleton of Henry V's wife Catherine de Valois, who died over two hundred years before, was on display – "the Bones firmly united, and thinly cloth'd with Flesh, the Scrapeings of tann'd Leather" – and Mr Pepys, it seems, gave her a hug:

I had the upper part of her body in my hands. And I did kiss her mouth, reflecting upon it that I did kiss a Queen, and that this was my birthday, 36 years old, that I did first kiss a Queen.

And so to bed . . .

24th
FEBRUARY

"Excuse me, Mr Speaker – my Theatre's on Fire"

It is rare for the House of Commons to consider adjourning in the middle of a debate because an MP's theatre is on fire, but it happened on this day in 1809. Richard Brinsley Sheridan was taking part in a debate on the Peninsular War when the news arrived that the Theatre Royal Drury Lane was in flames.

The adjournment was moved "in consequence of the extent of the calamity which the event just communicated to the House would bring upon a respectable individual, a Member of this House". Sheridan declined the compliment, but it was indeed a calamity for him; most of his personal possessions as well as the theatre were destroyed, and his livelihood was lost.

He was drowning his sorrows, "swallowing port by the tumblerful" according to one report, when a benevolent brewer, Samuel Whitbread, launched an appeal which raised £400,000 for a new theatre. Drury Lane reopened in 1812, but without Sheridan. Whitbread, no doubt deploring Sheridan's penchant for port instead of his own product, bought his interest and told him to stay away. So he kept on drinking, was arrested for debt, and died while writs were still being served.

That day in the Commons, in fact, proved to be R.B. Sheridan's last public appearance and the end of his career – but happily *The Rivals* lives on.

FEBRUARY 24TH
The theatre blaze that interrupted a Commons debate. R.B. Sheridan was speaking in the House when news came that his Theatre Royal was on fire

25th
FEBRUARY

*FEBRUARY 25TH
Hubert Booth's
vacuum cleaner – six
years ahead of
Mr Hoover*

The Man who Cleaned Up before the Hoover

Vacuum cleaners are often called "hoovers" these days, but by rights it is not the American Mr Hoover but an English engineer called Hubert Cecil Booth who should be immortalized in this way. Instead of "hoovering" the carpet you are actually "boothing" it.

Mr Booth got the idea of a vacuum cleaner six years ahead of Mr Hoover. He saw a device demonstrated for blowing away dust – but the dust soon settled again. How much better, he thought, to suck up the dust instead. He built a machine and it worked. On this day in 1902 he issued the prospectus of his Vacuum Cleaner Company Ltd.

The machine was somewhat big and clumsy, so he provided a door-to-door service – or rather, window-to-window, since he parked it outside and put a long hose through the windows. His most spectacular commission was cleaning the carpets in Westminster Abbey for the Coronation of Edward VII. The King was so impressed he bought two machines for Buckingham Palace and Windsor Castle.

As a result it became fashionable for society ladies to hold "vacuum-cleaner parties", on the same lines as Tupperware parties, at which the machines were demonstrated by Mr Booth's handsome salesmen.

In 1908 Hoover produced a portable upright cleaner and took over the domestic market – but by then you couldn't see Hubert Cecil Booth for dust . . .

26th
FEBRUARY

"Cor blast, tha' Horatio, he's a Good ol' Boy"

Lord Nelson's native county of Norfolk has honoured its most famous son in many ways, from erecting its own Nelson's Column at Great Yarmouth to naming pubs the Lord Nelson, or more simply, The Hero. But there is a notable example of Nelson reciprocating this affection, and honouring his native county. A Spanish naval officer's sword is on display in the Guildhall in Norwich, together with the letter which the then Captain Nelson sent to the Lord Mayor on this day in 1797.

Nelson was one of Sir John Jervis's captains at the Battle of Cape St Vincent. The much larger Spanish fleet was routed, and Nelson received the surrender of one of the captured ships. Its commander, in accordance with tradition, handed over his ceremonial sword.

*FEBRUARY 26TH
A Spanish rear-
admiral surrenders
his sword to Nelson –
who passed it on
to the Lord Mayor
of Norwich in his
native Norfolk*

This left Nelson with an extra ship, which was useful, and an extra ceremonial sword, which was not. Twelve days after the battle he sent it to the Lord Mayor of Norwich with this letter:

"Sir. Having the good fortune on the most glorious 15th February to become possessed of the sword of the Spanish Rear Admiral Don Xavier Francesco Wintheysen, in the way set forth in the paper transmitted herewith, and being Born in the County of Norfolk, I beg leave to present the sword to the City of Norwich, in order of its being preserved as a memorial of this event, and of my affection for my native county."

As they do say thereabouts – "He's a good ol' boy."

27th
FEBRUARY

The end of "The Most Haunted House" – or is it?

Borley Rectory in Essex, once described as the most haunted house in England, burned down on this day in 1939 – to the considerable relief, one imagines, of everybody concerned. It was built in 1863 across the route which a ghostly nun took on her regular outings, and she was obviously irritated by the obstruction. She stared through windows, wandered the grounds, and occasionally drove a phantom coach through the dining room, drawn by headless horses.

The psychic investigator Harry Price stayed at the Rectory in 1929, and the nun helpfully threw vases around, wrote messages, extracted keys from keyholes, and – less helpfully – hurled a candlestick at Mr Price's head. Borley Rectory's reputation was firmly established.

Successive rectors finally gave up trying

to live there, and Harry Price held another seance in the empty house on March 27th, 1938, at which a spirit voice announced that the Rectory would burn down that night. It did burn down when a lamp unaccountably fell off a table – exactly eleven months later.

That was not quite the end of the story. After the fire three passersby paused at the gate to look at the ruins – "and out of

nowhere came the most evil, filthy presence. We were surrounded by a moisty, misty something, which hid us from each other and terrified us."

Has the nun turned nasty?

28th
FEBRUARY

Another Great Idea for Solving the Irish Problem . . .

The institution of the Order of St Patrick, on this day in 1783, was one of countless attempts over the centuries to mollify the Irish. "It was prompted," wrote one historian, "by the recent appearances of a national Irish spirit which would no longer sit patiently under neglect and mismanagement."

FEBRUARY 27TH Borley Rectory was called "the most haunted house in England". Even after it burned down, there was "a most evil, filthy presence"

So instead of ending the neglect and mismanagement, the British Government decided to flatter some of the Irish peers by giving them an elegant new Order, complete with ceremonial dress and insignia on similar lines to the Order of the Garter. Its motto, optimistically, was "Quis Separabit?"

The Order was founded with fifteen "Companions", later increased to twenty-two. The hall of Dublin Castle was re-named St Patrick's Hall and used as their meeting place, and the principal symbols of the Order were the Cross of St Patrick, a golden harp and a shamrock. It was in fact just about as Irish as they could get. The only factor they missed out on was linking the Order with St Patrick's Day itself.

Two hundred years later the Order still technically survives. At the last count in 1968 the Order consisted of the Sovereign and two Knights – but there have been no new elections since 1924. It must go down in history as Another Great Idea for Solving the Irish Problem Which Didn't Quite Work Out.

FEBRUARY 28TH
The tattered banners of the Knights of St Patrick still hang in the cathedral in Dublin

29th
FEBRUARY

Glory Day for a Norfolk Admiral – No, not Nelson

This is an awkward sort of day, particularly for those born on it, who only have a birthday every fourth year. The prophet Job was one of them, and he "cursed the day he was born", though for very different reasons. But some believe it has been blighted ever since, not least St Hilarius, who found it anything but hilarious; he died on this day.

For Admiral Sir Arthur Knyvet Wilson, however, February 29th, 1884 was a day of glory. He was one of the few naval officers who not only won the Victoria Cross, but

won it on a Leap Day – not at sea, but in the desert. By a remarkable coincidence he was captain of the HMS *Hecla*, in which the first naval VC, Charles Lucas, was an officer thirty years before. But while Lucas saved his men by throwing a shell overboard just before it exploded, Wilson did so by holding off a horde of enemy Arabs singlehanded.

During the Sudanese campaign he served with the Naval Brigade, and his detachment was attacking an Arab stronghold at El Teb when the Arabs charged out to capture their gun. While his men dragged it to safety, "Captain Wilson sprang to the front and engaged in single combat with some of the enemy, and so protected the detachment until help came."

(Sir Arthur may also have held the record for the oldest and longest-serving naval officer. He was recalled to be First Sea Lord in the First World War, and finally retired at the age of 76. He was buried in his home town, Swaffham in Norfolk.

FEBRUARY 29TH
Norfolk has produced a number of naval heroes, but only Sir Arthur Knyvet Wilson won the VC – on a Leap Day

March

1st
MARCH

❧

Our first humble Printer was Quite Huge in Bruges

On this day in 1468 the Governor of the English in Bruges, the early equivalent of a British Consul, started to translate the "Recueil of the Histories of Troy" from the French, at the command of Margaret, Duchess of Burgundy, sister of Edward IV. It was a project which was to change his life and start a new era in communications. His name was William Caxton.

With his translation finished, Caxton was keen to have copies made as quickly as possible – certainly quicker than the usual

MARCH 1ST
Hold the front page, as William Caxton might have said. His famous printing press was in London, but it all started when he was Our Man in Bruges

copying by hand. He found a man in Bruges called Colard Mansion, who was trying out a new form of copying he had picked up in Germany and Holland, involving printing

with blocks and movable types. Caxton paid him to produce the first book ever printed in English.

Much impressed, the Governor returned home and went into business as a printer himself. It may have seemed slightly undignified for a wealthy man who had held high office to be setting type and getting covered in printing ink, but he also fancied himself as a writer, and he wanted to print his own books as much as anyone else's. So he set up his press – and the idea caught on.

2nd
MARCH

❧

"Wot, No Respect for St Chad?"

The name of St Chad, who died on this day in AD 672, came in for a certain amount of ridicule during the last World War. Anyone of that generation will remember the drawings of a bald-headed, long-nosed little chap with a question-mark growing out of his head, peering over a wall. The caption read: "Wot, no . . . ?" depending on what particular shortage we were complaining about at the time. He was the creation of the cartoonist "Chatt" – George Edward Chatterton – who adapted his nickname to Mr Chad.

Many people therefore have a rather bizarre mental picture of the real Chad, who was probably bald and may well have had a long nose, but spent little time peering over walls. He was one of England's earliest missionaries, with his headquarters at Lichfield. He became the patron saint of medicinal springs, and many pilgrims were cured at Chad's wells; the name Chadwell lives on around London and elsewhere. But according to the Royalists who defended Lichfield Cathedral during the Civil War, his powers extended further than that.

The attacking Parliamentarians were led by Lord Brooke, who tempted Providence before the battle by praying that, if his cause were unjust, he might die. He was not only tempting Providence, it seems, he was also tempting St Chad, because this happened on St Chad's Day in 1643, and after all this was his cathedral. The general had hardly got off his knees before a brace of musket bullets struck him down.

And somewhere a saintly voice may have murmured: "Wot, no respect?"

3rd

The Concerts that always have the Audience on their Feet

It is difficult to picture Sir Henry Wood without his beard, but presumably he did not have one when he was born on this day in 1869. It was certainly well in evidence when he conducted his first Promenade Concert in 1895, and it continued to be a familiar sight on the rostrum for the next half-century. These days it is immortalized on the bust in the Royal Albert Hall which gazes down imperiously – and sometimes, it seems, disapprovingly – on his successors.

Although the Proms are always associated with his name, the money for the first ones was put up by Dr George Cathcart, honorary laryngologist to the Royal Academy of Music. He lost two thousand pounds on the first season, equivalent to a hundred thousand today, but he still paid for an entire new set of lower-pitched instruments for the orchestra, to save vocal strain on the singers.

The idea of audiences "promenading" was not new. It was a common sight in the Champs Elysées in Paris sixty years before,

and a little later it was tried out in London's pleasure gardens. The difference with the Proms was that they were moved indoors.

These days, of course, they are presented under the wing of the BBC. Dr Cathcart may well have wished the Corporation had been around in 1895.

4th

The Charter that put the Penn in Pennsylvania

The Royal Charter which led to the creation of the State of Pennsylvania was granted by Charles II on this day in 1681 to William Penn, a Quaker who had earlier been imprisoned in the Tower for his beliefs. He was now authorized to establish a colony in North America.

He did not name Pennsylvania after himself, it is said, but after his father Admiral Sir William Penn, one of Cromwell's most successful commanders. Admiral Penn helped to defeat the little Royalist fleet of Prince Rupert in the closing stages of the Civil War. Later he captured Jamaica from the Spanish, and it became an English colony. As it already had a name, he had to wait for his son to start a colony from scratch before the name of Penn was immortalized on the map of the Western hemisphere.

The younger William has not, however, been forgotten in the gazetteers. The Buckinghamshire villages of Penn and Penn Street are close by the famous Quaker Meeting House and the burial ground where he was brought back home to be buried,

MARCH 3RD
Sir Henry Wood in one of his dramatic poses – but the lady violinists have seen it all before

MARCH 4TH
The Quaker Meeting House at Jordans in Buckinghamshire. William Penn is buried close by, with two of his wives and ten of his sixteen children

along with his first and second wives and ten of their sixteen children. The two villages which bear his name should be keen opponents on the cricket field – eager to establish, I like to think, which Penn is mightier on the sward.

5th
MARCH

Never mind the Whiskey – Pour us some Tin

In Victorian times it was believed that St Piran, patron saint of Cornish miners, whose day it is today, arrived from Ireland by floating across the Irish Sea on a millstone –

MARCH 5TH
The annual procession through the dunes to St Piran's oratory at Perranporth, now buried under the sand. Note the flags of Cornwall being carried by those taking part

and once that story had got around, many others crept into the legend books, as befits a good Irishman. He fed eighteen kings and their armies for eight days "with no larger provision than that which could be afforded him by three cows", and his early disciples included a boar, a fox, a badger, a wolf and a doe, in the best tradition of St Francis; when the boar died, he brought it back to life again.

Later historians discount all this, unfortunately; they say he's been mixed up with St Ciaran, and Piran actually arrived from Wales by more orthodox transport. But there is one Piran story which may well have an element of truth in it: how he made the discovery that brought prosperity to Cornwall.

He brought with him some Irish whiskey, and finished it off one night with a hermit friend. Next day he lit a fire to demonstrate the art of distilling. It was on a bed of black stones, and when they heated up, a silver liquid ran out – more precious even than whiskey. He had launched the Cornish tin-mining industry.

There are processions in his honour today, one in Truro, another at Perranporth to the site of his oratory in the dunes. After the sand buried it, a church was built by the Normans, but that is buried too. The Tynwarnhaule Cross marks the spot.

6th
MARCH

"I challenge anyone. Well, almost anyone"

The last Hereditary Grand Champion of England to challenge all comers on behalf of the Sovereign at a Coronation banquet died peacefully in his bed on this day in 1784. The Hon. John Dymoke, whose family has

Sacred to the Memory of
The Hon.ble JOHN DYMOKE,
of *Scrivelfby* in this County,
Champion of *ENGLAND*,
who performed that Service at the
Coronation of His Majefty GEORGE 3d
and whofe Body lieth interred
in a Vault near this Place:
He departed this Life March 6th 1784
Aged 52 Years.

held the title for generations, rode his horse into Westminster Hall after George III's Coronation, wearing full armour and flanked by his squires carrying his shield and lance.

The herald proclaimed: "If any person . . . shall deny or gainsay our Sovereign Lord, here is his Champion, who saith he lieth, and in the quarrel will adventure his life against him, on what day soever shall be appointed."

Then the Champion threw down his gauntlet – and crossed his fingers.

The title was instituted by William the Conqueror, who was no mean hand with a lance and shield himself, but perhaps felt he deserved a rest. Only once over the centuries has the challenge been accepted. At the banquet for William and Mary, an old woman on crutches appeared, picked up the gauntlet, threw down her own tattered glove, and fixed an hour for the contest next day.

The Champion did not keep the appointment, and nobody blamed him. In those days it was considered unwise to tangle with old women who can suddenly materialize in the middle of a heavily guarded Coronation banquet . . .

7th MARCH

He left us "Dignity and Impudence" – and Four Large Lions

The artist whose painting of a bloodhound and a Scots terrier sharing a kennel gave the English language a new phrase, with its title "Dignity and Impudence", was born on this day in 1802. Then, as now, the English doted on animals, and Sir Edwin Landseer made the most of it. As one patronizing critic commented: "His paintings provoked the same 'A-a-a-a-ah!' that resounds across the darkness of a cinema whenever a puppy or a kitten is given pride of place on the screen" – except that, in Victorian times, they really meant it.

Landseer could make even large wild animals look cuddly, and his dogs could be real tearjerkers. Few Victorian homes felt complete without "The Highland Shepherd's Chief Mourner" – a forlorn sheepdog nuzzling against the empty chair of his dead master.

His most familiar creations these days are the four lions at the foot of Nelson's Column in Trafalgar Square. He was part of a team headed by the versatile builder Sir Samuel Peto (he who built London's first public conveniences) and the sculptor of Nelson's statue, Edward Hodges Bailey. To my mind, though, the real stars of this enterprise were the fourteen stonemasons who actually built the column. When it was finished and before the statue was in place, they perched on top of it and ate their lunch, while enjoying the finest view in London – the same view that Lord Nelson has enjoyed ever since. "Dignity and Impudence"?

it, but on the long coach ride back to Kensington that evening it was jolted out of place again and had to be re-set.

Some days later, when the bandages were removed, the fracture had not mended and his arm was swollen. He became increasingly weak, in spite of some new medicaments involving powdered crabs'-eyes, and he died sixteen days after his encounter with the mole-hill.

The official cause of death was pleuro-pneumonia, but his old enemies the Jacobites gave the credit to the mole. They drank a special toast: "To the little gentleman in black velvet!"

M A R C H 8 T H
William III coming a cropper, thanks to the "little gentleman in black velvet". He only broke a collarbone, but it proved fatal

M A R C H 9 T H
A contemporary drawing of William Cobbett, perhaps planning his next scoop in the "Twopenny Trash"

8th
M A R C H

"To the Little Gentleman in Black Velvet!"

The only English king to be killed, albeit indirectly, by a mole – a real mole, that is, not a secret agent – died on this day in 1702. William III, the male half of the royal double act, William and Mary, was riding in the park near Hampton Court when his horse fell to her knees. "I tried to pull her up by the reins," he told the doctor afterwards, "but she fell first forwards and then sideways, and I fell on my right shoulder on the ground. It was odd because it was level ground."

But it was not completely level; the horse had stumbled on a mole-hill. The King only broke his collarbone and the doctor soon set

9th
M A R C H

The Earlier Hansard who preferred Twopenny Trash

The name of William Cobbett, who was born on this day in 1763, is generally linked with *Cobbett's Rural Rides*, a useful reference for travel writers who need a pithy eighteenth-century

quote about the English countryside and country towns. But Cobbett was primarily a political writer, who often ran into trouble with the libel laws and spent some time in prison.

Most notably, he was the first to publish a regular record of the proceedings in Parliament. *Cobbett's Parliamentary Debates* ran for nine years until it was taken over by Luke Hansard, printer to the House of Commons.

In due course it became known simply as "Hansard", but if we were still reading "Cobbett" it might be a lot more entertaining, because he included his own opinions of the debates as well. Instead of brief references such as "Cries of 'Shame!'" – which is as far as the staid writers of Hansard like to go – Cobbett would have printed what they really shouted, and added his own comment too: "The fellow is a liar and a villain, and well merits their opprobrium . . "

Certainly the *Weekly Register* which he published for over thirty years was so sensational at times that his opponents labelled it "Twopenny trash" – whereupon he started a new publication called *Twopenny Trash*, which sold by the thousands.

No, Mr Cobbett would not be writing Hansard today; more likely he would be editing the *Sun*.

10th
M A R C H

The First Mother's Day – but what about Mothering Sunday?

The religious festival of Mothering Sunday, on the fourth Sunday in Lent, has become

inextricably confused with the much more recent celebration of Mother's Day, which originated on this day in America in 1908.

Mothering Sunday, in pre-Reformation times, was when people returned to their mother church, and this developed into young women in service returning home to visit their mothers and take them flowers, traditionally violets. In the United States, however, Mother's Day started when a Miss Anna Jarvis, of Grafton, West Virginia, had the idea of holding a service of commemoration for her mother. All those present were given a carnation, Mrs Jarvis's favourite flower. So Mother's Day and Mothering Sunday had the common denominators of mothers and flowers, and somehow the two merged.

To add to the confusion, Mothering Sunday is also called Refreshment Sunday, because both the lessons for that day are devoted to food. The first is all about the banquet Joseph gave his brethren, the second is the feeding of the five thousand. This led to the eating of rich fruit cakes called simnel cakes, traditionally decorated with scallops – and simnel cakes became mixed up with mothers and flowers too.

As a final irony, now that every other person in England refers to Mothering

*MARCH 10TH
Mothering Sunday
should not be
confused with
Mothers' Day – but it
often is*

Sunday as Mother's Day, the Americans have moved their Mother's Day away from Lent altogether, to the second Sunday in May.

11th
MARCH

"Read (nearly) All About It" in the Courant

Britain's first successful daily newspaper was launched on this day in 1702. It was not exactly a newspaper as we know them, more of a leaflet, just a single page with two columns, but it did come out daily for six thousand issues, and it did contain news, though it was all from abroad and there was no comment column or editorial. With a humility rarely displayed by his modern successors, the editor of the *Daily Courant*, a Mr E. Mallet, gave an assurance that he would not express any opinions himself, "supposing other people to have sense enough to make reflections for themselves".

He also had an interesting explanation for the *Courant* not running to a double page. "It is confin'd to half the compass," he wrote, "to save the public at least half the impertinence of ordinary News-Papers." Which perhaps is why his paper flourished and the other News-Papers failed; Mr Mallet may have hit the nail on the head.

In due course Mr Mallet sold the *Courant* to Samuel Buckley, an established publisher with a less self-effacing approach; he later produced the *Spectator*, a much earlier version of the present magazine and never short of an opinion on almost anything. In 1735 the *Courant* was absorbed into Buckley's other newspaper, the *Gazette*, and its name disappeared; but its original location continued to be the heart of the

MARCH 11TH
The very first page of the very first daily newspaper

national newspaper industry until very recent times. Mr Mallet's premises were "Against the Ditch at Fleet Bridge" – better known today as Fleet Street.

12th
MARCH

A Saint – and a Blessing – not to be Sneezed At

Gregory the Great, or St Gregory, whose day this is, was a Father of the Church, one of the handful of early saints and scholars who set the pattern of Christian doctrine – and Christian music. It was he whose name lives on in the Gregorian chant.

He was also the first Pope to take an interest in Britain. It is said he saw two handsome fair-haired boys in the slave market, discovered where they came from, and decided that a place which produced such good-looking inhabitants deserved to know more about Christianity. He sent his representative Augustine to Britain, and for good measure, released the boys.

But this important and greatly revered figure of the sixth century Church has for me a rather particular distinction. It is believed he was the first person to say "God bless you" when somebody sneezed.

It was not just a polite reaction to cover the sneezer's embarrassment; he really meant it. In time of pestilence, a sneeze could indicate that disease had struck and was likely to be fatal. A saint's blessing in such circumstances was not to be sneezed at . . .

13th
MARCH

A First Test for Drivers: what is a Beleacon?

On this day in 1935, Britain, one of the last countries in Europe to introduce a driving test, finally got around to it – on a voluntary basis. The test became compulsory three months later. Thirty-four thousand people applied to become examiners – quite a large proportion of the nation's drivers. Just two hundred were selected – presumably those with the strongest nerves.

The Transport Minister who introduced the test was Leslie Hore-Belisha, whose name has been immortalized by the Belisha beacons he introduced the year before to indicate pedestrian crossings. The original orange globes were glass, which made them ideal targets for trophy-hunters and small

boys with stones. The current ones are plastic – and are still occasionally stolen or smashed.

The first proposed name for the beacon was "Beleacon", but a Hore-Belisha fan wrote to *The Times* urging that his name should not be tampered with in this way. It is as well, perhaps, that the first half of the minister's surname was not adopted; a Hore Beacon might give quite the wrong message . . .

14th
MARCH

The Young Men who gave birth at Suckling House

"Out of the mouths of babes and sucklings cometh forth wisdom" – and it was perhaps appropriate that Suckling House in Norwich was chosen on this day in 1927 for a meeting of young men who decided, in their wisdom, to form an organization called the Round Table. Its key factor was the age rule: no one over forty could join, and every member reaching that age had to retire whether he

MARCH 14TH
Louis Marchesi, founder of the Round Table movement, which inspired thousands of young men to "adopt, adapt, improve"

liked it or not. Its objects, in a nutshell, were fellowship and service.

The ninety men present formed Norwich Round Table No. 1. By the time it reached its silver jubilee there were four hundred Tables in Great Britain and Ireland; since then the number has gone into four figures, and the movement is worldwide.

It was not the idea of the Rotary Clubs, as many people assume, but of a young Rotarian, Louis Marchesi, universally known as Mark. When members of Norwich Rotary were asked to give a "My job" talk, Mark began: "There's just one thing I know better than anyone else in this room" – and hackles rose. But he continued: "I know what it feels like to be twenty-seven," and as he spoke, the idea crystallized of an independent organization for under-forties.

Many of the Rotarians, to their credit, were enthusiastic; others were not. It took two years and a speech by the then Prince of Wales – "The young business and professional men of this country must get together round the table" – for Round Table to be born at Suckling House.

15th
M A R C H

~∞~

The Day Mr Selfridge came to Town

Britain's first purpose-built West End department store opened on this day in 1909. Harry Gordon Selfridge, the son of a small Wisconsin shopkeeper who became a partner in the giant Marshall Field

organization in Chicago, brought his fortune to London and sank it into Selfridge's in Oxford Street. The store had a floor space of forty-two thousand square feet, which he later doubled as business boomed.

That was largely due to his imaginative publicity and advertising campaigns, which included the first radio commercial ever directed to a British audience. It was a fashion talk on Eiffel Tower Radio in 1925, organized by the aptly named Captain Leonard Plugge. Three listeners wrote in to say they had heard it.

Selfridge's main competitor was Whiteley's, in nearby Bayswater, which had been founded by William Whiteley more than forty years earlier. But that business started with a staff of three and gradually multiplied, with extra departments being added one by one. It did match Selfridge's advertising with the slogan "Anything from a Pin to an Elephant", but it never beat one Selfridge record. In 1948 a Mr Kevin Mellish queued in Oxford Street for eighteen days and one hour for the post-Christmas sales. He raised two thousand pounds for charity – and didn't buy a thing.

MARCH 15TH
Pillars of retailing wisdom. The imposing facade of the first purpose-built department store in London's West End – founded by an American

16th
M A R C H

One Norfolk Railway –
Two World Records

Tucked away in the rolling sugar beet and barley fields of North Norfolk is an unlikely double record-holder – the longest $10^1/_4$-inch narrow-gauge railway, and the smallest public railway, in the world. Its story started on this day in 1981, when a team of volunteer railway devotees, headed by Lieutenant-Commander Roy Francis RN (Retd), started work on constructing the Wells & Walsingham Light Railway.

They used the former trackbed of the British Rail line closed by Beeching in 1964. It was four miles of weeds and undergrowth, and one cutting had been used as a rubbish

MARCH 16TH
A veteran loco hauls another trainload from Wells to Walsingham in Norfolk, on the longest 10¼-inch narrow-gauge railway in the world

tip by the local Council for years, but the undergrowth was cleared, fresh ballast was laid, and twelve hundred lengths of track were put into place. As for the cutting, four days after the Council dumped its last load of refuse, Roy Francis and his team started clearing it out again, vastly helped by a digger-loader, two tipper lorries, and their drivers, all loaned by a local contractor, Ken Barnard.

Just a year later the first train steamed up the steep one-in-29 gradient through Barnard Cutting and into the record books. A regular passenger service has been running every summer since, and Commander Francis can still be found at the controls of the unique little engine, *The Norfolk Hero*. It is named after Nelson, who was born in these parts, but it is this latter-day commander who is the real hero of the Wells & Walsingham.

17th
M A R C H

The Bar with the
Underfloor Weeping

A love-sick girl called Juliet Tewsley hanged herself at Holywell in Cambridgeshire on this day in 1050, an event which might have long since been forgotten except that her gravestone is in the bar of Ye Olde Ferry Boat Inn.

Any inn which incorporates "Ye Olde" in its name can be slightly suspect, but the Ferry Boat really is Olde. It is said to date back to Saxon times, when the monks built it as a ferry house near their holy well; they may have preferred a glass of ale to holy water before they rowed across. Some records say they were selling the ale to all comers in 1068, by which time the hapless

Juliet had passed that way. She was waiting by the river to give her lover a bunch of flowers, but the inconsiderate fellow, named Tom Zoul, spurned the flowers and her too, so she hanged herself from a nearby tree. Because she was a suicide she could not be buried in consecrated ground, so they dug her grave close by the inn. Eventually either the inn was extended over it or they just ran short of flagstones, but her gravestone is now set in the floor of the bar.

Business is always brisk at the Ferry Boat on this particular day, not only because it is St Patrick's Day. Juliet, still weeping, may rise from her grave to see if her errant lover has dropped in for a drink.

The Case of the (probably) Wicked Stepmother

King Edward the Martyr was killed at his stepmother's hunting lodge at Corfe Gate, on the Isle of Purbeck, on this day in AD978. The sixteen-year-old king had been out riding and called at the lodge for a drink. While he was still mounted, a glass was put in his hand, and a dagger was put in his back.

The horse, startled by this unorthodox welcome, bolted away down the hillside, dragging Edward's body with it. Both of them mysteriously disappeared, but many months later some miraculous cures were reported in the vicinity of some reeds by the Wareham road, and Edward's body was found in a

MARCH 17TH
Customers at Ye Olde Ferry Boat Inn at Holywell in Cambridgeshire are not too worried by ye olde gravestone in the floor

MARCH 18TH
The ruins of Corfe Castle stand where King Edward the Martyr was murdered. His horse may still be around . . .

shallow grave, still perfectly preserved and bearing the wound from the dagger.

This made things a little tricky for his stepmother, who had merely announced he had died in a fall, and had put her own son Ethelred on the throne. Many historians have accused her of the murder, but nobody had the nerve to do so at the time. Her son was only ten and not ready to complain; he was, after all, Ethelred the Unready.

Edward's horse was never found, but it may still be seen on this day in the vicinity of Corfe Castle – the last key witness to the murder.

19th
MARCH

❦

Six Martyrs and a Wedding
Six Dorset farmworkers were sentenced to seven years' transportation on this day in 1834 because they had formed the first trade union and introduced collective bargaining for better wages. It had been successful for three years until the authorities found an obscure law they had broken. They became known as the Tolpuddle Martyrs, and there was such an outcry that they were pardoned two years after sentencing and allowed to return to England.

The sycamore tree under which they first met still stands – just – in the tiny village of Tolpuddle, and there are plaques on a cottage where one of them lived, and on the Methodist chapel where their leader worshipped.

They are also remembered, more obscurely, at St Andrew's Church, Greensted-juxta-Ongar, in Essex. The marriage register contains the signatures of James Brine, one of the Martyrs, and Elizabeth Standfield, the daughter of another. They were married

there in 1839 after the exiles had returned from Australia. If you find the register is inaccessible, their story is told in tapestry on some of the hassocks.

20th
MARCH

❦

A Miserable Memorial to a Misguided Man
Sir Thomas Tyrwhitt, who laid the foundation stone of Dartmoor Prison on this

MARCH 19TH
An elegant hassock in Greensted church, Essex, illustrates the romantic sequel to the story of the Tolpuddle Martyrs

MARCH 20TH
Dartmoor Prison is a reminder of an experiment using cheap labour which never quite worked

day in 1806, was an enthusiastic town planner with an eye to cheap labour. The town he planned was Princetown – or Prince's Town, as he originally called it, in honour of his friend the Prince Regent – and the cheap labour was supplied by French prisoners-of-war. He built the prison as their "construction camp"; its only luxuries were the cast-iron pillars from which they could hang their hammocks.

At one time there were nine thousand Frenchmen living there while they built Tyrwhitt's dream town – on one of the most isolated and exposed sites in Dartmoor, which the Prince Regent would probably not have been seen dead in. It had a corn mill, a brewery, a market – and of course a prison. Then to everyone's relief except Tyrwhitt's, the war ended, the prisoners went home, and Princetown virtually died.

Tyrwhitt had one more brainwave: to house poor children from London in the prison and teach them to dress flax. Nobody fancied it, least of all the children. He gave up his dream town and went abroad to die.

After being empty for thirty years, Dartmoor Prison was used to house long-term criminals. It continues to do so, a miserable memorial to a misguided man.

21st

When Archbishops and Monarchs fall out

Thomas à Becket is probably the best-known example of an Archbishop of Canterbury being killed on the orders of his sovereign, but a later archbishop, another Thomas, also fell foul of the monarch and died in a much more unpleasant way, on this day in 1556. The Martyrs' Memorial in Oxford marks the

spot where he and two bishops were burnt at the stake.

Thomas Cranmer had disavowed his Catholic faith under Henry VIII, and this naturally landed him in trouble when Henry's Catholic daughter Mary came to the throne. After months in prison, with his execution already arranged, he signed a recantation and turned Catholic again. They took him to St Mary the Virgin Church, Oxford, to be told the result.

The bad news was that the death sentence still stood. The good news was that, while he was burning at the stake, prayers would be said and a dirge would be sung in every church in Oxford.

So far, Cranmer's record for keeping faith with his faith – Catholic or Protestant – had been a little shaky, but now he made a final grand gesture. When ordered to recant his Protestantism publicly, he refused to do so. Instead, he announced that the offending hand which had signed the recantation would be the first to burn.

This time his faith did not waver. When the fire was lit around him, he plunged his right hand into the flames.

*MARCH 21ST
Another unhappy memorial, marking the site in Oxford where an archbishop and two bishops were martyred*

22nd

Art for the Nation – and a Duchess who kept her Head

Britain's first national art collection was founded on this day in 1824, when Parliament voted to spend £57,000 on thirty-eight paintings, left in the estate of a wealthy

23rd
MARCH

"We are getting weaker, and the end cannot be far"

The last entry in the diary of Captain Robert Falcon Scott was written on this day in 1912, a postscript to one of history's great heroic failures. Nearly two years earlier Scott and his companions had set off in the *Terra Nova* for the Antarctic, hoping to beat Amundsen to the South Pole. After marching nearly 350 miles across the ice they found that Amundsen had got there more than a month before.

On the long journey back they were hit repeatedly by blizzards. On March 17th Captain Oates, hardly able to walk, stumbled out of the tent to die, so his companions could travel faster, and for two days they made better progress. Then they were trapped again in their tent by another blizzard, only eleven miles from their base.

MARCH 22ND
The National Gallery, home of Britain's first national art collection – including a portrait of a Danish princess who shrewdly avoided becoming Henry VIII's fourth wife

MARCH 23RD
Captain Robert Falcon Scott, who never returned from his expedition to the South Pole. His last diary entry read: "It seems a pity, but I do not think I can write more"

merchant, John Angerstein. Subsequent purchases have worked out at a rather higher figure than fifteen hundred pounds a picture.

The collection was originally kept in Mr Angerstein's house in Pall Mall. It was re-located in Trafalgar Square in 1838, and since then the National Gallery has been enlarged four times.

Many of the exhibits are of course a lot older than the gallery. Hans Holbein the Younger's portrait of Duchess Christina of Denmark, for instance, was commissioned by Henry VIII; he had her in mind for his fourth wife after the death of Jane Seymour.

Christina, however, was not too keen, remembering how Anne Boleyn had fared. It is said she wrote to Henry saying that if she had been born with two heads, she would happily have placed one of them at the disposal of His Majesty. The King checked the portrait, saw she had only one, and crossed her off his list.

After four days, with the blizzard still raging, Scott knew it was all over.

"I do not regret this journey," he wrote, "which has shown that Englishmen can endure hardships, help one another, and meet death with as great fortitude as ever in the past. We took risks, we knew we took them; things have come out against us, and therefore we have no cause for complaint, but bow to the will of Providence, determined still to do our best to the last."

The entry ended simply: "It seems a pity, but I do not think I can write more."

24th
MARCH

The "White Waxy Solid" that went with a Bang; well, several

Polythene was discovered on this day in 1933 – and nobody knew what to do with it. Two ICI scientists, Reginald Gibson and Eric Fawcett, wanted to find out what happened when ethylene and benzaldehyde were put together under pressure. They produced a "white waxy solid" – and that was it.

Six years later another ICI chemist thought it might be a substitute for gutta-percha in insulating submarine cables. It actually did the job rather better, so it was decided to build a full-scale production plant – just in time for the Second World War.

Polythene was enormously useful for cables and radar parts, but there was a bizarre problem in manufacturing it. Unless production was stopped for a fortnight every couple of

years, the plant exploded. ICI found it was actually quicker, cheaper and simpler to let this happen and rebuild the plant with prefabricated parts rather than to lose two weeks' production, so it continued to blow up on a regular basis – after due warning of course – until a better system was devised in 1978.

Meanwhile a new use had been developed in the domestic market. The first polythene washing-up bowl was manufactured – between explosions – in 1948.

25th
MARCH

The Head that Came in from the Cold – eventually

The macabre travels of Oliver Cromwell's head, spanning three hundred years after his death, finally ended on this day in 1960, when it was buried at Sidney Sussex College, Cambridge, where he had once been a student.

MARCH 25TH Oliver Cromwell's head, after many travels, now rests in the chapel of his old Cambridge college

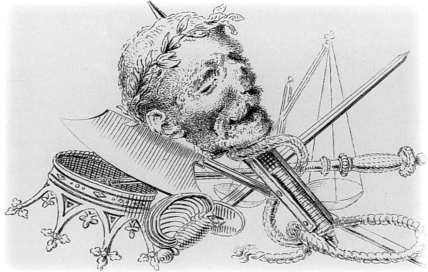

It was in 1661, a year after the monarchy was restored, that the Lord Protector's remains were dug up from his grave in Westminster Abbey and hauled on a sledge to Tyburn. The body was hung from the gallows for a day, then the head was severed, taken to Westminster Hall and impaled on a spike on the roof, while the body was flung in a pit, on the site where Marble Arch now stands.

For the next twenty-odd years Cromwell's head remained exposed to the elements on Westminster Hall, until a gale finally blew it down. A passing soldier recognized what it was – which must have been quite a feat by then – and sold it to a dealer. It passed from hand to hand among speculators and appeared in a number of museums until, mercifully, it was presented to his old Cambridge college and given a decent interment in the chapel. A discreet plaque records its presence.

that by the time it was finished, the Delaval who commissioned it had been dead for five years. Places like these earned him the epitaph: "Lay heavy on him, earth, for he laid many heavy loads on thee."

MARCH 26TH
Sir John Vanbrugh
was better at
designing stately
homes like
Chatsworth than
theatres

26th
MARCH

Maybe he should have stuck to Stately Homes

Sir John Vanbrugh, who died on this day in 1726, left some monumental memorials behind him. He built Castle Howard, the enormous country house much loved by film producers; Blenheim Palace, seat of the Dukes of Marlborough; and Seaton Delaval, the vast Palladian mansion in Northumberland which took so long to build

But this was only a part-time activity for Sir John. He was primarily a poet and dramatist, a leading figure in the Restoration theatrical world. Strangely, when he tried to combine his talents and build a theatre, it turned out to be a disaster.

In the early 1800s he persuaded thirty friends to subscribe a hundred pounds each towards a new theatre in the Haymarket; in return they got free tickets for life. That privilege turned out to be a mixed blessing – the Queen's Theatre was a very handsome building, but its ceiling was so high that the acoustics were appalling. As one critic wrote: "The articulate sounds of a speaking voice were drowned by the hollow reverberations of one word upon another."

The interior had to be rebuilt to make it usable – while Sir John went off to build another stately home.

27th
M A R C H

"Signor Marconi is very well satisfied"

The first international radio transmission was sent across the English Channel by Guglielmo Marconi – who else? – on this day in 1898. Marconi had taken out the first radio

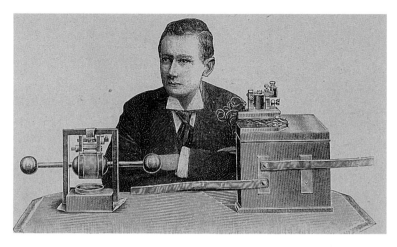

MARCH 27TH
The name of Marconi is always associated with the early days of radio, but he did not invent it, he just commercialised it

patent three years before, and he sent the first transatlantic radio signal three years later. It was his company that set up the first permanent wireless installation on the Isle of Wight, and his transmitter made the earliest regular broadcast. The name of Marconi is synonymous with the early days of radio – but he did not invent it, he just developed and commercialized it.

In fact Michael Faraday predicted the use of electro-magnetic waves in 1831, and a long-forgotten American called Mahlon Loomis was sending radio signals in Virginia in 1864.

Nevertheless *The Times* got quite excited – for *The Times* – over the cross-Channel radio link on this day, because it was used to carry a report from its Boulogne correspondent – the first news item to be sent by radio from one country to another. And their Boulogne

correspondent did Marconi proud:

"Communication between England and the Continent was set up yesterday morning by the Marconi system of wireless telegraphy . . . This message has been transmitted by the Marconi system . . . Signor Marconi is here conducting the trials and is very well satisfied with the results obtained."

As a shrewd business man with an eye for publicity, I'll bet he was.

28th
M A R C H

Viking Viragos – or a Saxon Muslim?

St Alkelda, whose day this is, was a victim of the Vikings – not the much-maligned, raping-and-pillaging menfolk, but two Viking women, who would seem to be just as heavy-handed as their husbands. It is said they strangled this Saxon princess because she would not renounce her Christian faith.

It happened near Middleham in Wensleydale, and the parish church is dedicated to St Alkelda as well as St Mary. When it was restored in the 1870s some bones were discovered which were pronounced to be hers. They were interred in the church, and by the font is a piece of the stone which is said to have marked her grave.

There is an alternative legend that Alkelda was beheaded by a tyrant called Muncius because she spurned his amorous advances – a much more routine fate for saintly princesses. On the other hand, the sceptics argue that Alkelda's name is very like the Saxon words "hal keld", meaning "well in a valley", and they point to a spring near the church.

MARCH 28TH
St Alkelda was a victim of the Vikings – not the menfolk, but two Viking women. A window in her church in Wensleydale shows them strangling her

But you could also argue that Alkelda sounds equally like Al Kadr, the night in Ramadan when Muslims say that Gabriel and the other angels descend to earth to reveal the decrees of God. Does that mean Alkelda was a Muslim?

No, I shall stick to those two Viking viragos.

MARCH 29TH
The memorial at Towton in North Yorkshire marking the site of the bloodiest battle ever fought on English soil

29th
MARCH

England's Bloodiest Battle – for Roses

The bloodiest battle ever fought on English soil took place in a snowstorm on this day – which happened to be Palm Sunday – in 1461. At Towton in North Yorkshire the Wars of the Roses culminated in this mass confrontation between the Yorkist army of Edward IV, thirty-six thousand strong, and forty thousand Lancastrians, supporters of Henry VI.

Yorkshiremen will not be surprised that the smaller force of Yorkists were the victors, but at an appalling cost. Estimates of the number who died on both sides range between twenty-eight and thirty-eight thousand.

Towton established Edward IV as king, but both he and Henry were on and off the throne, in and out of exile, and in and out of prison during the next ten years, until Henry was stabbed to death in the Tower of London. Edward, unusually for a monarch in those days, died in his bed, suffering from pneumonia.

As for the tens of thousands who died at Towton on their behalf, just a single cross on the battlefield marks where they fell.

30th
MARCH

The Winning Horse that was even Backed by the RSPCA

Anna Sewell, who was born in Great Yarmouth on this day in 1820, is the member of the Sewell family widely remembered as a children's writer, but it was her mother Mary whose children's books were far better known in her day.

Mrs Sewell did not start writing until she was sixty, but her little stories in poetry and prose, based on her Quaker background, found a new and untapped market; few writers had thought of catering for children in this way. One of her moral tales, *Mother's Last Words*, sold an astonishing million copies.

Anna started late too; she was fifty-seven when she wrote *Black Beauty*. It was not intended for children, but they loved it and sales boomed; there was not a dry eye in the nation's nurseries. I have a copy published

MARCH 30TH
The Sewell Barn Theatre in Norwich was owned by Anna Sewell's brother, and the locals may tell you this was where she stabled Black Beauty – if they see you coming . . .

in 1901, and even then it was in its fifty-seventh edition. At the last count, over thirty million had been sold worldwide. It received its final accolade when it was officially recommended by the RSPCA. But Anna never knew about all this fame; she died a year after writing it.

Did the horse really exist? The Sewell Barn Theatre in Norwich was formerly a barn owned by Anna's farming brother. The locals may well tell you this was where Black Beauty was stabled – but don't forget this is Norfolk . . .

so he published his translation of the *Rubáiyát* himself and gave copies away to his friends. His friends remained unexcited, so he unloaded the rest on a bookseller, who failed to sell them for a shilling and dumped them in his "fourpenny tray".

So much for the bad news. The good news was that the poet Rossetti was rummaging through the box when he found the *Rubáiyát*, invested fourpence and showed it to his even more influential literary friend Swinburne. It still took time to catch on, but nine years after it was first published by Fitzgerald, a publisher paid him to produce a new revised version – and it has been selling steadily ever since.

His moving finger having writ, Fitzgerald did not move on, but stayed in his native Suffolk. He was a familiar figure in Woodbridge: "a tall dreamy man, with straggling hair and slovenly in dress, wearing an ancient battered, black-banded shiny-edged tall hat, round which he would in windy weather tie a handkerchief to keep it in its place . . . in cold weather trailing a green and black or grey plaid shawl, in hot weather even walking barefoot with his boots slung to a stick . . ."

Just another average East Anglian . . .

31st

The Moving Finger Writes – but what about a Publisher?

MARCH 31ST
Edward Fitzgerald, looking unusually smart. In hot weather he liked to walk barefoot with his boots slung on a stick

The story of Edward Fitzgerald, who was born on this day in 1809, and the *Rubáiyát of Omar Khayyám* should hearten all aspiring writers. Many eventual bestsellers are rejected several times before being accepted by a publisher, but Fitzgerald never found a publisher at all –

APRIL

~

"Doorman, Hail me a Hackney, forsooth!"

On a day associated with practical jokes, a

APRIL 1ST
A tramp trying to hitch a ride, or a customer refusing to pay her fare? An intriguing scene from the early days of the hackney cab

Mr Garrard, known as "Gossip Garrard", might have been suspected of a leg-pull when he wrote from London to a friend in Ireland, one April 1st some three and a half centuries ago, to tell him that England's first taxi-rank had been established in the Strand.

"I cannot omit to mention any new thing that comes up amongst us," he wrote. "Here is one, Captain Baily. He hath been a sea-captain but now lives on the land about this city, where he tries experiments. He hath erected some four hackney coaches, put his men in a livery, and appointed them to stand at the Maypole in the Strand, giving them instructions at what rate to carry men into several parts of the town, where all day they may be had."

Captain Baily started his cab stand in 1634 with those four coaches. In three years the idea had become so popular that the number of hackney coaches in London was limited to fifty; they had to have licences issued by the King's Master of Horse.

Demand continued to increase. In 1652 the number went up to two hundred, ten years later it was four hundred. Captain Baily was on to a good thing.

Not everyone was happy. Lodging-house keepers on the main streets complained the noise was driving away their guests. Shopkeepers said their customers now drove straight past, and Thames watermen lost a lot of their trade. But the London cab was here to stay.

APRIL

~

The Only Job where you get Fired Every Day

There is one unexpected area of human endeavour in which women have been fired with more enthusiasm, one might say, than men. Being a human cannonball is not every young girl's idea of a good time, but presumably because they are generally slimmer and lighter they are better suited to being projectiles. They certainly seem to have led the field – which is entirely appropriate, since the patron saint of artillery is a woman, St Barbara.

A minor dispute exists over who achieved the feat first (though not feet first). According to one authority the first successful human cannonball (who knows how many failed?) was an American

APRIL 2ND
Blast-off time for the Human Cannonball, in the show that always went with a bang

performer known as "Lulu", who was actually a very small man called Eddie Rivers. But the first genuine woman to be blasted out of a gun was fired on this day in 1877 at the Westminster Aquarium in London – where I assume she had a safe splash-down in one of the tanks.

Her name was Zazel and she achieved a range of sixty feet. Her act proved so popular that her engagement was extended to two years, at the then substantial salary of £120 a week. And throughout her period of employment, of course, she was fired every day. . .

In spite of her explosive life-style, Zazel lived to a ripe old age. She died in 1937, sixty years after that first blast-off – of natural causes.

3rd
APRIL

His Monument lies Straight Ahead of you

Never mind Dick Whittington and his cat, the story of Percy Shaw and his cat's-eyes is just as romantic – and besides making him a fortune, it has saved thousands of lives.

Percy was the son of a dyer's labourer in Halifax who started work at thirteen, carrying bobbins of wool in a blanket mill. But he had an inventive turn of mind, and after learning welding and boilermaking he devised a mechanical pavement roller, using an old car engine, two radiators and three solid-tyred lorry wheels. Surprisingly, it worked – but his greatest success was yet to come.

He was driving from Bradford to Halifax one night, so the famous story goes, when his headlights were reflected by the eyes of a cat sitting on a fence-post, and he realized he

was heading for a sheer drop at the side of the road. Happily he survived, and so did the memory of that cat. He made his own version of cat's-eyes, with rubber pads which automatically polished the reflectors each time a car went over them.

He laid the first fifty, at his own expense,

on this day in 1934, at a notorious accident black-spot near Bradford. The accident rate dramatically decreased, and the Ministry of Transport took over.

Percy Shaw died in 1976. His monument is not exactly all around you, it lies straight ahead of you every time you get behind the wheel.

APRIL 3RD
Not the Creature from the Lagoon, just a close-up view of a cat's-eye

4th
APRIL

They stole Henrietta's Portrait – did Henrietta go along too?

Henrietta Nelson, who died on this day in 1815 at Yaxley Hall in Suffolk, made quite an impact on those who met her, as her portrait indicates – both before and after her death. She was an illegitimate daughter who was given a hard time by the family. She therefore insisted that, when she died, she should not be buried with the rest of them in the family vault, but in a mausoleum in the grounds of the Hall.

It rather spoilt the view – which perhaps was the intention – but she was left in peace until a new owner took over, who had no compunction in removing her remains to the vault and flattening the mausoleum.

This, it seems, made Henrietta somewhat restless, and she took to accompanying her portrait wherever it went. Successive owners and art galleries reported sightings, and often the portrait itself was said to change expression. One visitor was amazed by her look of disapproval and hostility, but after she had said some sympathetic words, the portrait seemed to display a kindly smile.

In October 1995 Henrietta had more cause to be irritated, and so did the portrait's owner, Mr Bryan Hall. Art thieves burgled his Norfolk home, tied and gagged him, and stole many treasures, including the portrait.

As I write, neither the robbers nor the portrait have been found. But I wonder, wherever they are – is Henrietta giving them hell?

APRIL 4TH
It is said the portrait of Henrietta Nelson can smile or glare, depending on how she feels. How does she look to you?

APRIL 5TH
John Stow was a hard-up historian who needed hand-outs from his friends. He is still handed a free quill pen each year

5th
A P R I L

"Pass me another Quill, Lord Mayor"

Each year, on or near this day, the Lord Mayor of London, or his representative, has the curious duty of giving a statue a new quill pen. He places it in the stone fingers of the figure seated on a tomb in the Church of St Andrew Undershaft, Leadenhall Street. It is all done with great ceremony. A distinguished historian gives a learned address, then removes last year's pen and hands the new one to the Lord Mayor, who passes it on to the statue. The whole procedure is called, logically enough, the Changing the Quill Ceremony, and it is in honour of the man who lies beneath the tomb, sixteenth-century historian John Stow.

Stow was a tailor by trade, and in due course became a Freeman of the Merchant Taylors' Company, but he gave up the day job to be a historian, and his *Survey of London* is a notable book of reference. Unfortunately there is less money in historical research than tailoring, and he fell on hard times.

In the last two years of his life King James granted him a Licence to Beg, which did not mean standing on street corners rattling a mug, but rather was meant to encourage his friends and admirers to help him out. Which perhaps is why, every year, they still give him a new quill pen.

6th
A P R I L

Get out of Bed, turn your Money – and Don't Look Down

The cuckoo makes its first appearance in our folklore on this day; in some parts of Britain it is considered to be unlucky to hear it before April 6th. In other areas they prefer to keep the earplugs in until their cuckoo fairs on April 14th or later, when legend has it that an old woman will appear and release the first safe-to-hear cuckoo from her basket. But once it has been heard – and the correspondence columns of *The Times* will tell you when – then the omens and superstitions come thick and fast.

It is particularly lucky, for instance, if you turn the money in your pocket when you first hear it, and particularly unlucky if you hear it in bed – presumably because you are not carrying any money. Worse still, if you are looking down at the ground at the

time, you will be dead within the year.

There are hints of course for would-be brides and grooms. If they remove their shoe at the sound of the cuckoo and find a hair inside, it will be the same colour as their future spouse's – which should narrow the field quite a bit. Also, the number of times the cuckoo goes "cuck-oo" represents the number of years before they get married. In the case of older folk, it tells them how many years they have to live.

So, what with supplying all this useful information and living up to all the other stories attached to it, small wonder the cuckoo has no time to build a nest.

7th
APRIL

That's not Santa up the Chimney – it's Dick Turpin

When Dick Turpin mounted the scaffold at York on this day in 1739, it is said that his last dashing gesture was to throw himself off the ladder, ahead of the official "drop". Far more likely, judging by his previous record, he just fell off.

Turpin was not of course the Robin Hood highwayman of legend, but a thoroughly unpleasant fellow, robbing and murdering travellers, stealing horses, and terrorizing old women in lonely farmhouses. He was finally captured, rather ignominiously, after shooting a gamecock.

Nevertheless the legends live on, not least at the Rose and Crown at Hempstead in Essex, where his father was landlord; at the Old Swan Inn at Woughton on the Green in Buckinghamshire, where he held up the coaches on Watling Street, and at the Cock Inn at Sibson in Leicestershire, where he used to hide.

Any inn must be grateful for a Dick Turpin connection – it is very good for business – but the Cock claims a particularly ingenious angle. It is said that, when pursued, Turpin would park his horse in the cellar and hide inside the chimney. A local historian reckons that is rather unlikely, since the Cock was owned by the Church at the time, and nor has any conclusive proof been found – hoofmarks in the cellar, or a highwayman's hat in the chimney. But that is what they say at the Cock, and who can prove them wrong?

APRIL 6TH
The cuckoo is so busy living up to all the stories about it, no wonder it has no time to build a nest

APRIL 7TH
The Cock at Sibson in Leicestershire, where Dick Turpin was said to hide his horse in the cellar and himself in the chimney

8th
APRIL

"You should be a Prizefighter, not a Fiddler"

The rags-to-riches-to-rags story of Jem Mace, champion bare-knuckle prizefighter and "father" of scientific boxing, who was born

on this day in 1831, would make a great film for Sylvester Stallone – if you can picture Mr Stallone as stocky, moustachioed, and with a broad Norfolk accent.

Jem, known as the "Swaffham Gypsy" because of his swarthy features, was the son of a village blacksmith. As a lad he joined in the friendly fisticuffs on the village green and developed his own boxing style, with a devastating straight left.

He also played the fiddle, and he was playing for coppers outside a Yarmouth pub when three sailors accosted him and one smashed his fiddle. Jem knocked the offender unconscious, flattened one of his friends, and the other ran away. Admiring spectators had a whip-round to buy another

fiddle, but one of them told him: "You've got more pluck and a punch in those maulies like the kick of a horse. You should be a prizefighter, not a fiddler."

Jem took his advice – and became world champion. He had over five hundred professional fights, some of forty rounds or more, toured America and Australia, made a fortune, and lost it. He had to go back to fiddle-playing outside pubs, caught a chill and died of pneumonia, aged 79. In the churchyard at Beeston in Norfolk, his home village, a marble cross "erected by a few of his old friends" is inscribed simply: "Jem Mace – Champion of the World."

APRIL 8TH
Jem Mace gave up playing the fiddle outside pubs to be bare-knuckle champion of the world

9th
APRIL

He eventually Cooked his Goose – but not enough

Francis Bacon, who died on this day in 1626, was a great scholar, philosopher and essayist – but not a terribly nice chap. When he was still a struggling but ambitious young lawyer, he was befriended by the Earl of Essex, who introduced him to influential friends and helped to launch his career. Years later, Essex was charged with high treason – and Bacon was one of the prosecuting counsel who sent him to his execution.

This singlemindedness (to put it generously) took him to the top of his profession, as Lord Chancellor under James I. In his spare time he wrote monumental learned works and books of essays, in which he made some visionary forecasts of future scientific developments. He propounded an

APRIL 9TH
Francis Bacon was a rather bad egg who cooked his goose – and had his chips

early version of the theory of the atom, and even foresaw the telephone: "a means to convey sounds in trunks and pipes to great distance".

However, in later years the other side of his character caught up with him. He was accused of taking bribes, admitted his guilt, and was declared unfit to hold any further office. He even had a spell in the Tower.

But his search after knowledge never flagged, and in the end it was his undoing. He ate a goose which had been stuffed with snow, to see if it had been preserved from decay – and died of typhoid.

The Chartists' other main project, creating idyllic rural communities for unemployed artisans, ended in failure; a Hertfordshire inn sign, "Land of Liberty, Peace and Plenty", is perhaps the only reminder. O'Connor himself ended up in an asylum. But their electoral reforms have long since become a reality, from secret ballots to male suffrage; the Tenth of April is still a date worth remembering.

APRIL 10TH
The Chartists had good ideas for electoral reform, but their "model villages" failed; just a pub sign survives

10th
APRIL

The March that Never Was – but it Worked

The Americans celebrate the Fourth of July, the French have the Fourteenth of July (Bastille Day), and in 1848 it looked as if the English might have an equivalent date to spell out, the Tenth of April. Or so the Government feared when it took quite extraordinary measures to protect the Palace of Westminster from a march bringing a monster petition for electoral reform. A large body of troops garrisoned the Houses of Parliament and other public buildings, cannon were drawn up on Westminster Bridge, and hundreds of civilians were sworn in as special constables to patrol the streets.

Actually the suspected revolutionaries were a fairly harmless group called the Chartists. Their leader, Feargus O'Connor, an Irish MP with a sense of humour, saw all these preparations and sent the petition in three taxi-cabs instead. What might have been a pitched battle in the heart of London ended in farce.

11th
APRIL

Back-paddling across the Channel – in a Blue Serge Suit

Captain Matthew Webb is credited in the record books with being the first man to swim the English Channel, but in fact Captain Paul Boyton beat him to it by four months – and he crossed the Channel on his back. (Rumour has it that a French prisoner swam from England to France and freedom about sixty years before; but that's another story.) Admittedly Captain Boyton was not entirely unaided; he had a small sail mounted in a socket attached to his foot, and a steering paddle to use as a rudder. But apart from that he did cross the Channel under his own steam, back-paddling with his hands, and he received the personal congratulations of Queen Victoria, who happened to be on the Isle of Wight at the time.

Captain Boyton was a member of the United States Atlantic Life Saving Service, and his exploit was partly to publicize an inflatable life-saving suit. To demonstrate that it was waterproof as well as buoyant, he wore an ordinary blue serge suit underneath.

He set off from Boulogne on this day in 1875, and was met halfway across by the steamer *Prince Ernst*, laden with journalists, who were much impressed by the lone back-paddler. Fortified by their encouragement and helpings of beef sandwiches and green tea, Captain Boyton reach North Foreland beach twenty-four hours after entering the water. I hope, before meeting the welcoming committee, he removed his inflatable gear and greeted them in his immaculate blue serge suit. James Bond, eat your heart out.

12th
APRIL

APRIL 12TH
Richard Smith's tombstone may sweat blood today, a reminder of a mocking that proved fatal

You can have the King's Shilling – or this Pike

The lot of a recruiting sergeant was not a happy one in the early years of the eighteenth century. To start with, their favourite ploy had been exposed. In order to get prospective recruits to "volunteer", by kissing the King's Shilling, they used to buy them a drink and put the shilling in the bottom of the mug. As the mug was made of pewter, the happy drinker did not spot it until he reached the last mouthful – and the shilling touched his lips.

Which is why, so they say, pewter mugs went out of fashion and young men would only drink out of glasses.

But for one recruiting sergeant who was trying to whip up some patriotic fervour at Hinckley in Leicestershire on this day in 1727, there was another drawback: Richard Smith.

Richard was the local wag, and poked fun at him, to the great delight of the crowd. The sergeant, realizing he had no hope of recruiting Richard, or indeed anyone else, ran him through with his pike.

The lad is buried in Hinckley churchyard, and his tombstone is said to sweat blood on this day each year. But I bet nobody ever poked fun at a recruiting sergeant again.

13th
APRIL

The "Turncoat Poet" who stopped Turning – and got Fired

John Dryden, the only Poet Laureate ever sacked from the job, died on this day in 1700. His dismissal had nothing to do with the quality of his poems; he just fell out with the King over religion.

This was distinctly out of character for Dryden. While his admirers called him "Glorious John", he is also known as the Turncoat Poet. In his early days he supported the Puritans, and when Cromwell died he wrote a poem in his defence:

His grandeur he derived from Heaven alone,
For he was great ere fortune made him so

But when Charles II was restored to the throne Dryden welcomed him as "His Sacred Majesty" and was appointed Poet Laureate as a result. Then along came James II, a Roman Catholic, and the former Puritan wrote a poem praising the Church of Rome and attacking the Church of England. It was only when the Protestant William III took over that Dryden gave up trying to adjust his

religious sails to the prevailing wind, and stood firm by his Catholic faith. He lost the Laureateship to his old enemy Thomas Shadwell.

When he died, however, he was given an impressive public funeral in Westminster Abbey. But as one of his critics gently observed: "None of his poems can be called an imperishable national possession." Maybe it wasn't just his religion that lost him his job after all.

APRIL 13TH
John Dryden may well look solemn; he was the only Poet Laureate to be sacked

14th
APRIL

"SS Titanic *ran into Iceberg. Sinking fast*"

On this day in 1912 a young operator in New York called David Sarnoff picked up a faint message from the SS *Olympic* in mid-Atlantic: "SS *Titanic* ran into iceberg. Sinking fast."

APRIL 14TH
How a contemporary artist portrayed the Titanic's fatal collision

It was the only source of information at that stage, and for the next three days and nights Sarnoff stayed tuned to the frequency, picking up the names of the survivors as they were rescued from the sea, while all other radio stations in New York were closed down by order of the President. Later came the names of the missing, over fifteen hundred of them.

Nine survivors are still alive, four in Britain, two in France and three in the States. A tenth, Beatrice Sandstron, died in Sweden in 1995, aged eighty-five; she was one of three hundred Scandinavian passengers on board.

Some fallacies grew up around the disaster. The band did not play "Nearer my God to Thee" as they went down but a hymn called "Autumn". And the millionaire Jacob Astor did not joke – thank goodness – "I ordered ice but this is ridiculous". But several sources quote Lew Grade's comment about his enormously expensive flop, *Raise the Titanic*: "It would have been cheaper to lower the Atlantic."

15th
APRIL

The First Car Ride for a Corpse – in a Car fit for a King

When William Drakeford's funeral procession set off from his home in Coventry on this day in 1901, it drove into motoring history. The body was carried in the first motor hearse to appear on the streets of Britain – and the days of black-plumed horses drawing glass-sided carriages were on their way out.

Mr Drakeford had worked for the Daimler Motor Company, and his employers adapted one of their larger products for the

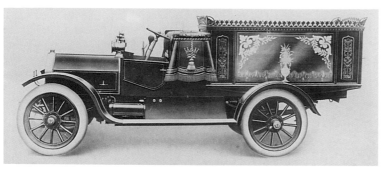

APRIL *15TH*
After a Daimler was adapted to take a coffin, the first purpose-built motor hearse was produced in 1909 for another Coventry firm, Pargetters

occasion. The *Motor-Car Journal* was sufficiently impressed to give it a special mention: "It was painted black, and the body of the car was draped with black cloth on either side, which gave it a very sombre appearance."

Daimler had already earned a place in the record books with another enterprising move. While the Prince of Wales, later Edward VII, was on a visit to Warwick Castle in 1898, the company shrewdly lent five of its cars for use by the guests, and thus when a member of the royal family was seen for the first time in England riding in a motor car, that car was a Daimler.

It did the trick; by the time the Prince became King he owned three of them. And they lasted well: one of them was entered by the Queen in the 1971 London-to-Brighton Rally.

APRIL *16TH*
Madame Marie Tussaud – but is it really her, or a waxwork?

16th
APRIL

If you want to Get Ahead, Get a Head

The woman whose wax death-masks of beheaded French aristocrats helped to found one of London's top tourist attractions died on this day in 1850.

Madame Marie Grosholtz Tussaud was taught wax modelling as a little girl in Paris, and became so proficient that Louis XVI brought her to court to teach the art to his youngest sister. With the coming of the French Revolution, her association with the royal family landed her in prison, and it is said she only saved herself from execution by modelling the heads of her former patrons – which were brought to her straight from the guillotine.

After the Revolution Madame Tussaud left France and went on tour with her waxworks collection, finally setting up her museum in London in 1838. A contemporary writer described how she would sit in the museum entrance, "a neat little figure hard to be distinguished in its calm primness from the counterfeits of humanity which it was the business of her life to fabricate."

She fabricated her last counterfeit of humanity in 1842, when she was in her eighties. It was a waxwork figure of herself.

17th
APRIL

"Sleepers awake!" – and Listen to the Sermon

On this day in 1725 a parishioner of Trysull in Staffordshire called John Rudge, perhaps fed up with the sound of snoring during the sermon, bequeathed twenty shillings a year to his church, "that a grave person might be employed to go about the church during sermon and keep the people awake."

The records show that a special stick was supplied to the successful applicant for this purpose. It had a fox's brush on one end and a knob on the other. As one historian explained: "With the former he gently tickled the faces of the female sleepers, while on the heads of their male compeers he bestowed with the knob a sensible rap." Presumably he needed to be a "grave person" to take this bizarre job seriously.

The bequest is still honoured at Trysull. Each year an entry is made in the church's accounts: "Sleepers awake: £1" – and a pound is duly handed to the verger. Happily the standard and duration of the sermons have improved since Mr Rudge's day – and anyway the rector says he is quite capable of delivering a good bellow from the pulpit if anyone starts nodding. So the pound is always returned to church funds.

However, if *your* church has a problem, why not try a stick with a fox's brush on one end and a knob on the other?

18th
A P R I L

"Psst! Want to Buy a Bridge, Guv'nor?"

Mr Ivan Luckin completed the sort of deal which is normally associated with April Fool's Day on this day in 1968: he sold London Bridge to an American.

Mr Luckin was not a master con-man but the genuine representative of the Court of Common Council of the Corporation of London. A replacement bridge had been built, and the Corporation wanted to dispose of the old one.

Over in Los Angeles Mr Robert McCulloch, head of the giant McCulloch Oil Corporation, offered $2,460,000, just over a million pounds – sight unseen. Luckin must have thought his luck was really in, and made the largest antique sale in history – ten thousand tons of it.

McCulloch had it shipped to America and re-assembled in Arizona as a tourist attraction, at a cost of another three million pounds. It was "re-dedicated", if that is the word, in 1971.

But was there an April Fool element in this sale after all? Because the story goes that McCulloch had mistaken London Bridge for the much more spectacular Tower Bridge. According to David Frost: "Instead of the picturesque Gothic towers and opening centre span which he'd thought he was buying, he'd got a perfectly ordinary-looking bridge which no tourist in his right mind would drive five miles to see."

Or is that just David having *us* on?

APRIL 18TH
London Bridge is not falling down, it is being taken down to ship to America. But did the buyer get an unpleasant surprise?

19th
A P R I L

The Primrose Path to Empire

This used to be known as Primrose Day, the anniversary of the death of Benjamin Disraeli on this day in 1881. Perhaps his greatest coup was to add the Suez Canal to

Britain's possessions by buying shares from the bankrupt Khedive of Egypt; and perhaps his most imaginative move was to make Queen Victoria Empress of India, to her considerable gratification. His ideas about Empire inspired the Primrose League; one of its main objects was "imperial ascendancy".

The League, formed after his death, was very popular during the years before the First World War; but times have changed.

APRIL 19TH
Queen Victoria sent a wreath of primroses to Disraeli's funeral – "his favourite flowers" – and Primrose Day was born

It took the primrose as its emblem because of the wreath of primroses sent to Disraeli's funeral with the note: "His favourite flowers from Osborne, a tribute of affection from Queen Victoria." April is certainly a good time for primroses, but nobody was aware of his particular liking for them; perhaps the Queen knew something they didn't.

Certainly it was she who insisted on him being awarded a peerage: he was created Lord Beaconsfield five years before he died. And it was well known that she much preferred him to his old opponent Gladstone. But Disraeli, it seems, knew just where he stood in her affections, judging by the comment he made when they both knew he was dying and she wanted to see him: "She would only ask me to take a message to Albert."

APRIL 20TH
The trial of the Tichborne Claimant, the aristocrat from Australia who turned out to be a butcher from Wapping

20th
A P R I L

~

The Claimant who lost his Case – but gave us a New Word

Roger Charles Tichborne, heir to an ancient Hampshire baronetcy and the substantial estate that went with it, set sail from Valparaiso on this day in 1854, bound for Jamaica. His ship went down somewhere off the South American coast, and all on board were feared lost, but his mother never gave up hope and offered a reward for news of his whereabouts.

Eleven years later "R.C. Tichborne" turned up from Wagga Wagga in Australia, and claimed not merely the reward but the title and the estate. Lady Tichborne was convinced he was her son, but the rest of the family – not surprisingly – disagreed. The Tichborne Claimant, as he came to be known, launched a civil law suit, but his claim was proved false; he turned out to be a butcher from Wapping called Arthur Orton.

Orton was charged with perjury, and in a trial which lasted ten months, the longest on record at that time, he was found guilty and sentenced to fourteen years' penal servitude.

There was a curious sequel to the Tichborne Case, which gave a new word to the English language. Orton was enormously fat, and years later a tiny music-hall comedian who had been very fat as a child was nicknamed Little Tichborne, or Little Tich for short. Since then, many other little people have to suffer being called a "titch".

APRIL 21ST
Charlotte Brontë –
pen-name Currer
Bell – wrote of "an
abominable spiced-
up indescribable
mess". In short,
Currer Bell thought
the curry
was hell . . .

21st
APRIL

❧

As a Food Critic too, Currer was Thorough

Charlotte Brontë, eldest of the Brontë sisters, was born on this day in 1816 at Haworth in West Yorkshire, where her father was the parson. When the three girls started writing they discreetly called themselves Currer, Ellis and Acton Bell; the Christian names had the right initials for Charlotte, Emily and Anne, but gave no indication of their sex. Many shrewd critics thought all their books were written by one person – a man.

The most famous novel by "Currer Bell" was *Jane Eyre*, but the story of Charlotte's own love life was almost as sad and romantic as Jane's. For ten years she was wooed by her father's assistant curate, the Rev. Arthur Bell Nicholls (was this where the "Bell" came from in Currer Bell?). She felt sorry for him but nothing more, and Mr Brontë sacked the poor chap for his pains.

However, they both relented; Mr Brontë reinstated him and Charlotte married him. A year later, in poor health and expecting their first child, Charlotte asked her husband to pray for her. "He will not separate us. We have been so happy." And then she died.

Charlotte's powerful emotions were not confined to her books, judging by her comment after an awful meal: "The humour I am in is worse than words can describe. I've had a hideous dinner of some abominable spiced-up indescribable mess, and it has exasperated me against the world at large!"

Egon Ronay could not have put it better.

22nd
APRIL

❧

The First Crash Course in Roller-skating

Any parents who have been badgered by their children for roller-skates must rue this day in 1823 when Robert John Tyers, a Piccadilly fruiterer, patented "an apparatus to be attached to boots . . . for the purpose of travelling or pleasure". His "Volitos" had five small wheels in a straight line, so they looked rather like wheeled ice-skates, which in fact date back to much earlier. Ice-skating was first noted by Samuel Pepys – who didn't miss much of what was going on – in December 1662: "To my Lord Sandwich's, and then over the Parks, where I first in my life, it being a great frost, did see people sliding with their skeates, which is a very pretty art."

Mr Tyers was not the first person to think of fitting wheels instead of blades on "skeates". As part of an entertainment, a Belgian musician called Joseph Merlin appeared in the ballroom at Carlisle House in London in 1760 wearing skates and playing a violin. Unfortunately he had no

APRIL 22ND
Victorian ladies
could look very
sedate on their roller-
skates (although the
top-hatted gent seems
to disapprove) but
some earlier attempts
were quite disastrous

control over his movements and skated straight into a very expensive mirror, doing considerable damage to the mirror, the violin, and himself. Thus roller-skating did not immediately catch on.

23rd
APRIL

The Garter Slipped – and got a Knee-jerk Reaction

The Most Noble Order of the Garter, Britain's highest order of knighthood, dates back to this St George's Day in 1348, when Edward III rescued a garter which had been shed by one of the ladies at a party. Her identity is not certain, but most historians plump for the Countess of Salisbury. What is certain, however, is what the King said when he noticed the nudges around him: "Honi soit qui mal y pense." And instead of embarrassing the lady by handing it back, or even trying to replace it, as some of his successors might have done, he gallantly tied the blue garter round his own knee.

The Order remains firmly male-

APRIL 23RD
The all-purpose
procession in
Stratford-upon-Avon
commemorates the
birth and death of
Shakespeare on St
George's Day

orientated. The only Lady of the Garter is the Queen, though her eldest daughter could have been if she were the heir-presumptive to the throne. Many notable commoners have been admitted to the Order, including Winston Churchill, but one who missed out was William Shakespeare, even though he managed to be born and to die on St George's Day. All three occasions are celebrated on this date at Stratford-upon-Avon.

St George himself, who is generally believed to have been a Roman officer martyred in the fourth century, probably didn't qualify for a KG anyway. . .

24th

APRIL

A Midnight Preview of the Dear Due-to-be-departed

This is St Mark's Eve, when the more ghoulish-minded would lurk in churchyards at midnight, hoping to see the spirits of those who would die during the coming year. For the full effect it was necessary to be there for three hours, on three successive years. A procession of spirits would then troop into the church – those which failed to return were the doomed ones.

At Burton in 1634 the watchers saw five apparitions, three of whom they recognized – and those three duly died. The fourth was an old man they did not know. During the year an elderly messenger brought a message for the squire, was taken ill and died too. The fifth was a baby – and sure enough, a local woman had a baby which died in childbirth.

There are local variations. At Whittlesford in Cambridgeshire, for instance, the spirits due to depart this life headed for

APRIL 24TH
In Whittlesford churchyard on St Mark's Eve the spirits due to depart this life enter their future graves. If a watcher falls asleep, he dies too. Or so they say . . .

their future graves and disappeared into the ground. And if a watcher fell asleep during the vigil, he died too.

But it is not all doom and ghoul on St Mark's Eve. This is when girls can identify their future husbands, if they missed out on St Agnes' Eve on January 20th. They must bake a Dumb Cake – in complete silence, of course – made from one eggshell-full of salt, another of flour and a third of barley meal, baked before the fire. At midnight, their lover would come and have a nibble . . .

25th

APRIL

"The Cups that Cheer" – but did he need Something Stronger?

William Cowper, who gave us "the cups that cheer but do not inebriate", died on this day in 1800 at Dereham in Norfolk. Maybe he should have drunk more tea himself, or better still, a glass of the other, because William was a sad, sad man. He had his first spell in an asylum in his twenties, then joined a religious group called the Evangelical Revival, which should have helped but merely made him sadder. They were very strong on eternal Hellfire, and the poor chap constantly worried about the welfare of his soul.

He settled in Olney in Buckinghamshire and friends rallied round. The local rector was a reformed slave trader, who must have developed strong powers of persuasion in his previous calling, and managed to rouse William into writing some comparatively

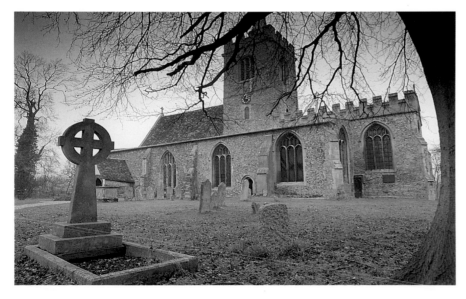

cheerful hymns. He even wrote "The Ballad of John Gilpin", a rollicking comic poem which Stanley Holloway would have enjoyed reciting. His major work, five thousand lines of blank verse under the daunting title *The Task*, was hailed by the critics.

But it all ended in tears. He moved to Dereham with his old friend Mary Unwin, but again his depression overcame him, and Mary had a stroke and died. She was buried at midnight in order not to upset him further, and when he died soon afterwards he was buried at midnight too – a sombre end to a sombre story.

26th
A P R I L

Sunday Athletics – the Idea that Ran and Ran

Sport on Sunday has been a bone of contention since the Reformation, and one of the earliest instances of the Crown giving its official blessing to a Sabbath sports meeting occurred on this day in 1569. The applicant was an out-of-work London poulterer called John Seconton, who must have had friends in high places, because a message went out from Queen Elizabeth to all mayors, sheriffs, constables and other head officers within the county of Middlesex.

"John Seconton," it said, "being a poor man, having four small children and fallen into decay, is licensed to have and use some plays and games at or upon several Sundays, for his better relief, comfort and sustentation."

The "plays and games" ranged from leaping, running and wrestling to "throwing of the sledge" and "pitching of the bar" – presumably the Elizabethan equivalent of

the hammer and the javelin. The licence stated that four or five "discreet and substantial officers" should be present – "we considering that great resort of people is like to come thereunto."

I expect they did, because these may have been our first officially approved athletics meetings. But I wonder if the four or five officers were able to cope with the "Keep Sunday Sacred" pickets on the gates . . .

27th
A P R I L

Lots of "Order! Order!" – and fewer Proposals

Six hundred and sixteen years, almost to the day, after the first Speaker of the House of Commons took office, the first woman Speaker was elected on this day in 1992 – and her earliest predecessor, Sir Peter de la Mare, would have been slightly startled to

*A P R I L 27 T H
The Tiller Girls go through their paces. Can you spot the Speaker of the House of Commons?*

know that she was an ex-chorus girl. She is of course Betty Boothroyd, Labour MP for West Bromwich, whose commanding cry of "Order! Order!" – sometimes accompanied by a wry smile – has become familiar to every television viewer.

Britain was well behind the field in appointing women Speakers, and, needless to say, a Scandinavian country was at the head of it: Miina Sillanpaa became Speaker of the Finnish Diet in 1936.

At that time we had only just got around to letting a woman loose in an aeroplane as an air hostess, although American airlines had been employing them for years. Our trailblazer was nineteen-year-old Daphne Kearley, whose qualifications had to include typing. In addition to her other duties she was expected to take dictation from business passengers and have the documents typed by the time they landed.

She also had to fend off the advances of over-amorous males under her care; she was said to have had three hundred proposals in the first year. This is one problem at least which Madame Speaker does not have to face.

I assume . . .

28th
A P R I L

Captain Cook and his Globe-trotting Goat

When Captain Cook made his historic round-the-world voyage to the South Seas he had a number of distinguished passengers on board. They included astronomers, a natural history expert, a botanist, three artists – and a goat.

It is not clear what role the goat played. As a pet, perhaps, or a ship's mascot, or in the last resort an emergency ration. But we know it was not unused to the seafaring life. This was its second circumnavigation of the globe; it had sailed on board a previous discovery ship, the *Dolphin*, under a Captain Wallis, but no details are recorded.

However, when the goat completed its second voyage and followed Captain Cook ashore, it shared in the general adulation. The King made Cook a commander and sent him off to sea again, but the Lords of the Admiralty felt the goat had done its bit, and granted it the privileges of an in-pensioner at Greenwich Hospital.

Unfortunately for the goat – though perhaps the other pensioners weren't too sorry – it died before the necessary warrant was signed, on this day in 1772. The much-travelled animal did however have the chance to wear a silver collar bearing a Latin couplet written by the great Dr Johnson:

Perpetui ambita bis terra praemia lactis
Hac habet, altrici capra secunda Jovis.

Meaning roughly: "This globe-trotting goat has been around a bit, by Jove!"

29th
A P R I L

Beecham and his Sometimes Bitter Pills

Sir Thomas Beecham, described by one of his friends as "Falstaff, Puck and Malvolio all mixed up" – his enemies put it rather more strongly – was born on this day in 1879, and became known almost as much for his acid comments as his musicianship. He was a

superb conductor, but he did not hesitate to express his feelings about those he worked with.

To one member of the orchestra he observed: "We cannot expect you to be with us all the time, but perhaps you would be good enough to keep in touch now and again." And when a new leader of the violins pointed out gently that they could not see his beat he roared: "Beat! What do you think I am – a bloody metronome?"

He was equally scathing about his fellow conductors. "Why do we engage at our concerts so many third-rate foreign conductors," he once asked, "when we have so many second-rate ones of our own?" Singers were not spared; he told one soprano her singing reminded him of a cart running downhill with the brake on. But another who was rehearsing the dying Mimi in *La Bohème* was treated more gently. After he had asked her to sing louder, she told him it was difficult to give of one's best in a prone position.

"I seem to recollect," said Sir Thomas Beecham, "I have given some of my best performances in that position."

APRIL 29TH
Sir Thomas Beecham – "Falstaff, Puck and Malvolio all mixed up". He conducted too

APRIL 30TH
The Aaron Manby, Britain's first iron steamship, apparently needed guy ropes to steady that amazing funnel – but it worked

Never mind I.K. Brunel, Spare a Thought for Aaron Manby

The imposing name of Isambard Kingdom Brunel is probably the first one that comes to mind – if you can remember it all – in connection with the early days of steamships. Among those he designed was the *Great Britain*, the first Atlantic liner to be built of iron and powered by steam, and it got a great deal of publicity; it is still revered by maritime steam buffs. But Britain's first iron steamship was built twenty-odd years earlier by a little-known ironmaster with a less resonant name, Aaron Manby. It was completed, without any great excitement, on this day in 1822.

The *Aaron Manby*, as he immodestly christened it, was built not in a shipyard but at his ironworks at Tipton in the West Midlands, about as far from the sea as you can get. It weighed 116 tons, much too large to sail along the canals and a distinctly abnormal load for a horse and cart. So Aaron transported the iron plates in sections to Rotherhithe for assembly.

After trials on the Thames to convince the sceptics that an iron steamship could float, the *Aaron Manby* made its maiden voyage across the Channel. There were no passengers on this historic crossing, it just carried in its cargo some of Aaron's best-quality export iron – in case the French wanted to have a go too.

ROYAL FESTIVAL HALL

May

The 'Appy Antics of the 'Opeful 'Oss

Of all the curious ceremonies and characters connected with May Day – Green Men and garlands, May Queens and maypoles, Morris dancers and milkmaids – the Padstow 'Obby 'Oss is perhaps the weirdest. Originally only one 'Oss paraded through the small town but about a hundred years ago a rival, the New 'Oss, began to challenge the original 'Oss on its streets.

Today the supporters of the two factions, wearing red or blue, seem equally divided and it needs careful planning to keep the two parades apart. Inevitably they become more boisterous as the day goes on but complete

MAY 1ST
The Padstow 'Obby
'Oss 'as its hannual
houting . . .

mayhem would break out if ever the two 'Osses met.

The 'Osses – strange figures shaped like mobile bell-tents six feet in diameter, with masked heads protruding – duck and weave as they follow the "Teasers" who dance in front, goading them with decorated staffs and distracting the beasts from capturing maidens underneath their enormous skirts. Legend has it that this was all part of a pagan fertility rite, and a maiden captured in this way would become pregnant. Presumably that rather depended on who was inside the 'Oss . . .

The Unauthorized Versions might have been more Fun

King James' Bible, the Authorized Version, which is still in general use, was published on this day in 1611, the work of forty-seven eminent scholars over a period of four years. Their achievement was not so much in editing it as agreeing on a final version. Jeremiah Radcliffe, Rector of Orwell in Cambridgeshire, was one of them, and if all of them looked as forceful as his effigy in the parish church does, there must have been some lively debates.

They had a number of earlier versions to work on, among them the "Breeches Bible", in which Adam and Eve "sowed figge-tree leaves together and made themselves breeches", and Coverdale's "Bug Bible", in which a psalm gives the assurance that "thou shalt not nede to be afrayed for any bugges by night". The Authorized Version has changed this to "terror by night", thus depriving the pesticide industry of a useful slogan.

MAY 2ND
Jeremiah Radcliffe,
Rector of Orwell in
Cambridgeshire,
helped to produce the
Authorized Version of
the Bible – and cut
out some rather jolly
misprints in the
process

In spite of their efforts, errors still crept in. Twenty years later, the so-called "Wicked Bible" appeared on the bookstalls. It omitted "not" from the seventh commandment so that it read: "Thou shalt commit adultery." The printers were fined £300 and went bust as a result. But their successors got their own back in 1702 with a Bible in which King David complained: "Printers have persecuted me without a cause." It should have been "princes" but the printers got away with it.

they produced the plans showing where the doorway should have been. Instead, the space had been filled by offices for the security guards. Peter Moro admitted that, because of all the changes that had been made to their original design, he had not visited the Hall for years; it was "too painful".

By now, happily, renovations should be complete, much of the clutter which had been added over the years should have gone, and the long-lost doorway should at last be in place.

3rd
MAY

The Hall that was Built "Back to Front"

King George VI opened the Festival of Britain from the steps of St Paul's Cathedral on this day in 1951, one hundred years and two days after his great-grandmother, Queen Victoria, opened the Great Exhibition in the Crystal Palace.

MAY 3RD
The Royal Festival Hall on London's South Bank had to wait over forty years to get its "front door" – at the back

The Skylon came and went, and so did many other Festival features, but the Royal Festival Hall on London's South Bank survives. It was only in 1995, however, that an enterprising arts director in charge of renovating the building discovered that it was "back to front". There should have been a large main entrance at the back of the Hall, but because of a rush to get the work finished in time for the Festival, it had been omitted.

He tracked down the original London County Council architects, Sir Leslie Martin and Peter Moro, both in their eighties, and

4th
MAY

If you can't Win at Epsom, try to come Second at Kiplingcotes

The Derby Stakes, greatest of England's five Classics and the Blue Riband of the Turf, was first run on this day in 1780. It was named after the twelfth Earl of Derby, a year after he had established the Oaks. He and Sir Charles Bunbury are said to have tossed a coin to see whose name should be attached to it; Lord Derby won the toss, but Sir Charles's horse Diomid won the race.

The Derby (which could so easily have been the Bunbury) is limited to three-year-old colts and fillies, so the same horse cannot win twice, but that does not apply to jockeys or owners. Lester Piggott was first past the post nine times during a period of thirty years, and the Aga Khan equalled the record of the third Earl of Egremont one hundred and fifty years earlier by owning five Derby winners.

These days it is run in June, and Derby Day at Epsom is a major social occasion, but they probably have just as much fun at the Kiplingcotes Derby in North Yorkshire,

MAY 4TH
Derby Day at Epsom
might have been
Bunbury Day if Lord
Derby had lost the
toss

Britain's oldest flat race, founded in 1519. It is run over four miles instead of a mile and a half, there is no formal race-course, just narrow lanes through the countryside – and under its eccentric rules the second prize is often worth more than the first . . .

5th
M A Y

For Ferrers, the First "Drop"; For the Prosecutor, just the Ticket

When the fourth Earl Ferrers was driven from the Tower of London to Tyburn in his own landau on this day in 1760 to be hanged as a felon, he notched up a "first" and a "last" in the history of capital punishment. He was the last English nobleman to be executed by

MAY 5TH
A hanging at Tyburn
was a great crowd-
puller – but that was
little consolation to
the star of the show

hanging, and the first person to be hanged by what was then the new technology. Instead of what one historian describes as "the barbarous cart, ladder and medieval three-cornered gibbet", there was a platform with a trap-door, the familiar "Hangman's Drop".

The Drop was still being used when the last criminal was hanged at Tyburn in 1783. John Austin was convicted of robbery with violence, and duly had his appointment with "the Lord of the Manor of Tyburn", as the common hangman was called. A "Tyburn ticket", however, was not a euphemism for the death sentence, but an actual ticket, awarded to prosecutors who had achieved a capital conviction. This exempted them from any duties within the parish where the crime was committed. Tyburn tickets could be bought and sold, or handed down, and as late as 1856 a Tyburn ticket-holder successfully applied for exemption from serving on a jury.

The village of Tyburn is now Marylebone, and the site of the gallows is marked by three brass triangles in the pavement at the junction of the Edgware and Bayswater roads.

6th
M A Y

He Ran into the Record Books – and then into Trouble

The four-minute mile was described as the Everest of athletics, "a challenge to the human spirit", by the first man to achieve it on this day in 1954, Roger Bannister. After long and careful planning and training, he ran the mile at Oxford in 3 minutes 59.4 seconds. It was another twenty-three years before the record was beaten by Sebastian Coe, who clipped ten seconds off Bannister's

MAY 6TH
Roger Bannister completing his record-breaking four-minute mile in 1954

time; in 1985 Steve Cram got the time down to 3 minutes 46.3 seconds.

Bannister was twenty-five when he became the first four-minute miler. Since then he has been knighted and become a distinguished physiologist, but he is still deeply interested in athletics. In 1995 he predicted that the mile would be run in 3.5 minutes – and much more controversially, he suggested that the dominance of blacks in sprint events was due to their innate biological advantages. Immediately, as one commentator put it, "he provoked a predictable flurry in the nesting boxes of Political Correctness". Sociologists attacked him for demeaning blacks' achievements, while other scientists backed him up with figures on weight–power ratios.

Talk about running on eggshells . . .

7th

MAY

MAY 7TH
The sinking of the Lusitania (on the right) is remembered in Swaffham Prior's memorial window

When they Sank the Lusitania, did they Shoot themselves in the Foot?

Of all the ships sunk by the Germans during the First World War, perhaps the most significant was the *Lusitania*, an unarmed Cunard liner torpedoed by a German submarine off the Irish coast on this day in 1915. Certainly the consequences were so far-reaching they may have altered the course of the war.

When the *Lusitania* went down, two thousand two hundred lives were lost, including those of 124 Americans. The impact on public opinion in the United States was tremendous, and many historians believe that it was this disaster that was the deciding factor in bringing America into the war.

After the war ended, the *Lusitania* remained in the forefront of many people's memories, not least the artist who designed the controversial war-memorial windows in St Mary's Church at Swaffham Prior in Cambridgeshire. Not everyone approved of the way it featured tanks, Zeppelins, howitzers, fighter planes and other weapons of war. Even the church guidebook is rather scathing: "The windows are in appalling taste, but fascinating as curios."

But the windows also depict dramatic incidents in the war, and in a prominent position, sinking majestically below the waves, is the S.S. *Lusitania* – fifty-odd miles from the nearest sea.

8th

MAY

Forget the Fur and Flora – it Started with the Stone from Hell

A lot of confusion has grown up around the famous Furry Dance, which is held on this day, or close to it, at Helston in Cornwall. It has nothing to do with fur, of course, nor indeed with flora, in spite of the Victorians re-naming it the Floral Dance. The name is derived from *feriae*, Latin for festivals or holidays, and it probably goes back to pagan times, when the month of May was a peak period for singing and dancing in the streets. On the other hand, it could also be connected with the Middle English word *ferrie*, meaning a church festival, and is not pagan at all.

Much more entertaining than all this scholarly speculation, however, is the traditional story of how Helston got its name, as well as its dance. The Devil was flying home with a boulder to block the entrance to Hell – we are not told whether it was to keep the bad guys in or the good guys out – when he was intercepted by St Michael, out on a recce. "Archangel One-Five!" the Devil may well have cried, and jettisoned his load to gain height. "Hell's Stone" dropped to earth, where Helston now stands, and it is safely preserved, so they say, in the wall of the Angel Hotel.

So the Furry Dance is held on this day with St Michael in mind – though, surprisingly, Marks & Spencer have still not cashed in on the publicity.

MAY 8TH
The Furry Dance, re-named the Floral Dance – but nothing to do with fur or flora

9th
M A Y

A Jolly Good Excuse for a Party – that's the Punch Line

Three or four hundred Punch and Judy men – or "Professors", as they prefer to be called – congregate on this day, or close to it, at St Paul's Church, Covent Garden, to celebrate the "birthday" of Mr Punch. Some Punch professors are ordained clergymen, and at

MAY 9TH
A flurry of Punches at the birthday celebrations

the service are likely to give slightly anarchical sermons in the best Punch tradition. The garden by the church is then the scene of impromptu shows and learned discourses on, for instance, how to make the jaws of puppet crocodiles function more menacingly.

The date of the "birthday" is based on a passing reference in Samuel Pepys's diaries, and it was only put in the Professors' diaries about twenty years ago, when someone discovered that Pepys wrote, on May 9th, 1662: "Thence to see a puppet play that is within the rayles there [Covent Garden], which is very pretty, the best that ever I saw, and a great resort of gallants."

And that was it. No mention of Punch by name, nor his birthday. On the other hand, it is known that the puppeteer at Covent Garden at the time was an Italian, Signor Bologna, and the play may well have been *Polichinello*, which is not too unlike Punch. The plot of the Punch and Judy Show is attributed to another Italian of that era, Silvio Fierillo, who could have asked his mate Bologna to give Punch his debut on that day.

Anyway, it's a jolly good excuse for a party.

10th

MAY

But it's the Way you Say it that Counts

When three hundred German bombers raided London on this night in 1941 one of

their direct hits was on the House of Commons. As the debris was being cleared, Winston Churchill suggested that one damaged archway should be left as it stood, as a reminder to future generations of "those who kept the bridge in days of old". It became known as the Churchill Arch.

That particular Churchillian comment had an obvious classical allusion. Others have been credited entirely to his own splendid powers of oratory, but it was not unknown for him to borrow other speakers' phrases. The famous reference to an "Iron Curtain" descending across Europe is always associated with him, but half a dozen people had already used it, from the Queen of the Belgians in 1914 to Lord Conesford just the month before. Similarly the "blood, toil, tears and sweat" which he offered when he became prime minister was adapted from John Donne's "tears or sweat or blood", Byron's "blood, sweat and tear-wrung", and Gladstone's "blood and tears".

His lesser-known *bon mot* about Blenheim Palace, however, is entirely original – so far as I know. "I took two very important decisions here, to be born and to be married." (He proposed in the summerhouse.) "I am happily content with the decisions I took on both these occasions."

MAY 10TH
Churchill wanted a bomb-damaged arch at the Commons preserved as a reminder to future generations

11th

MAY

The Prime Minister who made History the Hard Way

The name of Spencer Perceval hardly ranks alongside Walpole, Gladstone, Disraeli and Churchill in the list of most notable prime ministers, but he does have a rather special place in history. More than one prime minister has suffered character assassination, but on this day in 1812 Mr Perceval became the only one to be actually assassinated.

He was shot in the chest at close quarters in the lobby of the House of Commons. His assailant was a bankrupt called John Bellingham, who apparently bore a grudge against the British Government for failing to give him adequate

MAY 11TH
Spencer Perceval left no reminders, but made history all the same; he was the only Prime Minister to be assassinated

support when he was arrested for debt in St Petersburg.

He pleaded not guilty and said that he had nothing against Spencer Perceval personally, but that was small consolation for the Prime Minister or his family. After a trial which only lasted a day, he was hanged at Newgate.

Five days after the murder *The Times* reported that a mining engineer named John Williams had foreseen it in a dream. But that didn't do Mr Perceval much good either.

12th

MAY

Great TV – but did it spot the Bishop on the King's Robe?

The Coronation of King George VI on this day in 1937 was not only a "first" for the central figure, who had never expected to be king anyway, but also for one of his loyal subjects, Mr Freddie Grisewood, who commentated at the first major outside-broadcast by the BBC's new Television Service. Some local OBs had been made from the grounds of Alexandra Palace, where the Service was based, but these were no more complicated, or exciting, than a gentleman demonstrating golf swings, a simulated sheepdog trial, or a parade of old cars.

The Coronation produced the first really mass audience. Fifty thousand people watched, and had their first close-up of the King waving directly to them from the Coronation coach – he had fortunately been told beforehand where to look.

What the cameras did not always spot were the occasional hiccups during the service. The King noted wryly in his diary afterwards that one of the clergy in the procession fainted, and when the Archbishop held the form of service for him to read, his thumb covered the words of the oath. Finally, "as I turned after leaving the Coronation Chair I was brought up all standing, owing to one of the Bishops treading on my robe. I had to tell him to get off it pretty sharply!"

MAY 12TH
George VI's Coronation drew the first mass TV audience – but how many spotted the Archbishop's thumb covering the Oath?

13th

MAY

Garlands for the Sea God – but they didn't Work

Most tourists go to Abbotsbury in Dorset to see the great tithe-barn, dating back to the eleventh-century abbey which gave the village its name, or the famous swannery which was founded by the monks who lived there. On this day of the year, however, they can see another reminder of past glories, from the days when Abbotsbury was a notable fishing port.

This is Garland Day, when a garland of flowers for each boat in the fishing fleet was carried in procession round the streets to mark the first day of the mackerel-fishing season. The garlands were blessed, then handed over to the skippers to be taken out to sea and thrown into the waves.

The ceremony presumably dates back to pagan times, when the flowers were cast on the waters to persuade the sea god to provide more fish. Unfortunately it didn't work. The mackerel forsook this area in the early years of this century, and the fishing fleet has dispersed – but Garland Day is still observed. Instead of tossing the garlands into the sea, however, they are placed on the war memorial or in the churchyard, as a less pagan tribute to the dead.

MAY 13TH
On Garland Day at Abbotsbury the flowers were thrown into the sea to ensure plenty of fish. Alas, they didn't work – but they still make the garlands

a thought for an eight-year-old boy called James Phipps, who on this day in 1796 was used as Jenner's guinea-pig in his first vaccination experiment.

In fact inoculations with smallpox "matter" had been carried out in Britain for at least a century. The good news was that it often cured the patient; the bad news was that it made them contagious and could sometimes start an epidemic. It was banned by Act of Parliament in 1840, but by then Dr Jenner had come up with his alternative idea.

There was a tradition in his native Gloucestershire that dairymaids who caught cowpox by milking diseased cows could not catch smallpox – so he decided to test it. Enter the hapless James Phipps – whether voluntarily, or supplied by his parents for their own reasons, is not generally recorded. Jenner gave him the cowpox virus, then six weeks later inoculated him with human smallpox – and nothing happened.

This may not have been the first vaccination; a Bridport doctor is said to have

14th

MAY

Well done, Dr Jenner – but don't forget James Phipps

Edward Jenner is generally given all the credit for introducing vaccination, but spare

MAY 14TH
Edward Jenner got a statue and a place in medical history for introducing vaccination; young James Phipps just got the vaccination

carried one out successfully on a local butcher. But it was Jenner who invented the name, based on *vaccinia*, Latin for cowpox, and shrewdly publicized his results. So Jenner became famous – and James lived to be a guinea-pig another day.

15th

In the End it was the Levellers who were Levelled

In recent years a procession has taken place through Burford in Oxfordshire on this day to commemorate the execution in 1649 of three mutineers in Cromwell's army. They were supporters of the Levellers, a group of radicals who were eventually crushed by Cromwell.

The Levellers had a variety of causes, ranging from a more democratic electoral system to the restoration of common land to the peasantry. In the army they wanted a levelling of the ranks and an end to

MAY 15TH
The plaque to the Leveller mutineers who were executed in Burford churchyard, while their comrades had to watch from the church roof

To the Memory of Three Levellers
Cornet THOMPSON
Corporal PERKINS
Private CHURCH
Executed and buried in this Churchyard
17th May 1649

Cromwell's campaign in Ireland. "Have we the right," they asked, "to deprive people of the land God and nature has given them and impose laws without their consent?" They were not the only ones who have asked that question over the centuries, but their efforts came to nothing; it was the Levellers who were levelled.

The mutineers were certainly against the

Irish campaign, not for any profound ethical reasons – they just wanted to go home. They also wanted the back pay they were owed. Three hundred of them marched from Salisbury to meet comrades at Banbury, but loyal troops cut them off and defeated them at Burford. The leaders were court-martialled on the spot and sentenced to death. Cornet Thompson, Corporal Perkins and Private Church were executed in the churchyard, while the rest were forced to watch from the church roof.

And none of them ever did get their back pay.

16th

When Mary, Queen of Scots left her Luck behind

Mary Stuart, Queen of Scots, spent her last three days of freedom at Workington Hall in Cumbria, the ancestral home of the Curwens, after landing as a fugitive from Scotland on this day in 1568. Her Scottish army had been defeated by the Protestant Lords of Scotland, and she came to England to seek help from her cousin, Queen Elizabeth.

"I entreat you to send for me as soon as possible, for I am in a pitiable condition," she wrote. "If it please you to have compassion on my great misfortunes, permit me to come and bewail them to you."

Elizabeth, however, was not too keen on helping the Catholic claimant to her throne. She sent the Governor of Carlisle to arrest her and her entourage, "that not any of them escape from you until you have had knowledge of our further pleasure" – which turned out to be nineteen years' imprisonment, and execution.

17th
MAY

A Cathedral of Brick and Copper – and a Stone from Jerusalem

The first cathedral to be built on a new site in the south of England since the Reformation was consecrated on this day in 1961 – twenty-five years after the foundation stone was laid. Work had to stop on the Cathedral of the Holy Spirit at Guildford because of the Second World War, and it was not resumed until 1952.

The decision to build it followed the division of the diocese of Winchester into three parts, with two new dioceses being formed, Portsmouth and Guildford. The first Bishop of Guildford was enthroned in Holy Trinity Church, but it was considered unsuitable for permanent cathedral status. A site was chosen on Stag Hill, just outside the town, and Sir Edward Maufe designed it in what was described as "simplified Gothic",

MAY 16TH
When Mary, Queen of Scots sheltered at Workington Hall she gave her host a wine cup, "The Luck of Workington". But it seems to have run out

Before she left, Mary gave Sir Henry Curwen a small agate wine cup as a token of gratitude. It became known as the Luck of Workington and was handed down to each generation. But the Hall is now in ruins, and the whereabouts of the cup are uncertain. The last Curwen moved to Belle Isle in Windermere, then to an unknown address in London, taking it with her. Enquiries have been made, but alas – no Luck.

MAY 17TH
Guildford Cathedral was the first to be built on a new site in the south of England since the Reformation. The style is "simplified Gothic" – with a copper roof

though the Goths might be inclined to quibble. It is built of bricks from local clay, and the roof is copper. They would appreciate, however, the Bishop's throne of gilded oak, made and assembled on the spot by one craftsman.

While it was being built the crypt functioned as the parish church and was used for services. An inscribed stone brought from Jerusalem "witnesseth" this information – rather quaint wording, perhaps, for an otherwise very modern cathedral.

18th
MAY

"The Smell that Rises is no Smell of Roses"

Henry II, first of the Plantagenet kings of England, was married at Bordeaux on this day in 1152 to the Duke of Aquitaine's daughter, Eleanor. She was eleven years his senior, and twenty years later Henry still had a few wild oats to sow, it would seem, when along came a young lady who has been immortalized as "the Fair Rosamund".

Henry spotted her while she was still being taught by the nuns at Godstow, near Oxford. He was so captivated that he built a house for her near his palace at Woodstock, where Queen Eleanor was in residence. In order that never the twain should meet, he had a maze built around Rosamund's house, and it proved such a successful deterrent that he was able to father two children there, so it is said, before Eleanor found her way in, using a length of silken thread.

"The Queen came to Rosamund," wrote an early historian, "and so dealt with her that she lived not long after."

She was buried at Godstow in 1177, with a singularly unflattering epitaph which Eleanor might well have composed:

Here Rose the graced, not Rose the chaste, reposes;
The smell that rises is no smell of roses.

The evidence for some of this story is a little sketchy, but a labyrinth in Blenheim Park, not far from Woodstock, is still known as Rosamund's Bower.

19th
MAY

When the Devil Put his Hoof in it – Twice

St Dunstan, whose day this is, has been given the credit for making horseshoes lucky, and turning the Tunbridge Wells spa water red. Both achievements are connected with encounters he had with the Devil while working as a blacksmith at Mayfield in Sussex, in the days before he became Archbishop of Canterbury.

In one encounter the Devil asked him to shoe his "single hoof". Dunstan spotted who he was, tied him to the wall, and banged nails into his cloven hoof until he promised

MAY 18TH
The ruins of Godstow nunnery, where Henry II's "Rose the graced, not Rose the chaste" reposes

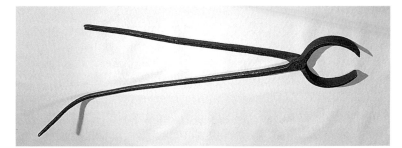

20th

MAY

The Lights all Shine for Trinity – Bar One

Henry VIII spared a moment from his matrimonial problems on this day in 1514 to grant a charter to the Guild of Shipmen and Mariners "in honour of the most blessed Trinitie" – and Trinity House was born. At first it was only authorized to ensure that qualified people piloted vessels in English rivers, but during Elizabeth's reign its powers were extended to erect "sea marks".

However, most "sea marks" or lighthouses around the coast continued to be privately owned. It could be a lucrative business; in some cases ships had to pay a toll whenever they sailed past one – even if it was broad daylight at the time. The key lighthouses at the North and South Forelands in Kent, for instance, which helped mariners avoid the Goodwin Sands, were owned by the Directors of Greenwich Hospital, and must have been nice little earners. It was not until 1816 that all were in effect nationalized and transferred to Trinity House.

Today it owns and manages a hundred lighthouses, twenty-odd light-vessels and seven hundred buoys. The notable exception is Happisburgh lighthouse in Norfolk. In the 1980s Trinity House said it was superfluous; the locals said it was not. There was a petition, an appeal to Prince Philip as Master of Trinity House, and a strenuous campaign. It all worked – and so does the lighthouse, now managed by a local trust.

MAY 19TH
St Dunstan used these tweezers, it is said, to seize the Devil by the nose – which was particularly clever, because they probably weren't made until after his death

MAY 20TH
Trinity House may not look very maritime, but it is the HQ for a hundred lighthouses, twenty-odd light vessels and seven hundred buoys

never to enter premises displaying a horseshoe on the door.

Once released, however, the Devil dreamed up a more cunning ploy. He revisited the smithy, this time disguised as a beautiful girl, and tried to lead Dunstan astray. The saintly blacksmith was not deceived, largely because of the pair of hooves sticking out from below the girl's dress, and he seized her by the nose with a pair of red-hot tongs. When the Devil was released he flew to Tunbridge Wells and plunged his sizzling nose into the water to cool it off; hence the red-tinted water and the faint smell of sulphur.

The convent at Mayfield has a pair of tongs which it is said Dunstan used. Only a spoilsport would argue that they were probably made in the twelfth century, well after Dunstan's death.

21st

The Duke who launched the Canal Age – above Ground and Below

Francis Egerton, Duke of Bridgewater, was born on this day in 1736, and he was still only twenty-five when he opened his Bridgewater Canal and triggered off the Canal Age in Britain. He had noted the success of canals in Europe and commissioned James Brindley to build one between his family's coal mines at Worsley and the customers in Manchester.

Its most spectacular feature was the aqueduct which carried it forty feet above the River Irwell. When the Manchester Ship Canal was built over a century later, the original aqueduct was replaced by a swing one, another revolutionary idea, which allowed unlimited headroom for the ships beneath.

Even more remarkable in some ways were the underground canals which the Duke installed in his mines. There was a network of them at various levels, connected by inclined planes, so the tub boats could be moved from level to level.

It was this network, not the Bridgewater itself, which most excited one canal enthusiast at the time: "Gentlemen come to see our eighth wonder of the world – the subterraneous navigation cut by the great Mr Brindley, who handles rocks as easily as you would plum pies, and makes the four elements subservient to his will."

Yes, but it was the enterprising young Duke of Bridgewater who had the inspiration, risked the investment – and made the fortune.

22nd

How Baronets got Bloodstained Hands

The first eighteen baronets were created on this day in 1611 by James I, not so much to do them honour as to do them out of some cash; each new baronet had to pay a thousand pounds to the Crown. It was the bright idea of the Earl of Salisbury, who needed the money "for the amelioration of the province of Ulster" – which has a familiar ring. When King James baulked at asking money for titles, Lord Salisbury told him crisply:

"Tush, sire, you want the money, it will do you good. The honour will do the gentry very little harm."

In addition to the lump sum, the baronets also had to be wealthy enough to provide thirty men, if called upon, to serve in the Army in Ulster – "ready to hazard life in preventing rebellion in its native chiefs".

In recognition of this Ulster connection,

MAY 22ND
The Red Hand of Ulster on baronets' coats of arms has prompted some gruesome legends

MAY 21ST
The Bridgewater Canal which started the Canal Age really did bridge water – originally it crossed the River Irwell, later the Ship Canal

they were allowed to incorporate in their arms the symbolic Red Hand of Ulster. This has caused some confusion over the centuries and all manner of gruesome crimes have been attributed to baronets involving bloodstained hands. They range from impaling a cook on his own spit to murdering an unco-operative pantry boy. They are mostly untrue – but they do make jolly good stories.

23rd
MAY

What a Pity Captain Kidd never met Perry Mason

The notorious Captain Kidd was hanged in chains at Execution Dock, Wapping, in East London, on this day in 1701, on charges of piracy and murder which have since been proved quite unjustified. He was in fact a reputable privateer, authorized by William III to attack the French and seize pirates, and it was never proved otherwise at his trial. Perry Mason would have cleared him in a trice . . .

William Kidd, the son of a Scottish clergyman, had his own ship stolen by his crew in the West Indies while he was ashore. On his return the King sent him off in a new ship, the *Adventure*, to arrest certain pirates along the New England coast.

Nothing was heard of him for two years, but rumours circulated that he had turned pirate himself, so when he showed up in New York he was sent home in chains. On the piracy charge he was accused of taking two ships owned by the friendly Great Mogul, but quite recently the Public Record Office found documents proving they belonged to the French and were therefore lawful prizes.

The murder charge related to a mutinous gunner whom he knocked down with a bucket – a not unusual incident in those days – but the man unexpectedly died. Captain Kidd has been labelled as a murderous pirate ever since.

24th
MAY

The Day Sir Henry really Rang the Bells

John Henry Brodribb, better known as Henry Irving, became the first actor to receive a knighthood on this day in 1895. He had refused the honour twelve years before, but accepted it this time because he felt his profession needed "official recognition". Theatrical knighthoods have come fairly thick and fast ever since.

Irving was the son of a hard-up Somerset shopkeeper. He started his stage career playing bit-parts in Sunderland, with no pay for the first month, then twenty-five shillings a week, all of which he sent home to his parents. By the time he was twenty-eight he had played nearly six hundred roles in the

MAY 24TH "The bells, the bells . . ." They gave Henry Irving a headache – and helped him to a knighthood

provinces, but had yet to make a real impact in London. Then came *The Bells* at the Lyceum Theatre, with Irving playing the conscience-haunted burgomaster. "The bells, the bells . . . " has been parodied often, but it made him a star. One of his American tours netted £123,000 in six months – a phenomenal figure at the time.

He was playing Don Quixote at the Lyceum when his knighthood became known. One of his lines was: "Knighthood sits like a halo round my head", to which the supporting player replied: "But Master, you have never been knighted." Amid the loud applause, I hope there was a traditional cry of "Oh yes he has!"

25th
M A Y

MAY 25TH
Charles II lands at Dover to claim his throne. He could probably do with an aspirin too

A Right Royal Channel Crossing; no Need for Duty-frees

Charles II set foot on English soil for the first time after the Civil War when he landed at Dover on this day in 1660, following what sounds like a highly convivial Channel crossing. The details were recorded faithfully by the young Clerk of the Acts of the King's Ships, who had organized the collection of the King and his family from Holland: one Samuel Pepys.

He had hastily adapted the ship on the outward journey to be worthy of its royal passengers. Under Cromwell it had been called the *Naseby*; it was rechristened the *Royal Charles*. The figurehead, representing Cromwell in belligerent pose, was replaced by a less controversial Neptune, and the austere interior was smartened up with elegant draperies and furnishings.

The work completed, Pepys had a high old time with the crew in The Hague while the royal party got ready. On one night, he reports with great honesty, he was so drunk that when he awoke he mistook the sunrise for the sunset. On the voyage itself Charles and his entourage were in equally merry mood, and there were two days of feasting and celebration until they anchored off Dover. Pepys went ashore in a boat with the King's dog, which relieved itself en route – "and which made us laugh and me think that a king and all that belonged to him are just as others are."

And thus the Restoration began.

26th
M A Y

Show me the Wey to go Home – to Portsmouth

The dream of the third Earl of Egremont to create an alternative route by water from London to Portsmouth became a reality on this day in 1823, when the final link in the network of waterways was opened, the Portsmouth and Arun Canal.

The Wey and Arun Canal, linking the two rivers, had already been completed, so

barges could sail up the Thames from the Port of London into the River Wey, head south along the Wey & Arun to Arundel, and use the new canal to reach Chichester or Chichester Harbour, where a passage had been dredged to Portsea Island. A short stretch of canal across the island then took them to Portsmouth.

Lord Egremont led a procession of decorated barges along the new canal for the inaugural celebrations at Chichester Basin. One eyewitness reported: "It was a pretty sight, the vessels being towed down with scores of people on the decks, bands playing and flags flying."

But the new route never caught on. The cost and time involved in passing through all the locks made the sea passage much more attractive, and the coming of the railways was the final blow. After just twenty-five years, sections of the canals started closing; the last commercial barge was laid up in 1888.

However, the railways have closed, the Wey & Arun is being restored by volunteers, there is deep water in Chichester Basin – so who knows . . .

Atlantic for the fastest crossing, from the French *Normandie*, and it remained with her until the American liner *United States* set a faster time in 1952.

She was used as a troopship during the war, and although she was never hit by the enemy she did collide with her escort cruiser and three hundred lives were lost.

After her "retirement" in 1967, life continued to be eventful. She was taken to Long Beach, California, and turned into a floating hotel, much patronized by wedding parties in particular – a thousand weddings a year were held in her chapel.

Although her outward appearance was little changed, a large area inside was opened up and cleared of decks to create an exhibition hall. This seemed a good idea at

27th
MAY

The Blue Riband of the Atlantic must seem a long time ago

The *Queen Mary* set sail with two thousand passengers on her maiden voyage across the Atlantic on this day in 1936, two years after she was launched by her namesake. Two years later she won the Blue Riband of the

the time, but when she changed hands and business fell off, it was found she could not be moved because she was no longer seaworthy.

Fortunately a new owner took over in 1992 and preserved her as a tourist attraction. But for the grand old lady, the Blue Riband of the Atlantic must seem a long, long time ago.

28th
MAY

What Really Happened on the Night before Sole Bay?

There is more than one account of how the British commanders prepared for the Battle of Sole Bay, which took place on this day in 1672 off the Suffolk coast. James, Duke of York, spent the previous night ashore in Southwold, at a house called Cammels, now Sutherland House, and, according to one writer, his Vice-admiral the Earl of Sandwich slept there too, although another says he spent the night on board ship.

Either way, the main attraction at the house appears to have been a sixteen-year-

old red-haired servant girl, who is said to have descended from her attic during the night to the guest bedrooms on the floor below. As a result, the Duke – and possibly the Earl, if he was there – rejoined the Fleet rather late, allowing the Dutch to sail into the bay and wreak havoc.

In the end, neither side was entirely victorious, but the Earl of Sandwich had to take to the water after his ship caught fire, and his body was picked up a fortnight later. The Duke's flagship was so badly damaged it had to be abandoned, but he survived.

And it seems the servant girl survived too – not only in legend but also in Sutherland House. On the eve of the anniversary of the battle a red-haired girl has been seen looking from the window of a first-floor bedroom, footsteps have been heard descending from the attic, doors have unaccountably opened and shut, and other strange manifestations have occurred. So what really did happen on the night before Sole Bay?

29th
MAY

The Village that wasn't Grovelly over Grovely

For Royalists this is Oak Apple Day, when they celebrate Charles II's escape in the Boscobel Oak and his subsequent restoration to the throne, but at Great Wishford in Wiltshire it has a different significance. In 1603 the local landowner, the Earl of Pembroke, closed a road to create Wilton Park and cut off the villagers' access to Grovely Forest, where they got their firewood. Far from being grovelly, they protested so strongly that their right was confirmed to gather "all kinde of deade snapping woode, Boughs and Sticks" – so long as they exercised

MAY 28TH
Sutherland House,
Southwold, haunted
by the ghost of a
red-head

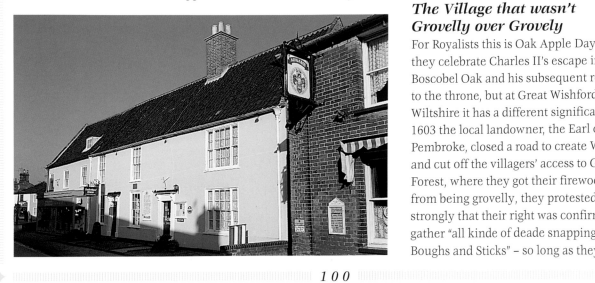

MAY 29TH
*The good ladies of
Great Wishford
celebrate their
ancient right to
gather wood from
Grovely Forest*

It has also been the tradition for four women in Victorian costume to take boughs to Salisbury Cathedral, six miles away, and indulge in much shouting and dancing before the High Altar, but these days the celebration is more muted. In Great Wishford itself, however, they let the joy be unconfin'd.

30th
MAY

"Gravedigger! Follow those Oxen!"

St Walstan, son of King Benedict of East Anglia and patron saint of agricultural workers, died on this day in 1016 and was given, at his own request, a rather bizarre funeral. Although highly born, he spent all his life labouring in the fields at Taverham in Norfolk, healing his fellow workers, giving all he had to the poor, and being generally saintly. He asked that, when he died, his body should be put on a farm cart drawn by two oxen, and he was to be buried wherever they stopped.

the privilege once a year.

So on this day, oak boughs are cut in the forest and carried through the village with triumphant cries of "Grovely! Grovely!" A banner also announces "Unity is Strength" but this sounds like a more recent addition.

Some of the wood is used to decorate the streets, and one decorated branch, called the Marriage Bough, is hauled to the top of the church tower, to bring good luck and many children to couples who are married there in the coming year.

They did pause briefly in Costessey Wood, but not long enough, apparently, to qualify as a stop, though a well sprang up on the spot. They continued to Bawburgh, a few miles south of Norwich, and legend has it that the oxen, just to make the situation quite clear, actually hauled the cart through the solid wall of the church and parked inside. More likely, the church was built later over his grave.

Here again a well sprang up, and it became a place of pilgrimage until Henry VIII stopped all that sort of thing and had the shrine demolished. A service is still held at the well, however, on or near this day.

1989 was designated in Norfolk as the

MAY 30TH
*It may look modern,
but this is where St
Walstan's body was
taken by his two
free-range oxen*

Year of St Walstan. Was it just a coincidence that Norfolk then enjoyed the best summer for a decade?

31st
M A Y

A Devil of a Way to Spend her Wedding Night

There are many tales of souls being sold to the Devil, but few more dramatic than the tale of Evelyn Lady Montefiore Carew, whose soul was sold by her scheming mother in exchange for a love philtre – and who had it claimed by the Devil on this day in 1742.

Her mother was determined to marry off Evelyn to the incredibly wealthy Sir Godfrey Haslitt of Bastwick Place, in the Norfolk Broads. Sir Godfrey, however, was notoriously impervious to women's charms, and even the lovely Evelyn failed to stir him, until her mother acquired a potent aphrodisiac for her to slip into his punch, in return for pledging both their souls.

Sir Godfrey drank the laced punch and was immediately enthralled. He and Evelyn were married in Norwich Cathedral on this day, and the wedding guests returned to Bastwick Place for the wedding feast. The bishop was due to join them, and rather belatedly a coach arrived at midnight with a figure in mitre and cope, and several cloaked companions.

When the cloaks were flung aside, skeletons were revealed, and the skeletal "bishop" flung the bride into the coach and drove off in a cloud of sulphurous smoke, still in his canonicals. As the coach hurtled across Potter Heigham Bridge it struck the parapet, smashed to pieces, and fell into the river in a fountain of flame – a spectacle which is repeated, so they say, every year on this night.

Beat that, Dr Faustus.

MAY 31ST
A peaceful holiday scene on the Norfolk Broads, but every year, so they say, a phantom coach manned by skeletons crashes over Potter Heigham bridge

June

1st

J U N E

❧

No one Ducks out of a Drink at the Duck Feast – Mr Fowle Sees to that

The Duck Feast, which is held on or close to this day at Charlton St Peter in Wiltshire, conjures up visions of fragrant roast duck, but the name originates from the Rev. Stephen Duck, an eighteenth-century cleric and scholar with local connections, who bequeathed land to the village – Duck's Acre, no less – to provide income for an annual meal in his memory.

It was originally intended for married farmworkers, but there are not so many of them about these days and the qualification has been waived. However, the three farmworkers who do attend, out of the total of thirty-two diners, are considered the only genuine Ducks. Women are admitted – but only to serve the meal.

JUNE 1ST
The current Chief Duck at Charlton St Peter's Duck Feast is happily a Mr Fowle

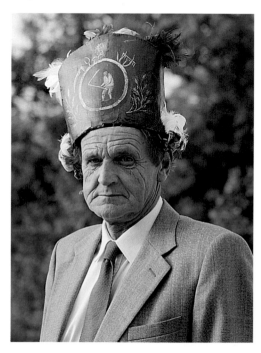

The Feast is held at the Cat Inn – there is no Duck Inn within range – and the central feature is the Duck Goblet, which has to be drained by each man present, or he pays a fine. It holds five-eighths of a pint, so much depends on its contents . . .

The toast is "To the Reverend Duck and the first Lord Palmerston". They were apparently great friends, and indeed some say it was Palmerston who gave the land. The Feast is presided over by the Chief Duck, who wears a hat decorated with duck feathers. By a happy chance, the current Chief Duck is a Mr Fowle.

2nd

J U N E

❧

The Night that Soham nearly Disappeared

Soham, a little Cambridgeshire town on the edge of the Fens where St Felix was buried in AD634, owed its survival on this day in 1944 to the courage of a little group of railwaymen who carried out one of the less publicized acts of heroism of the Second World War.

Soham lies on what used to be the London and North Eastern Railway. An ammunition train was passing through the town in the early hours when one of the waggons caught fire. The engine driver, Ben Gimbert, and his fireman, James Nightall, uncoupled the burning waggon from the rest of the train and started to haul it away, hoping to reach open country.

They had only travelled a hundred yards, however, when it exploded, killing the fireman and a signalman on duty in his box beside the track. Ben Gimbert was seriously injured, but survived; the guard on the train escaped with shock.

The explosion destroyed the station and

caused considerable local damage, but the wagon had been moved far enough along the track to prevent it affecting the rest of the ammunition train. As the citation said when the medals were awarded – one of them the George Cross: "The devotion to duty of these brave men saved the town from grave destruction."

St Felix, incidentally, had already been moved to safety – eleven centuries before. His remains were taken to Ramsey when Soham Abbey was destroyed by the Danes.

3rd
J U N E

J U N E 3RD
William Harvey demonstrates the circulation of blood to Charles I

He found out about Blood Circulating – but could he Cure the Gout?

William Harvey, the slightly eccentric doctor who stopped his gout troubling him at night by sitting on the roof in his nightshirt with his legs in a pail of cold water, died on this day in 1657, having proved and published a notable medical discovery – not just a cure for gout, but the whole concept of blood circulating in the body.

Harvey was a student at Caius College, newly re-founded by John Caius who was physician to three monarchs, and in due course he took over Caius's royal practice and became physician to the ill-fated Charles I. But he was still able to fit in his scientific studies with his royal duties, and as an old man, while left in charge of the young princes, he studied a learned book, with the Battle of Edgehill being fought not far away.

In his earlier days he would hurry home from Court to his rooms at Oxford, where a helpful professor kept hens in a bedroom for him. He was able to crack the eggs they were sitting on to see how the infant chicks were developing. Like Newton and his apple, Harvey learned a lot from the simplest processes of nature.

Incidentally his treatment for gout did work, if only temporarily. After sitting on the roof until his legs were almost frozen, "he betook himself to his stove, and so 'twas gone". But somehow it never caught on.

4th
J U N E

Jolly Boating Weather – and their Bodies between their Knees

The boys of Eton College hope for jolly boating weather on this day, while they swing, swing together, with their bodies between their knees. It makes them sound like contortionists (or something worse), but these are the words of the Eton boating song, not mine, composed for this occasion.

They are celebrating George III's birthday in 1738. First there are "Speeches", when senior boys in knee-breeches read out passages of literature, then the Procession of Boats, when the boys' boaters are decorated with flowers and period dress is worn by the crews. The dress has remained unchanged since 1814, based on the naval uniform of the day. The most impressive figure is one of the smallest, the cox of the leading boat, who wears the uniform of an admiral.

Each boat was traditionally sponsored by a Royal Navy ship, whose name and flag were adopted. The trickiest part of the procession is when the crews stand up in their boats, with their oars held vertically aloft. The coxes also stand to attention and salute with drawn swords. Compared with this balancing feat, the actual boating must seem fairly simple – as they swing, swing together with their bodies between their knees.

5th
JUNE

"The First European" – and the First Christmas Tree?

St Boniface, "the first European", Saxon monk, missionary and martyr, was killed on this day in AD755 by a band of heathen tribesmen during one of his expeditions through what is now Germany and Holland. The day is remembered throughout Europe, and particularly in his birthplace, Crediton, where the Boniface Festival is held every three years.

Boniface was actually called Wunfrith by his Crediton parents. The new name, meaning "maker of good", was given him by

JUNE 4TH
Jolly good balancing weather – Etonians celebrate George III's birthday

Pope Gregory II, who made him Bishop of all Germany east of the Rhine. He later became Archbishop and King of the Franks. And as well as introducing Christianity to a large part of Europe, he is also credited with introducing the Christmas tree.

Legend has it he chopped down the Oak of Thor, a sacred pagan tree, in front of a crowd of hostile tribesmen, to demonstrate

JUNE 5TH
Each year, beautiful Crediton church is transformed by the elaborate displays of its flower festival

that it was powerless. A fir tree grew up in the roots, and he took this as a new symbol of Christianity.

"This humble tree's wood is used to build your homes; let Christ be at the centre of your household. Its leaves remain evergreen in the darkest days; let Christ be your constant light. Its boughs reach out to embrace, and its top points to heaven; let Christ be your Comfort and Guide."

It is the wrong time of year to have Christmas trees at the Crediton Festival, but they do have a jolly good flower festival in the parish church.

6th
J U N E

Where Journey's End reached Journey's End – at the Journey's End

Robert Cedric Sheriff was born on this day in 1896, which made him eligible for service in the British Army as a young man during the First World War. As a result, he wrote a play which made the name of R.C. Sheriff familiar to generations of playgoers. He wrote other plays too, but none achieved the success of *Journey's End*.

It is entirely set in a front-line dug-out in France in 1918, and all the characters are men. This is not an obvious blueprint for success, but when he finished it in 1928 the public was ready for an honest and accurate portrayal of life in the trenches, and *Journey's End* ran for nearly two years in the West End before being played all over the world. As one critic wrote: "Few accounts of the circumstances of war are as sincerely recorded, and for that reason as genuinely moving, as Journey's End."

It also gained the rare distinction, for a play, of having an inn named after it. The Journey's End at Ringmore in Devon was originally the New Inn – which, like most New Inns, is actually very old – until Mr Sheriff moved in to write the final scenes.

The peaceful setting of the inn could hardly have provided a greater contrast to the setting of his play.

JUNE 6TH
Journey's End – a good name for a pub, and a play

7th
J U N E

Kings on a Campsite – but Butlin's was never like this

Summit meetings may still have their share of dress uniforms, guards of honour and even the odd twenty-one-gun salute, but for sheer extravagance there has been nothing to match this day in 1520, when Henry VIII crossed the Channel to have a top-level meeting with his opposite number, Francis I. Their countries had been at loggerheads and the conference was called to see if they could

JUNE 7TH
The Field of the Cloth of Gold in all its splendour – with a fly-past by the local dragon

bury their differences and form a common front against the Germans; European history is inclined to repeat itself . . .

They met on an up-market campsite in Northern France, with the two Courts trying to outdo each other in the magnificence of their clothes and accoutrements. The tents were richly embroidered inside and out, the horses could hardly move for all their elaborate trimmings, and the monarchs themselves were positively dazzling.

As it turned out, they needn't have bothered. No alliance emerged, and they all went home as suspicious of each other as when they arrived. But at least an elegant new phrase was created for the history books, to describe their meeting: The Field of the Cloth of Gold.

was given his farm, then returned to England and wrote *Rights of Man*, which advocated, among other things, the abolition of the monarchy; he was accused of sedition and exiled. In France he drafted a new Constitution for the Revolution, but then argued that Louis XVI should be spared from the guillotine; he was jailed, then deported, and went back to America a disillusioned man.

His home town of Thetford in Norfolk has a statue and a hotel named after him, but it was only in 1995 that the first Thomas Paine Day was held there on this date by the Thomas Paine Society, 186 years after his death – and even then, the Society had no local members. Poor Tom always did seem to make enemies more easily than friends.

8th
J U N E

JUNE 8TH
It looks as if he's brandishing a weapon, but for Tom Paine the pen was mightier

A Great Radical Thinker, but to many, just a Paine

Thomas Paine, the Radical English writer who campaigned for complete American independence from Britain and coined the phrase "The United States of America", died on this day in 1809 in New York, and was buried on the farm he had been given by George Washington. His bones were brought back to England, but no one knows where they are. Paine had the knack of antagonizing authority and being sacked, jailed or exiled as a result. He started as an Excise officer and wrote a pamphlet calling for better salaries; he was fired. He went to America, supported the Revolution and

9th
J U N E

The Navy Hits Rock Bottom – in every Sense

According to Naval historians, this was the day of the Royal Navy's greatest shame, the day that marked the nadir of British seapower. It was on June 9th, 1667, that the Dutch Admiral de Ruyter sailed up the Thames estuary unhindered to capture Sheerness, burn and sink many of the Fleet's finest ships, and finally take the flagship *Royal Charles* as it lay in the River Medway.

It was blamed on inadequate funding and general neglect of the Navy, under the high-living Charles II. Earlier we had done rather well against the Dutch, either defeating them or gaining an honourable draw. Then the Fleet was laid up and fell into decay, crews deserted because their pay vouchers were not honoured, morale hit rock bottom – and de Ruyter took his chance. As he sailed

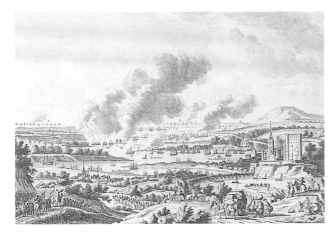

up the estuary destroying the unmanned and unprotected ships, their commander, Lord Albemarle, could only watch "with impotent rage and shame".

Samuel Pepys was watching too. He reported that the voices of English deserters were heard from the Dutch ships. They shouted: "We did heretofore fight for tickets (vouchers); now we fight for dollars!" It seems doubtful the average deckhand used words like "heretofore", but Pepys got the gist of it correctly.

De Ruyter had the Thames to himself for four days until Albemarle managed to strengthen the shore batteries sufficiently to see him off. So Albemarle got what little credit there was – plus a street named after him in Mayfair – while Charles got the blame, the Dutch got the glory – and the Navy got a very red face.

10th
JUNE

Rowing went Up-market – and the Boat Race went Down-river

The first University Boat Race was held on this day in 1829, not on the course between Putney and Mortlake which we know today, but from Hambledon Lock to Henley Bridge. It became so popular that it developed in ten years into a fullscale regatta, and when the Prince Consort became a regular patron it was called Henley Royal Regatta – and the Boat Race itself moved to a less exotic venue downstream.

This meant that the coxes no longer enjoyed a view of the splendid masks of Neptune and Isis on the side of Henley Bridge as they approached the finish line. They were sculpted by a woman called Anne Damer, who it is said had a close relationship with the Emperor Napoleon; but of course such matters are not mentioned at Henley-on-Thames.

It was more than a hundred years before women took part in the Boat Race. Susan Brown launched the new era when she coxed the winning Oxford boats in 1981 and

JUNE 9TH
Embarrassing times indeed for the English navy – Sheerness is captured by Dutch forces, under the command of Admiral de Ruyter

JUNE 10TH
The finishing line for the first University Boat Race – not Mortlake, but Henley-on-Thames

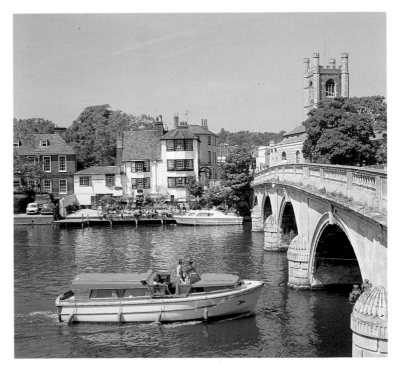

1982. Far from it being unusual for a student to take part more than once, some are around long enough to compete year after year. The record is held by Boris Rankov, either a devoted seeker after knowledge or a very slow learner, who turned out for Oxford six times. He must have been pretty good; they won every time.

11th

Hay-ho, Hay-ho, it's off to Hell we Go

Long, long ago, when Darlington in Durham had farms, a local farmworker had a very unpleasant experience on this day, St Barnabas' Day. The saint's symbol is a rake, not necessarily because he worked on the land himself, but because this is the time of hay-harvest. Indeed, this was the longest day before the calendar changed in the eighteenth century, and it used to be known as Barnaby Bright – "the longest day and the shortest night".

Surprisingly, Barnabas had a strong antipathy to anyone bringing in the hay on his day, and the Darlington farmworker was no exception. As he drove his waggon and horses to the hayfield – or possibly from it – the ground opened up beneath him, and he was sucked into two great holes full of water – waggon, horses, the lot.

The holes are still known as Hell's Kettles, and when the water is clear, the waggon and horses are said to be visible on the bottom. Alas, the water rarely is that clear, but for those determined to see them, legend has it that the farmworker conveniently reappears with his waggon each St Barnabas' Day, and re-enacts his disastrous plunge.

"Stop kicking that Football and take a Bow"

Archery has survived in England since the days when King Harold got that arrow in his eye, but there was a period when it might have died out altogether, and a royal edict had to be issued to make sure it continued. On this day in 1349, Edward III sent an "epistle" to the sheriffs of London, ordering them to proclaim that every able-bodied man must spend his spare time with a bow and

*JUNE 12TH
English archers putting their skills to good effect on the battlefield at Crécy*

arrow – "the said skill being as it were wholly laid aside".

On the face of it, this order seems astonishing. Only three years earlier, English archers had played the main role in winning the Battle of Crécy. Their arrows killed thirty thousand Frenchmen, while the men-at-arms only had to stand and watch. But then came the Black Death, and the English were more interested in keeping themselves alive than killing the French. Archery was pretty low on their priority list.

So other sports were banned by the King. Football, cockfighting, even throwing stones were condemned as "vain plays which have no profit in them"; it had to be the bow.

The ploy worked. The archers got back their skills and helped to win the Hundred Years' War. And in their spare time the English still enjoy their archery – but they play a little football too . . .

13th
JUNE

❧

Never Mind the Dancing Dog, what about Lucy?

The great treasure of Gatcombe Church on the Isle of Wight is the solid oak effigy of Edward Estur, who fought in the Crusades. It is said the little dog at his feet comes to life each summer and dances on its hind legs, which is intriguing enough. But an even stranger story than a ghostly performing dog is attached to the effigy, and to this day.

In the 1800s a beautiful young woman called Lucy Lightfoot developed an obsession for Estur's effigy and visited it daily. On this day in 1831, she tied up her mare in the porch as usual and went inside. Moments later a violent storm broke, and

JUNE 13TH
The oak effigy of Edward Estur in Gatcombe church, central figure in a strange love story spanning five centuries

there was a total eclipse of the sun. When it was over the horse was still in the porch, but Lucy was never seen again. A dagger had unaccountably been torn from the effigy's hand and lay in fragments on the altar.

Thirty-odd years later a local antiquarian found a fourteenth-century manuscript written by a fellow Crusader who met Edward Estur in Cyprus, accompanied by a woman. He and Estur went to Palestine, where Edward was wounded in the head, lost his memory, and was shipped home, quite forgetting the woman in Cyprus. She waited for him for three years, then married a fisherman and never came back to England.

Her name, according to the manuscript, was Lucy Lightfoot.

14th
JUNE

❧

The Archbishop and Chancellor who Shared the Same Skull

Simon Tybald, who combined the duties of Archbishop of Canterbury and Chancellor of England, and was equally hated in both capacities, was beheaded on this day in 1381, as one of the high points in the Peasants' Revolt. He was hiding in the Tower at the time, but they dragged him out and executed him.

As Archbishop he excommunicated John Ball, the parson who campaigned on behalf of the poor; as Chancellor he introduced a crushing poll tax on labourers which was even more unpopular than its recent counterpart. These two measures were largely responsible for sparking off the revolt, led by Wat Tyler. Tybald promptly urged Richard II to deal ruthlessly with the "barefoot rebels", and indeed the King did, but not before they had dealt ruthlessly with the Chancellor-Archbishop.

In earlier times, when he was simply Bishop Simon of Sudbury in Suffolk, Tybald rebuilt St Gregory's Church there, and after his execution his severed head was taken back to it. But it was not buried; the skull still glowers balefully at any passing peasants who venture into the vestry.

JUNE 14TH
Bishop Simon Tybald left Sudbury in Suffolk to become Archbishop and Chancellor. Only his head returned; it is still in St Gregory's Church

15th
JUNE

"The Fleet's Lit Up!" – and so of course was Tommy

For thousands of BBC listeners the celebrations following the Coronation of George VI were greatly enlivened on this night in 1937 when Lieutenant-Commander Thomas Woodrooffe uttered into the microphone, with a certain lack of clarity, the phrase which earned him a special place in the annals of broadcasting: "The Fleet's lit up!"

Indeed it was. The Navy had assembled at Spithead for a royal review and the illuminations looked spectacular. Unfortunately Tommy Woodrooffe had been

entertained a little too liberally on board his old ship, and was manifestly illuminated too. After he had repeated the phrase a few times, with increasing conviction but less and less coherence, London faded him out – and Fleet Street had a field day.

The BBC was still under the austere control of Sir John Reith, and nothing like this had ever happened before – though it has occasionally happened since. The official excuse was "technical difficulties" but nobody was deceived. Woodrooffe, normally a very competent broadcaster, was suspended for six weeks and gently vanished into obscurity, but he has not been forgotten. How many BBC men since have thought, "There but for the grace of God . . ."?

I know at least one . . .

16th
JUNE

Did Lord Lovell Die – or did he do a Lord Lucan?

The Battle of Stoke in Nottinghamshire on this day in 1487 marked the end of Lambert Simnel's bid to take the throne from Henry VII on the grounds that he was the rightful successor to Richard III. On the losing side was Francis, first and last Viscount Lovell. He had supported Richard and escaped to the Continent after the Battle of Bosworth. After the Battle of Stoke he escaped again, this time – so it is said – to the family seat at Minster Lovell in Oxfordshire, only to meet a much more unpleasant end than a quick death on the battlefield.

He hid in a secret room at

JUNE 16TH
The ruins of Minster Lovell Hall in Oxfordshire, where a skeleton was found in a secret chamber. Was it Lord Lovell or just a stand-in?

Minster Lovell Hall, giving a faithful servant the key with instructions to keep him fed and watered until things quietened down. Some say the servant died and the key was lost, others that he was not all that faithful after all. Either way, Lord Lovell was left inside with the door locked. When work was being done on the Hall in 1708, a skeleton was discovered in the secret room.

That is the story, but it may only have been developed to explain the skeleton. The bones disintegrated before they could be identified, and even the secret room does not exist any more; the Hall has been in ruins for years.

It is equally possible that Lord Lovell escaped to the Continent for a second time, and successfully disappeared. If my name was Lovell, I think I'd check my family tree for a French connection.

17th
J U N E

He was Martyred – but still Held his Head High

St Nectan, whose day this is, landed near Hartland Point in North Devon during the sixth century and settled, according to ancient records, "in a valley of marvellous beauty and pleasant with the abundance of the trees which grew thickly there . . . which has in its recesses a fountain of never-failing water."

He built a hut near the fountain, "in which place is now the church dedicated in his name, in which his body was buried, and the town which is now called Stowes", and there lived an unblemished life, making many converts. But his real fame came after his death. When his two cows were stolen he pursued the robbers, hoping perhaps to

JUNE 17TH
St Nectan's Glen, where the saint laid his head – after he was beheaded

convert them as well as retrieve the cows, but instead they cut off his head.

"Then the venerable martyr of Christ, taking his head in his own hands, carried it for about half a mile to the fountain where he lived, and there laid it down, smeared all over with blood, on a certain stone, and the bloody traces of that murder and of the miracle still remain marked on that stone."

The traces are not so clear these days, but Nectan's name lives on at "the town called Stowes" – now a village called Stowe – and in other parts of the West Country where his fame spread: the saint who was beheaded, but kept his head.

18th
J U N E

The Day when the Breeches Boys went into Long Trousers

The British infantry survived two dramatic experiences on this day, albeit in different years. One was the Battle of Waterloo, in 1815; the other, exactly eight years later, was the first time they wore trousers.

I hasten to say that they did not fight at Waterloo naked below the waist. The trousers were "in lieu of other nether garments" – normally breeches with coloured stockings, leggings or gaiters. That did not apply of course to the Scottish regiments, who sartorially, as in other ways, were a law unto themselves.

In 1823 the Duke of York, as commander-in-chief, issued the following fashion guide to his men: "His Majesty has been pleased to approve of the discontinuance of breeches, leggings and shoes as part of the clothing of the infantry soldier, and of blue-grey cloth trousers and half-boots being substituted."

I hope Sergeant William Dyke of Clifton Hampden in Oxfordshire was still around by then to enjoy his new trousers. He had the distinction of firing the first shot in the Battle of Waterloo, but rarely gets a mention – perhaps because he fired it accidentally. He was court-martialled as a result, but happily the victorious Duke of Wellington granted him a pardon.

machinery. But it is also the placental membrane which sometimes adheres to the heads of new-born babies, and was regarded as a sign of good luck.

It was particularly effective against drowning, which must have been good news for baby James. The bad news was an equally popular belief in those days that "he that is born to be hanged shall never be drowned". So did that mean, in effect, "out of the water and into the noose?" Actually James died in his bed from Bright's Disease at the age of 58.

As to that little problem of James One and Six (we used to call him Eighteen-Pence in the days of old money), here's a clue. His maternal great-grandmother's brother was Henry VIII. Simple really . . .

JUNE 19TH
James I was born with a caul on his head, but in later years he preferred a very tall hat

19th

Safe from Close Calls – because he had a Close Caul

When baby James was born to Mary, Queen of Scots and Lord Darnley on this day in 1566, he was destined to become not only a headache for history pupils – how many of us can explain off-hand how he was simultaneously James VI of Scotland and James I of England? – but also a very good swimmer. Or so one presumes, because he was born with a caul on his head, which traditionally meant he would never drown.

A caul was originally a snood, which we would now call a hairnet, very popular during the last war among women factory-workers for keeping their hair out of the

20th

The Ock Mayor is only a Mock-Mayor, but he gets the Ock's Ox

Some towns and villages used to have a mock-Mayor to lead their annual revelries, but Abingdon in Oxfordshire is the only place which still elects its "Ock-Mayor", the

JUNE 20TH
The newly installed Mayor of Ock Street

Mayor of Ock Street, on the Saturday which falls on or before this day. A voting box is put outside the Cross Keys in Ock Street, and all the street's residents are eligible to vote. Candidates are usually past or present dancers in the Abingdon Morris, though it is not an essential qualification. If the winner is up to it, however, he becomes the Squire or Captain of the Morris.

The Mayor is chaired up and down Ock Street, after being invested with his regalia, which includes a sash, a sword, a collecting-box (always useful) and the Ock Street Horns. Tradition has it that in 1700 a farmer confusingly called Morris – not the originator of the Morris dancers, who were around much earlier – presented a black ox for the town to roast, and a fight started over who should have the horns.

The men of Ock Street, apparently a belligerent lot, challenged the rest, and a very unpleasant free-for-all ensued, involving sticks, stones and blazing torches. Ock Street carried off the horns, and they have been Ock's Ox ever since. These days, happily, the horns are a signal for dancing instead of fighting.

21st
JUNE

"A Pretty Staggering Count for a Victorian Spinster" – by George!

One might think that any woman reputed to have had four sexual liaisons, three serious flirtations and one failed love affair before running away with a married man and then, when he died, marrying a man twenty years her junior, would be rather proud of her attractiveness, and her womanhood. But Mary Anne Evans described herself as "a withered cabbage in a flower garden", and

when she started writing she assumed a man's name. Today the George Eliot Society gathers in Westminster Abbey around her memorial stone to lay a wreath and read from her works.

This aspect of her private life is not likely to be referred to, but as one modern reviewer comments: "It was a pretty staggering count for a Victorian spinster." He adds: "A late developer, she did not start writing fiction until she was nearing forty." Hardly a late developer, surely? Perhaps she was just too busy.

When she did start, her novels became highly successful, but her *nom de plume* did not fool Charles Dickens, for one. After reading her first published book, *Scenes from Clerical Life*, he wrote to a friend: "If George Eliot is not a woman I'll eat my hat!"

At least ten of "George's" men-friends could confirm he was right.

22nd
JUNE

Practice-bomb a Cathedral? Never let it be Cedd's

The oldest cathedral in Britain was re-consecrated on this day by the Bishop of Chelmsford, some thirteen centuries after it was built by St Cedd, the first Bishop of the East Saxons, in about AD654. It is at Bradwell-on-Sea in Essex.

The plain rectangular building, some fifty feet long and twenty feet wide, looks more like a barn than a cathedral, and indeed it was used as such for several years until it was identified; there is still the outline of the big doorway that was knocked

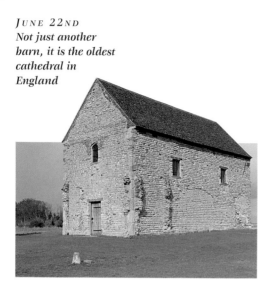

Not just another barn, it is the oldest cathedral in England

November 5th. The idea was not only to provide protection against witches and noxious dragons, which were inclined to go on the prowl on this night, but also to ensure the well-being of the sun as it reached its highest point and started its descent to the horizon over the next six months.

However, this was a little too esoteric for non-sunworshippers, and it was the anti-witch element that kept the Midsummer Eve fires burning over the centuries. The tradition is still observed in Cornwall, where a chain of fires is lit on hillsides from Land's End to the Tamar. More daring youngsters are wont to leap through the flames, if their elders don't stop them in time. Originally this was meant to purify them from the influence of the Devil; now it's just for the hell of it.

One traditional ploy for thwarting the Evil One is less often observed these days, to most people's relief. Rotting bones used to be thrown on the fire, in order to create unpleasant fumes which no self-respecting witch could bear. The "bone-fires" may have died out, but the name, slightly adapted, still survives – and back-garden bonfires can be just as exasperating to the neighbours, even without the bones.

J U N E 24TH
Mazey Day in Penzance. Purists of tradition may scoff, but the tourists love it

in the side wall so a waggon could enter. But there are still the original stones which Bishop Cedd made use of, from the former Roman fort on the site, and it is called the Chapel of St Peter's-on-the-Wall, a reminder of the Roman wall that used to stand there.

The building stands alone on a desolate stretch of the Essex coast; the wooden Saxon huts which once surrounded it have long since disappeared. It might well have disappeared too during the last war, had it not been for a fortuitous chance encounter between the rector and the local RAF station commander. The CO mentioned that his pilots were due to have a little bombing practice that day. "We're going to take out that old barn by the beach . . ."

23rd
J U N E

~

They Kept the Bone-fires Burning – and gave the Bonfire its Name
Midsummer Eve was the traditional night for lighting bonfires in Britain long before Guy Fawkes provided a counter-attraction on

J U N E 23RD
Celebrations round a "bone-fire" on Midsummer Eve

24th
JUNE

Those Hazy, Crazy, Mazey Days of Summer

The Festival of Golowan, marking this Feast of St John, was revived in Penzance in 1991

as just a one-day event, but in the next few years it developed into two weeks of celebrations which would probably quite overwhelm the simple folk who danced round their bonfire centuries ago. Fireworks, a torchlight procession, marching bands, Breton musicians and dancers from Kurdistan and Tibet, a fair on the quayside, sailing craft filling the harbour, and the Serpent dances featuring Penglas, the Penzance 'Obby 'Oss – it's all there, a triumph of tradition combined with tourism.

The main festivities are on Mazey Day, a name taken from a traditional Cornish dance, but the ingredients go far beyond that. The organizers, however, are quite unabashed:

"Purists of tradition may scoff, but unimprisoned by the past, the new Golowan has successfully and unashamedly brought together the best of the old with the best of the new, celebrating the past and the present with new imagery and ritual."

And forty thousand tourists can't be wrong.

25th
JUNE

Smooth Crossings and Smooth Lawns – Thanks to Two Tin Cans and a Hoover

In the great tradition of amateur inventors, Sir Christopher Cockerell started with two tin cans. It was the third ingredient that was different: a vacuum cleaner, which he used in reverse, to blow instead of suck.

The smaller can, with the lid removed, was fitted inside the larger one, which was open at both ends, and they were put on the nozzle of the cleaner. The nozzle was held by a clamp, facing downwards on to a pair of kitchen scales. When the cleaner was switched on, the air was forced between the sides of the two cans and blew the scales

JUNE 25TH
An early flight of
SR-N1, as visualized
by a contemporary
Italian illustrator

down until they registered a pressure of three pounds – three times as much as the vacuum's normal pressure.

The principle of the Hovercraft was born.

Cockcroft was an electronic engineer, but his hobby was building boats, and in conjunction with Saunders-Roe, famous for their flying boats, they designed another kind of flying boat which could use this form of power. The SR-N1 made its first flight from Cowes on the Isle of Wight on this day in 1959, hovering nine inches above the water; a month later it flew across the Channel.

Four years after that, the two tin cans and the Hoover brought relief to countless weary gardeners. The first Hovermower took off across the lawns of Britain.

window, hoping to win the thousand-pound reward on the duke's head. Instead of hitting him, however, he hit the ceiling. During recent restoration work a beam was uncovered with lead shot in it, which may or may not confirm the story.

The duke, according to a local ballad, found the incident rather amusing:

> . . . he gaily turned him round,
> And said, "My man, you've missed your mark
> And lost your thousand pound!"

So much for the good news. The bad news came ten days later – at Sedgemoor.

JUNE 26TH
The musket ball that missed the Duke of Monmouth. That arrow makes sure you don't miss the musket ball

26th
JUNE

The Assassin Missed him – but the Bad News came Later

The Duke of Monmouth, illegitimate son of Charles II and pretender to the Throne, had a narrow escape on this day in 1685 at Norton St Philip in Somerset. It was an early example of a contract killer – who missed.

The duke had had a disappointing couple of days. Having mustered the local peasantry he had marched to Bristol, hoping to get there before the King's army arrived, but he was too late. He turned towards Bath, but that was held by the King's men too – and when he hopefully sent a trumpeter to demand their surrender, the poor chap was promptly killed.

So Monmouth turned back and camped his men at Norton St Philip, while he and his officers moved into the George Hotel. He was in his bedroom when the would-be assassin took a pot at him through the

27th
JUNE

The First Woman Leader Writer and the Coronation Hags

Harriet Martineau, who died on this day in 1876, was the first woman journalist in Britain to get a major job on a London newspaper: she became a leader writer on the *Daily News* in 1852.

She had been a prolific writer ever since her early days in Norfolk, campaigning for social reform and later the abolition of the slave trade. She managed to get a seat in Westminster Abbey for Queen Victoria's Coronation, though she actually balanced on the rail behind it to get a better view, which not many people would do in Westminster Abbey today, let along a woman in the 1830s.

JUNE 27TH
Harriet Martineau looks benign, but she had a wide range of dislikes, from the slave trade to coronations

One wonders why she bothered, because she was fairly scathing about the whole affair – particularly the ladies.

"Old hags, with their dyed or false hair drawn up to the top of the head to allow the putting on of the coronet, had their necks and arms bare and glittering with diamonds – and those necks were so brown and wrinkled as to make one sick; or dusted over with white powder which was worse than what it disguised."

And she summed up the Coronation itself: "It strengthened instead of relaxing my sense of the unreal character of the monarchy in England . . . There was such a mixing up of the Queen and the God, such homage to both, and adulation so alike in kind and degree that, when one came to think of it, it made one's blood run cold."

Small wonder she became a leader writer.

28th
JUNE

"Why do the Heathen Rage?" Why indeed . . .

The Littleport Martyrs did not make such an impact on history as the Tolpuddle Martyrs, perhaps because the details did not filter far beyond the Fens, but they were martyrs nonetheless, victims of a period of oppression and acute poverty in the nineteenth century from which no one emerged with any great credit.

It was due partly to the lack of jobs for the thousands of soldiers returning from the Napoleonic Wars, and partly to the enclosure of common land, which robbed country folk of their livelihood. In the Fens they had to watch grain being taken away to distant markets while their own children starved.

They stayed alive by poaching, and when they were caught, they no longer stayed alive.

In 1816 an angry mob marched from Littleport to Ely, taking with them Fenland's equivalent to heavy artillery, a cart carrying four long punt-guns, but they were never fired. After rampaging round the streets for a bit, they all went home.

The military came, arrested eighty men and took them before judges in Ely, appointed by the Bishop, as was his right. Five of them were hanged at Mill Pits, Ely, on this day in 1816, ostensibly for poaching; five were transported, and the rest were jailed. The Bishop returned to the Cathedral with the choir singing: "Why do the heathen rage . . . "

There was a sequel to the hangings. The man who supplied the cart to the gallows was drowned in his own cesspit, and the carpenter involved was found stuffed into a waterpipe. The heathen, it seems, still raged.

JUNE 28TH
The plaque to the Littleport Martyrs at St Mary's Church, Ely. The choir sang "Why do the heathen rage . . ."

29th
JUNE

Thirteen Men went to Mow – after they'd had a Ball

A medieval lottery on the lines of the draw for the FA Cup used to take place at Yarnton in Oxfordshire until the 1970s on the Monday following this day, St Peter's Day. A draw was made for the mowing rights on meadows called West Mead and Pixey Mead, and it involved thirteen ancient balls made of wood from a holly-tree. Each was inscribed with the name of a plot on the

meadows – names like Parry and Watts, which probably belonged to the original tenants, back in the eleventh century.

The draw took place at the Grapes Inn, and there was much merry-making and feasting. The lucky winners headed for the meadows, cut their initials into the turf of their plots, and started mowing.

These days, however, the conservationists have taken over, and the meadows are an official conservation area, with wild flowers and birds and bees taking precedence over the mowers. The Mead Balls have gone into retirement, in the care of the Head Meadsman of the Mead, farmer Pat Shurmur – one of the few men outside the film industry who can hold a hollywood ball . . .

hands were added later. At first it was only used for petty thieves and cheats, but from the seventeenth century it was extended to political offenders, and some famous heads were inserted in the central hole.

The best known, perhaps, was Daniel Defoe, who was a political pamphleteer before getting round to *Robinson Crusoe*. He was sentenced to three days in the pillory for writing what was considered a seditious pamphlet, but to the irritation of the authorities the sympathetic crowd pelted him with garlands instead of garbage, and had quite a party round the pillory, drinking his health.

One of the few surviving pillories is at Coleshill in Warwickshire. Its last occupant was a tramp who posed in it for a photographer in 1895.

30th

You Put your Right Hand in – and Your Left – and Your Head

On this day in 1837 an Act of Parliament ended the use of the pillory in the United Kingdom, a device that for the luckier ones only meant a period of undignified discomfort, but for more unpopular offenders could mean a painful roughing-up from the crowd, which occasionally proved fatal. A contemporary writer called it "a mode of punishment so barbarous, and at the same time so indefinite in its severity, that we can only wonder it should not have been extinguished long before". Even so, it continued to be a legal punishment in parts of the United States until 1905.

The pillory came to England from the Continent before the Norman Conquest in the form of a "stretchneck", which had just a hole for the head; the other two for the

July

1st

Over Six Hundred Thousand Casualties – and an Historic Hole

This was not going to be a good day in 1916 for a hundred and twenty thousand men serving under General Douglas Haig, but he

JULY 1ST
A war artist's impression of the Battle of the Somme; the reality was far worse

assured them it would be quite a picnic. "The wire has never been so well cut, nor the artillery preparations so thorough."

He was wrong on both counts, but one of his brigadier-generals was even more blasé. He told his officers: "You'll be able to go over the top with just a walking stick – you won't need rifles . . . You'll find the Germans all dead; not even a rat will have survived."

He was wrong too, but they were foolish enough to believe him. Some just carried their swagger sticks, one had an umbrella, another nonchalantly kicked a football as they climbed out of the trenches and went to their deaths.

Twenty-one thousand men were killed in the first half-hour, tangled up in the uncut barbed wire, as the Germans emerged

from their undamaged concrete bunkers and mowed them down. As the day progressed, casualties reached 57,470 – nearly half the initial Allied force. By the end of the battle, over six hundred thousand finished up dead or wounded.

General Haig finished up a field-marshal.

One other person benefited from the carnage. Over sixty years later a French farmer was paid a substantial sum for a hole in the ground, ninety feet deep and three hundred across, which was said to have "historic interest". It was made by British sappers on this day, the opening day of the infamous Battle of the Somme.

2nd

Cromwell Stayed Asleep after Marston Moor – and Lived to Win the War

The Battle of Marston Moor on this day in 1644 was very different from the start of the Battle of the Somme on July 1st. It lasted only three hours and the winning Parliamentarians lost only three hundred men. However, the victorious Oliver Cromwell was wounded, and headed for nearby Ripley Castle to recover in comfort.

JULY 2ND
Ripley Castle sees rather more action nowadays than it ever did during the Civil War

Slightly ahead of him was the castle's owner, Sir William Ingilby, an ardent Royalist, who took refuge in a secret room while Lady Ingilby reluctantly entertained Cromwell in the library.

It was not the first time the Ingilby family had been on the losing side. One of them was a Roman Catholic priest under the Protestant Queen Elizabeth, and finished up on the block. An earlier Sir William was accused of conspiring in the Gunpowder Plot, but all the witnesses mysteriously refused to testify, and he was cleared of all charges – including one of bribing witnesses.

Lady Ingilby had her own way of surviving. Throughout the night, it is said, she kept guard on the sleeping Cromwell with two loaded pistols, in case he wandered into the wrong room. Happily he went on sleeping, or she might have changed the course of history.

Ripley Castle survived too. It is still owned and occupied by the Ingilbys, but at last they are on the winning side. They run it as a successful centre for conferences, receptions, open-air concerts – and re-creations of the Battle of Marston Moor.

JULY 4TH
Not a latter-day Nero, playing while the Bale burns, just part of the celebrations

to such an extent that dogs are inclined to go mad. Nowadays the term "hot dog" has quite a different meaning, but Noel Coward may have had the dog-days in mind when he wrote about mad dogs and Englishmen going out in the midday sun...

There is no connection, incidentally, with the dog-watch, which lasts for two hours instead of the standard four. It was introduced so that seamen could vary their hours of duty, and has nothing to do with dog-stars or dogs. The term is probably a corruption of docked-watch, meaning a shortened one, or it might have been a dodge-watch. Anyone who turns up late for it, however, is definitely in the dog-house.

3rd
JULY

Every Dog has its Day – and this is when they Begin

The dog-days start on this day and last until August 11th. The Romans reckoned these were the hottest days of the year, and they probably are in Rome, but the English climate is less consistent.

According to the Romans, the dog-days were not hot just by chance. This is the period when the dog-star Sirius rises with the sun, thus adding to the heat it gave out –

4th
JULY

Whether it's Sun-worship or Independence Day – Let's have a Bale

Midsummer's Eve, the traditional night for making merry, was officially moved back eleven days when the calendar was changed in the eighteenth century, but one or two rural areas still hold a celebration on this night, Old Midsummer's Eve. One village where the tradition survives is Whalton in Northumberland, where they still hold the Whalton Bale on July 4th.

It is an occasion for Morris dancing and sword-dancing on the village green round an enormous bonfire, while Northumbrian pipers play, the children frolic, and the non-participants enjoy the odd glass of ale.

The Bale has no connection with straw. It comes from the Anglo-Saxon word *bael*, which simply means a bonfire, but like many of these old customs there is a pagan element too. "Bale" could also derive from the sun-god Baal, and the celebration could be based on pagan sun-worship.

Such considerations probably do not occur to any American tourists in the neighbourhood. They are more likely to assume they have come across some kindred spirits celebrating Independence Day.

5th
J U L Y

Cromwell Cut Down the Original, but the Appleton Thorn Survives

The thorn tree said to have grown from Joseph of Arimathea's staff after he thrust it into the ground at Glastonbury was cut down in Cromwell's time because it was considered an idolatrous image, but cuttings had already been taken from it and planted in the neighbourhood. One of them was taken hundreds of miles northwards to Cheshire and planted in the village of Appleton, which is now just off the M56 motorway. And there the custom grew up of "bawming the thorn" on this day.

"Bawming" does not appear in the dictionaries these days. It originally meant "anointing", but it is not really practicable to anoint a thorn tree, no matter how sacred its

origins may be, so instead it was decorated with ribbons and flowers. The occasion developed into an excuse for more general festivities, with dancing, sideshows, and plenty of ale – to such an extent that proceedings had to be toned down because they became too rowdy.

JULY 5TH
Some may think that making a fuss of an old thorn tree is barmy, but not the inhabitants of Appleton

Happily the thorn tree survived all this, with the assistance of protective railings. It still stands close by the village inn – which is called, predictably, the Appleton Thorn.

6th
J U L Y

After Sedgemoor, a Shepherd with the Order of the Garter

The last pitched battle on English soil took place on this day in 1685 at Sedgemoor in Dorset. It marked the end of the Duke of Monmouth's attempt to take the throne from James II. His hastily assembled force of countryfolk was routed by the King's army, and Monmouth himself was discovered three days afterwards, ignominiously hiding

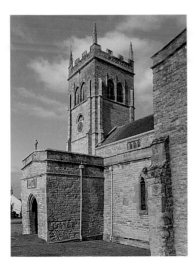

JULY 6TH
Chedzoy church is
said to have provided
some useful
stonework for
Monmouth's men to
sharpen their
weapons before
Sedgemoor; it did
them little good

in a ditch. He was disguised as a shepherd, but what rather gave him away was the Star of the Order of the Garter which he had kept for old times' sake under his smock.

He was taken to the nearest magistrate, sent to the Tower of London, and in spite of begging James for mercy he was beheaded on Tower Hill within a week.

Among the few reminders of the battle are some marks on a buttress of Chedzoy church, possibly made by Monmouth's men sharpening their weapons, and an ash tree said to grow where Monmouth was captured, and still known as Monmouth's Ash.

But there have been less tangible reminders too – strange balls of light, phantom horsemen, ghostly troopers, even Monmouth himself fleeing through the lanes. And about a century ago a farmer reported hearing what he first thought was a drunk, crying "Come over and fight", which could have been the last of Monmouth's men being mown down by cannon from across the river.

On the other hand, maybe the farmer was right the first time.

7th
JULY

∾

The Elizabethan Mansion that Mary Built – when it came to the Clunch

JULY 7TH
The bedchamber at
Sawston Hall where
Mary Tudor had an
early alarm call

Sawston Hall in Cambridgeshire has two unusual distinctions. It is the only Elizabethan mansion in the country to be built of clunch, the hard chalk which was once a popular building material in East Anglia. It is also probably the only Elizabethan mansion built by Queen Mary – which sounds a contradiction in terms, but according to legend she built it to replace one that was burnt down after she had sheltered there on this night in 1553.

Mary Tudor was being pursued by the Duke of Northumberland, who wanted to put Lady Jane Grey on the throne. The Huddlestones of Sawston Hall, a Roman Catholic family, gave her refuge overnight, until a party of Northumberland's men was spotted at dawn. Mary made her getaway, disguised it is said as a milkmaid, and her thwarted pursuers burned down the Hall as a punishment. Once Mary had been established as Queen, she rebuilt it for the loyal Huddlestones.

Experts date the Hall between 1553 and 1584, which just about tallies with this; Mary died in 1558. One must assume, I suppose, that the priest's hole under the staircase for hiding Catholics was added later, since they had no need to hide in Mary's time.

Whatever its age, the Hall remained the Huddlestones' home for the next four centuries – and many say the ghost of Queen Mary remained there too.

8th

A White Horse – or a White Elephant?

The Kilburn Feast, which starts on this day if a Sunday, or the nearest Sunday after it, is similar in many ways to traditional festivities in other Yorkshire villages, but it has one asset which few others can boast, a White Horse three hundred feet long and over two hundred feet wide. One of the high spots of the Feast – literally – is a foot-race up to the Horse on its limestone scar overlooking the Vale of York.

Unfortunately the limestone means that the Horse is a dirty grey rather than white – and the maintenance problems are enormous. The gravelly surface easily wears

away, it is very difficult to paint, and materials like chalk and chippings are soon washed off.

The Horse was the idea in 1857 of a local man, Thomas Taylor, who saw the Uffington White Horse and decided Kilburn should have one too. The village schoolmaster drew up the plans and the schoolchildren helped create it. Then Mr Taylor shrewdly emigrated to Australia, leaving local volunteers to groom his Horse ever since.

It has had its vicissitudes – jokers once pegged rows of black bin-liners on it to turn it into a zebra – but the Kilburn White Horse Association tries to keep it in trim, particularly at the time of the Kilburn Feast foot-race. Non-runners can take the hundred and fifty steps to the Horse's back.

9th

Come and Drum them up the Channel, Sir Francis!

The most famous game of bowls in history was played on this day in 1588, and it produced an equally famous one-liner: "Time enough to win this game and beat the Spaniards too!"

Every schoolboy used to be told how Sir Francis Drake duly finished the game on Plymouth Hoe, then went off to defeat the Armada. But alas, it may never have happened. According to a recent biographer: "Of all the great English sea-dogs, Drake's career is the most heavily barnacled with myths" – and this was one of them.

Apparently the first time this game of bowls was mentioned was in 1736, a century and a half later, and his neatly turned bon mot was probably invented by another biographer in 1835. As for his heroic

JULY 9TH
"Time enough to win this game" – unless the other player drops his wood on Drake's foot

JULY 8TH
The Kilburn White Horse – well, off-white perhaps, but still well groomed

circumnavigation of the globe, he only did it to loot unsuspecting and unprotected Spanish settlements and ships.

The famous "Drake's Drum" was merely invented by Sir Henry Newbolt to inspire the Victorians, and "Drake's Prayer" was written to strengthen morale during the last war. Even a plaque Drake set up in what is now California, naming it New Albion and claiming it for Queen Elizabeth, has turned out to be a nineteenth-century fake.

But never mind his attackers, he's still a hero to me. And it wouldn't surprise me if one day he quit the port of Heaven, and drummed them up the Channel as he drummed them long ago . . .

two hours, ten shillings for the next two hours, and two pounds after that.

This mixed blessing, like so many others, came to us from the States, where strangely the idea of parking meters was devised by a journalist, thirty-odd years before. The editor of an Oklahoma newspaper was made chairman of a committee to consider new ways of controlling parking, and this is what he came up with.

Traffic wardens appeared in London two years after the meters, and the first one to issue a parking ticket was a Mr Frank Shaw, who rather marred this historic moment by his unfortunate choice of culprit. He put the ticket on a Ford Popular illegally parked outside a West End hotel – but the driver turned out to be a doctor who had been called urgently to treat a guest with a heart attack.

Happily the magistrates had a heart too; they waived the fine.

JULY 10TH
A familiar sight in English towns and cities – but the idea came from an American

10th
J U L Y

Enter the Parking Meter – the new Curb on the Kerb

A modest milestone in British motoring history was passed on this day in 1958, when drivers had their first encounter with a parking meter. Over six hundred of them sprouted in the streets of Mayfair in London, planted there by Westminster City Council. The charge was sixpence an hour for the first

11th
J U L Y

The Oldest Shylock in the Business, at 99

England's oldest professional actor, Charles Macklin, who made his farewell appearance as Shylock in his hundredth year, died on this day in 1797 at the age of 106.

Macklin was an Irishman who came to London as a barman, joined a company of strolling players and became a regular performer at Drury Lane. He revived its

JULY 11TH
*Charles Macklin went
on to be the oldest
Shylock in the
business*

the audience, and asked them to allow his
understudy to take his place."

Like some current performers, perhaps,
he should have quit while he was winning . . .

12th
J U L Y

The Day the Catholics Remember at Padley Hall

The persecution of Roman Catholics under
Queen Elizabeth came late to the North of
England. For more than thirty years of her
reign, there were no executions north of the
Thames Valley – and indeed one northern
MP said that in his part of the country "it was
more dangerous to be a Protestant than a
Papist".

But when persecution did come it came,
one might say, with a vengeance, and in
Derbyshire it reached its peak on this day in
1588, when the Earl of Shrewsbury led his
men to Padley Hall near Grindleford, home
of the Catholic Fitzherberts, to arrest John
Fitzherbert on suspicion of sheltering
Catholic priests. To his delight, he found two
priests there, Nicholas Garlick and Robert
Ludlam. He arrested all three, plus
Fitzherbert's family and estate workers.

flagging fortunes when he suggested giving
the *Merchant of Venice* its first performance
for forty years, with himself playing Shylock.
The management was unenthusiastic, but
decided the box-office receipts could not sink
any lower. The play was an enormous
success, and, as Shylock, "Macklin marked a
new epoch in the conception of this character,
and it was the climax of his own art."

Or as Pope put it, more succinctly: "This
was the Jew, that Shakespeare drew".

Macklin went on performing in London
and the provinces, in the same league as
David Garrick, until May 7th,
1789, when he stepped on to the
stage for the last time as
Shylock. A biographer wrote:
"Even at that very great age he
was physically capable of
performing the part with
considerable vigour, but his
mental powers were almost
gone. In the second act, his
memory totally failing him, he
with great grace and solemnity
came forward and apologized to

The priests joined another one, Richard Simpson, who was already in Derby Gaol. The three were found guilty of high treason and executed on Derby Bridge. John Fitzgerald died in prison two years later, and his brother Thomas died in the Tower a year after that. His children spent long periods in custody.

Padley Hall is now in ruins, but the chapel survives, and each year on the Sunday nearest this day there is a pilgrimage of priests – eighteen took part in 1995 – and a commemorative service for the Padley Martyrs.

JULY 13TH
Children from the John Clare School at Helpston lay "cushions" of flowers around the Peasant Poet's grave

13th
J U L Y

From Potboy to Peasant Poet – Clare was there

John Clare, the "Peasant Poet", was born on this day in 1793 at Helpston, in what is now Cambridgeshire, and each year the John Clare Society meets at the Bluebell Inn, where he was once a potboy, while the village holds various celebrations in his memory. One of them is the Cushion Ceremony, when children from the local John Clare School take "cushions" of flowers to the church and lay them round his grave.

Clare was born in the thatched cottage next to the Bluebell, and started work as a ploughboy when he was twelve. A year later he went to work at the inn, and had to make regular night-time journeys to the next village to pick up flour, along supposedly haunted lanes. To keep up his spirits he composed verses and recited them aloud as he walked.

At twenty-seven, after working as a gardener and a lime-burner, he had his first poems published, and became a literary celebrity – partly because of his novelty value as a "peasant poet". But after a while interest faded, his writings became less popular, and he suffered depression and delusions. He spent his last twenty-three years in an asylum.

His memorial in Helpston has a verse expressing his longing to return there – "To turn me back and wander home to die, among nearest friends my latest breath resign, and in the churchyard with my kindred lie."

At least the last of those wishes was granted.

14th
J U L Y

Even after he Died, Iron Mad Wilkinson left a Will of Iron

John "Iron Mad" Wilkinson, who died on this day in 1808, was one of the foremost ironmasters of his day, much involved in building some of the earliest iron boats. He did not earn his nickname because of that – though many people did believe it was crazy to expect iron to float. He was just madly

*July 14th
"Iron Mad"
Wilkinson's iron
memorial – and no,
the inscription does
not say "Rust in
Peace"*

enthusiastic about the uses to which iron could be put, and no one was too surprised when he asked to be buried in an iron coffin, with an iron memorial over the grave. He left, in fact, a will of iron . . .

As he died in the West Midlands and wished to be buried in his home village of Lindale in Cumbria, this involved some problems for the undertaker – particularly, carrying such a heavy load across Morecambe Sands, the short cut to Cumbria – but he was duly interred, and a twenty-ton iron obelisk, an early example of box casting, was erected over the grave.

Unfortunately it was struck by lightning, a hazard which even Iron Mad Wilkinson might have foreseen, and it lay neglected in a shrubbery before being restored and re-erected. A plaque records that "his different works in various parts of the United Kingdom are lasting testimonials to his unceasing labours".

It might have added – as some jokers have suggested – "Rust in Peace".

15th
J U L Y

It'll Rain for Forty Days – as Sure as Eggs are Eggs

*July 15th
St Swithun's shrine
in Winchester
Cathedral: eggs mark
the spot*

St Swithun, Bishop of Winchester, enjoyed the rain so much that he asked to be buried outdoors instead of inside the Minster, "that the sweet rain of Heaven might fall upon my grave" – and he was so upset when the monks later tried to transfer his remains after he was canonized that he caused the skies to weep for forty days. And thus: "St Swithun's Day, if thou dost rain, For forty days it will remain."

The monks, however, were undeterred, and on this day in AD971 they moved him into the cathedral choir, where his shrine remains today. There is nothing about it to recall the wet summer of '71, but another legend attached to St Swithun does get acknowledged. The story goes that a farmer's wife was taking a basket of eggs to market when a short-sighted monk bumped into her outside the Minster, and she dropped the lot. Swithun happened to be passing, and might well have lectured her on the folly of putting all her eggs in one basket. Instead he miraculously re-inserted the eggs into their shells, and sent her on her way. It is not known what he said to the monk . . .

That is why the tall candlesticks at each corner of his shrine incorporate carved golden eggshells – which could give the cathedral guides a useful one-liner if they are asked where St Swithun is: "Eggs mark the spot."

Well, perhaps not.

16th

J U L Y

Hob-Nob with the Giant?
Yes, but no one knows why

This is the Feast of St Osmund, when the saint's bones were transferred from Old

JULY 16TH
Hob-nob hob-nobs
with the Giant,
Salisbury's answer to
Little and Large

Sarum to Salisbury Cathedral in 1457 – and at one time that was a good excuse for parading Salisbury's Giant through the streets, with Hob-Nob the hobby-horse clearing the way and snapping at the crowd. This kind of pseudo-religious celebration

was banned during the Reformation, and many Giants in other cities were destroyed, but the Salisbury Giant survived, and since the eighteenth century he and Hob-Nob have re-appeared on the streets at times of great rejoicing.

The Giant is twelve feet high, but one man can carry it – with an effort. The head could date back to the fifteenth century, when it was the pageant figure of the Salisbury Guild of Tailors. When the Guild died out in the last century the museum bought the Giant for thirty shillings.

The Giant and Hob-Nob have always been a double act, the original Little and Large, but nobody is sure why. The Giant used to be called St Christopher, while Hob-Nob might represent the dragon slain by St George, Maybe one day the theologians will work out a logical link between the two. Meanwhile the Giant hob-nobs with Hob-Nob in the comfort of Salisbury Museum.

17th

J U L Y

Singer, you are Treading where
the Saint has Trod . . .

No, the sewing-machine was not invented by Mr Singer, even though his name has always been associated with them. It was not an American but a Londoner who patented the idea on this day in 1790, some twenty years before Mr Singer was even born.

Thomas Saint was a cabinet-maker by trade but an inventor by inclination, and patented various ideas for improving boots and shoes as well as a machine for sewing thread. Unfortunately none of his ideas was developed commercially, and his patents were only re-discovered in 1874 – by which time Isaac Singer had cornered the market.

Even so, Singer was not the first in the commercial field. An obscure French tailor called Barthélemy Thimmonier built a prototype in 1829, when Singer was still a teenager, and sold eighty machines to a Paris clothing factory. The workers saw their jobs in danger and promptly wrecked them. Thimmonier salvaged just one, and exhibited it at fairs to make a few bob until he could go into production again.

JULY 17TH
Saint invented the sewing-machine, but Singer had it sewn up

By then, however, Singer had produced the first domestic sewing machine in the States, and from then on he reaped where Saint and Thimmonier had sewn.

arches all varying in height and width; though one writer has unkindly compared it to a herd of elephants crossing the Tweed.

The crowning takes place by the river, under the shadow of the new bridge, an unromantic concrete creation built to carry the heavier traffic. Various festivities then follow, including the Salmon Feast, which traditionally features an unusual combination of salmon, gooseberry tarts and tea. Everyone has a very jolly time – except, of course, the salmon.

18th
J U L Y

A Feast Fit for a Saint – Salmon and Gooseberry Tart

This is St Boisil's Day, an Irish saint who was Bishop of Melrose in the seventh century. He seems to have made less impact than most, and only two churches in the country are dedicated to him, but one of these is at Tweedmouth, just across the Tweed from Berwick, and the annual ceremony of crowning the Salmon Queen is held on or near this day, on a convenient Thursday.

The ceremony was revived in 1945 after a gap of several years, and it has been brought up-to-date by inviting a television personality to crown the Salmon Queen. She is first piped across the oldest of the three bridges that link Tweedmouth with Berwick. It is also the most attractive, with its fifteen

19th
J U L Y

Hooray, Up She Rises – after 400 Years

The *Mary Rose*, pride of Henry VIII's fleet, capsized and sank in the Solent on this day in 1545, with the loss of seven hundred lives – nearly everyone on board. It was watched from the shore by a weeping King – though, true to character, he also took the opportunity of comforting and consoling Lady Carew, wife of the vice-admiral.

JULY 18TH
The Salmon Queen of
Tweedmouth and her
attendants, looking
forward to their
salmon and
gooseberry tart

The popular theory about the disaster is that this was her maiden voyage, and the water rushed in through the low, open gunports which had been provided to accommodate the new-style cannon. This does not quite tally with the official records, which say she was built in Portsmouth between 1509 and 1511, and had served in the Navy for over thirty years before this happened. Perhaps the gunports had just been added, and the new cannon made the ship top-heavy – or maybe everyone rushed to one side of the deck to see the King, and she tipped over . . .

Whatever the cause, the *Mary Rose* stayed on the seabed for four hundred years, until being located again in the 1960s. Over a period of years the hull was excavated and brought to the surface, a remarkable achievement by archaeologists and engineers. It was towed to Portsmouth Docks in 1982, and the Mary Rose Trust has preserved it safely ever since.

JULY 19TH
The wreck that came in from the cold: the carefully preserved remains of the **Mary Rose**

20th

J U L Y

If you want to Get a Head – Give a Bribe

The story of Sir Thomas More's head is one of those bizarre legends which have a sound basis in fact. Henry VIII's former chancellor refused to accept his marriage to Anne Boleyn, and although Sir Thomas was a favourite of the King he was tried and beheaded, and his head was impaled on a pole on London Bridge.

The legend runs that his eldest daughter, Margaret Roper, resolved to retrieve it. On this day in 1535, a fortnight after her father's head had been put on display, she passed under London Bridge in a boat and exclaimed: "That head hath lain many a time in my lap, would to God it would fall into my lap as I pass under." And it did.

It may have been an answer to prayer, but more likely she bribed a guard to throw it down to her, and then claimed it was a miracle in order to cover his tracks. She was later arrested, even though she had gained, one might say, a head start, but she was unrepentant. She spent a short time in prison, presumably on a charge of being in unlawful possession of a head, but she was allowed, surprisingly, to keep it.

When she died nine years later it was buried with her in the family vault at St Dunstan's, Canterbury. King Henry, it seemed, was not too bothered. By then he had seen off four more wives and several more executions, so what was one head – More or less?

21st
J U L Y

Pierce-Eye became Percy, and Harry became Hotspur

The Percys, Earls and Dukes of Northumberland, have dominated the county since the days when Robert de Mowbray, according to legend, leaned down from the walls of Alnwick Castle after the besieging King Malcolm of Scotland had demanded the keys, offered them to him on the end of his lance, then thrust the lance into the King's eye. De Mowbray became known as "Pierce-eye", and the Percys have held the castle against all comers ever since.

On this day in 1403, however, they suffered their greatest defeat when their forces were routed by Henry IV at the Battle of Shrewsbury. They were led by Henry Percy, son of the Duke of Northumberland and known to his friends as Harry Hotspur, because of what they called his impetuosity and his critics called uncontrolled temper.

The medieval arch of Hotspur Tower at the southern entrance to Alnwick is a permanent reminder.

Back at the scene of his death, Battlefield Church just outside Shrewsbury has a peal of bells which ring out, according to a local jingle, "Hold up your shields". But the advice came too late for Harry Hotspur.

JULY 21ST
Battlefield Church, on the site of the Battle of Shrewsbury, where the bells are said to peal out "Hold Up Your Shields". Unfortunately Harry Hotspur didn't

22nd
J U L Y

The Dean who Called the Lord a "Shoving Leopard"

The Rev. William Archibald Spooner, who was born on this day in 1844, would no doubt like to be remembered as a distinguished dean of New College, Oxford, but his name lives on for quite a different reason, thanks to a curious little failing of his which afforded constant entertainment to his colleagues and students.

JULY 22ND
The Reverend William Spooner, who was inclined to sytch swyllables . . .

The official word for it is metathesis, the transposing of letters or syllables in spoken words, but most English grammar books call it a spoonerism, because Dr Spooner was its most prolific exponent. His listeners may have been confused at first by comments like "The Lord is a shoving leopard", but once they realized he meant "a loving shepherd" they soon got the hang of it, even with more obscure observations such as this: "We all know what it is to have a half-warmed fish within us."

Spoonerisms are in the same field as malapropisms, but not quite the same. Sheridan's Mrs Malaprop in *The Rivals*, unlike Dr Spooner, had only a little learning where long words were concerned, and it could prove a dangerous thing. Her classic was perhaps: "As headstrong as an allegory on the banks of the Nile!"

Dr Spooner's problem was probably just absentmindedness – but I suspect, once he realized the effect his spoonerisms had, he slipped in one or two on purpose. He was, after all, a fright bellow.

23rd
J U L Y

The "General" who Sallied forth to found the Sally Ann

On this day in 1865 a former Methodist preacher set up his own separate mission in one of the poorest areas of London. It developed into what is now known throughout the world as the Salvation Army, though the name was not given to it until some thirteen years later.

William Booth was a native of Birmingham who joined the Methodists when he was thirteen, and he was already making his mark as a fiery preacher when he was still in his teens. He moved to London when he was twenty, left the Methodist church a few years later, and in due course set up his mission in Whitechapel, providing physical as well as spiritual comfort to the poor and homeless of the East End.

JULY 23RD
General William Booth, founder of an Army that still marches on

"General" Booth became the commanding officer of an army whose uniform is now as familiar to the public as those of the regular Services – though the Victorian poke-bonnets of the "lasses" have no military counterpart. The general himself lived on into his eighties, a splendid figure in his flowing beard and high-necked "Sally Ann" tunic.

"The enthusiastic singing, often accompanied by a brass band, has not appealed to Christians of more restrained tastes," wrote one cautious critic. But that was forty years ago; these days it is the "restrained" Christians who seem to be losing their appeal . . .

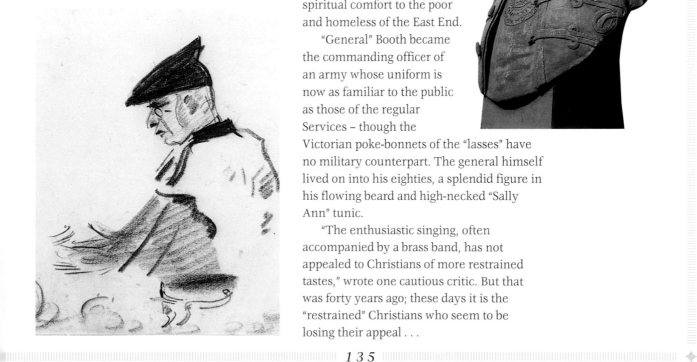

24th
J U L Y

When Britain's first Black-out ended, and Pitt's Pictures came down

A little more light was shed into the life of the average British taxpayer on this day in 1851, when the much-hated Window Tax was abolished. Until then, even better-off people built houses with the minimum number of windows – though the shrewder ones, anticipating this day, put only one thickness of bricks where windows could be installed if and when the tax was revoked. Poorer ones were inclined to brick up what windows they had, making their gloomy tenements even gloomier. These bricked-up windows – and there are still plenty of them about in older houses – became known as Pitt's Pictures, as William Pitt the Younger increased the tax and accelerated the process.

The Window Tax followed an earlier one on fireplaces, the Hearth Tax. Under Charles II, who was always glad of an extra few bob, two shillings a year was levied on every fireplace in houses which were worth more than an annual rent of twenty shillings. The difficulty of assessing a house's value accurately, and the time involved in entering every house to count the fireplaces, must have made the Hearth Tax even more complicated to enforce than its more recent successors, and it lasted only for a couple of decades. Then they started counting windows instead, and Britain's first black-out began . . .

25th
J U L Y

A Pagan Fertility Rite gets Hit for Six

A pagan version of the Ashes is played every year on this day, St James's Day, during the Ebernoe Horn Fair in West Sussex. A cricket

JULY 25TH
A pagan version of the Ashes, competed for each year at Ebernow Horn Fair

match takes place between two local teams, Ebernoe and Lurgashall, while a black ram is roasted on a spit. At lunchtime the players eat roast lamb, and after the match the horns are presented to the highest run-scorer on the winning side.

It is a rare combination of two traditional rural activities, one of them probably dating back to pagan times, when ram's horns were considered to be a great aphrodisiac and the Horn Fair was a fertility ritual.

When the custom was revived in its present form in 1865, the ram was roasted in a pit of embers with the head projecting over the side so the horns would not get singed. This procedure hardly conforms to modern EC standards, so the sheep is roasted without its head, and the horns are dressed separately.

The Wadey family has roasted the ram for three generations, and by a happy chance the current roaster, Ivan Wadey, is also president of Ebernoe Cricket Club. The other family involved is Lord Egremont's, who owns the land; they always provide the sheep.

minute or more, and spluttering and shouting when at last his great white head bobbed dripping on the surface".

These days his great white head would probably be taken off by a powerboat propeller, and the railway came anyway. But Norwich is still a fine city . . .

26th
JULY

JULY 26TH
George Borrow's home in Norwich – but he spent most of his time on the road

"A Fine City" – to Borrow from Borrow

George Borrow, author, traveller, champion of gypsies and hater of railways, died on this day in 1881, leaving behind *Lavengro*, *Romany Rye*, *Bible in Spain*, and four words frequently quoted in his native Norfolk, a Borrow phrase much borrowed since: "A fine city, Norwich". He actually wrote "A fine old city", but in these days of creating a virile image to attract new investment and industry, "old" is not a buzz-word.

Borrow started his travels when he was still at school. He persuaded three other boys to run away with him, but they were all caught and as ringleader he got a whipping. This merely seemed to whet his appetite for travel, and he spent much of his life on the road, enjoying the company of the gypsies and taking notes for his books.

He spent his later years in a big house by Oulton Broad, annoying his neighbours by encouraging gypsies to camp on his land, and trying to stop a railway being built across it. He developed various eccentricities, like leaping into the Broad fully clothed, "staying under water for a

27th
JULY

The Mill that Commemorates "A Harvest of Wisdom"

The large windmill at Shipley in West Sussex has an unusual distinction. It is not only the best-preserved smockmill in the county, but also a memorial. Over the door a tablet reads: "Let this be a memorial to Hilaire Belloc, who garnered a harvest of wisdom and sympathy for young and old."

JULY 27TH
A very English memorial to a very English Frenchman: Hilaire Belloc's windmill at Shipley

It may seem odd that such a very English feature of the countryside should commemorate a man who was born in France, on this day in 1870, but Belloc was educated in England, continued to live here, and became a British citizen in 1902. He even became a Member of Parliament, but was not impressed and did not stand again.

While he was an MP he bought the house at Shipley, "King's Land", where he spent the rest of his days. The mill stands in its grounds, and he started its restoration, in between writing a remarkable range of books: histories, biographies, travel books, essays, comic verses for children, and poems which extolled the English countryside in general, and English pubs in particular.

For me, his two most memorable titles are those of his two volumes of early essays. The first is *On Nothing*; the sequel is *On Something*. Which covers – everything . . .

28th
J U L Y

It Started with Sir Thomas – and Finally came to the Crunch

The name of Sir Thomas Harriot is not as familiar as that of Sir Walter Raleigh, but in one respect he is of equal importance. On this day in 1586, the same year that Sir Walter brought home the first leaves of tobacco, Sir Thomas brought home the first potato – and in due course changed the eating habits of the nation.

Sir Walter has been credited with discovering the potato too. It has been suggested that he acquired some in Virginia and planted them on his land in Ireland, thus laying the foundation for future famines, a year before Sir Thomas arrived back from Columbia with his. Historians,

however, point out that the potato did not appear in Virginia for another century or more, and when it did, it was imported from Ireland . . .

So Sir Thomas is the genuine potato pioneer, to whom we owe our staple vegetable, whether boiled or mashed or roasted. Three centuries or so later it

achieved a new surge of popularity when a different method was devised for preparing it. The idea came from a Red Indian chef, of all unlikely people, spread across the Atlantic to France, where "french fries" were already established, and was brought to England in 1913 by a Mr Carter.

And then one of Mr Carter's employees with an equally mundane name, Mr Smith, started out on his own, and Smith's Crisps started crunching their way into our lives.

JULY 28TH
"So what do you do with these, chaps – shred them and smoke them?" The discovery of the potato . . .

JULY 29TH
William Wilberforce became famous as an anti-slavery campaigner – but others were there too

29th
JULY

Wilberforce was Great, but Granville and Zachary were there too

William Wilberforce, who died on this day in 1833, is remembered as the outstanding figure in the anti-slavery campaign. He was an MP at twenty-one, spent some time travelling abroad, and came back appalled by the slave trade. For twenty years he introduced Bill after Bill in the House, and an Act was finally passed in 1807, repressing the British slave trade. Just after his death another Act freed all slaves in the British Empire.

But Wilberforce would not expect all the credit. While he campaigned in Parliament, others campaigned in the streets and the courts. Granville Sharp, for instance, was a self-taught law clerk who on one occasion served a writ on a ship's captain who had chained an escaped slave to the mast; then he spent three days in court arguing that the slave was a man and not a chattel. The slave was freed, and from then on – years ahead of Wilberforce's Act – any slave who set foot on English soil became a free man.

Zachary Macaulay, Lord Macaulay's father, wrote pamphlets and helped to found the Anti-Slavery Society. Another founder was Thomas Clarkson, a Cambridge student who studied slavery to write a winning Latin essay, and was horrified by what he discovered. And so on.

Wilberforce did a great job – but Granville, Zachary, Thomas and the rest were there too.

30th
JULY

How about Gray's Elegy on a Fire Escape?

If ever a poet gained his reputation on a single poem it was Thomas Gray, who died on this day in 1771. The curfew, as every schoolboy used to know, tolls the knell of parting day, the lowing herd goes over the lea and the ploughman homeward plods to tea – more or less – but that's about it. Many may have believed it was called *Graze Elegy*, all about cattle and sheep, and never realized there was actually a chap called Gray.

He was in fact a retiring fellow, so much so that it is said he turned down an invitation to be Poet Laureate, though it seems surprising he was ever offered the job on the strength of one poem. He spent most of his life, and wrote his other few poems, within the precincts of Cambridge University, no doubt hoping for peace and quiet.

He did not always get it. Gray was terrified of fire, and outside his second-floor

JULY 30TH
Thomas Gray's second-floor window at Peterhouse College, where he always had a rope ready in case of fire

window in Peterhouse College he had a hook with a rope attached, so he could make a speedy escape if the building caught fire. Knowing his phobia, playful students put a tub of water under his window, then set fire to some wet straw. Gray smelt the smoke and duly slid down the rope into the tub of water, to the great delight of the spectators.

Gray's *Elegy on a Fire Escape* would have made interesting reading . . .

31st
J U L Y

"Victims so pure Heaven saw well pleased – and snatched them"

A memorial stone at Stanton Harcourt Church in Oxfordshire, with an epitaph written by Alexander Pope, is a reminder of a tragic and bizarre accident which happened on this day in 1718.

John Hewet and Sarah Drew, both in their twenties, had been in love for some

time, and that morning they had just obtained permission from Sarah's parents to marry. As they worked in the harvest fields together, a storm burst overhead. Sarah was terrified and collapsed in a faint on a heap of barley, and John, still by her side, was raking the barley together to protect her from the rain when there was a loud crash, "as if the heavens had split asunder".

Nearby farmworkers rushed to the spot. "They perceived the barley all in a smoke," the story goes, "then spied the faithful pair, John with one arm around Sarah's neck, the other held over her as if to screen her from the lightning. They were struck dead, and stiffened in this tender posture."

It was a tale to move any poet, and Pope happened to be staying with the squire, Lord Harcourt. His first epitaph was so obscure that his host suggested the locals would never understand it. I hope they fared better with the second:

> *Think not by rigorous judgment seized*
> *A pair so faithful could expire;*
> *Victims so pure Heaven saw well pleased*
> *And snatched them in eternal fire . . .*

JULY 31ST
The memorial at Stanton Harcourt to "an industrious young man and virtuous maid . . . who were both in one instant killed by lightning"

NEAR THIS PLACE LIE THE BODIES OF
JOHN HEWET AND SARAH DREW
AN INDUSTRIOUS YOUNG MAN AND
VIRTUOUS MAIDEN OF THIS PARISH
CONTRACTED IN MARRIAGE
WHO BEING WITH MANY OTHERS AT HARVEST
WORK, WERE BOTH IN ONE INSTANT KILLED
BY LIGHTNING ON THE LAST DAY OF JULY
1718.

Think not by rigorous judgment seizd   Live well & fear no sudden fate
A Pair so faithful could expire;   When God calls virtue to the grave
Victims so pure Heav'n saw well pleasd   Alike tis Justice soon or late
And snatchd them in cœleftial fire.   Mercy alike to kill or save

virtue unmovd can hear the Call
And face the Flash that melts the Ball.

FLORENCE NIGHTINGALE.
1820 - 1910

August

who came to London and went into management at the Drury Lane Theatre and the Haymarket. A devoted Whig, he was delighted when George I came to the throne and his party came into their own, so he founded the race to mark the King's accession on this day in 1714. The first race was probably held the following year.

He organized them himself until his death in 1721, then left money "to provide a Badge of Silver, a Livery on which the Badge is to be put, and a guinea for making up the suit of livery and buttons and appurtenances to it".

In recent years apprentice watermen have been thin on the water and the rules have been slightly stretched, but the race has been kept going with Doggett enthusiasm.

2nd
A U G U S T

Did the Arrow Ricochet or was it a Contract Job?
The death of "William Rufus", King William II, while out hunting in the New Forest on this day in 1100, remains an unsolved mystery. The official verdict was accidental death – an arrow shot by one of his companions, Walter Tyrrel, is supposed to have glanced off a deer and pierced his heart. Later investigators have worked out, however, that Tyrrel was too far away even to see the King, and if his arrow had hit a stag it would simply have dropped to the ground.

More likely it was a political assassination, with William's

AUGUST 1ST
Doggett's Coat and Badge, awarded in the earliest competitive rowing event in England

AUGUST 2ND
The Rufus Stone marks the spot where William II died in the New Forest. Was it murder or accidental death? The jury is still out

1st
A U G U S T

After 280-odd Years, the Rowers still show Doggett Enthusiasm
The earliest competitive rowing event in England, and probably the oldest continuous sporting event of any kind, takes place on or near this day (depending on the tides) on the Thames between London Bridge and Chelsea. The rowers are six Freemen of the Watermen's Company who have just come out of their apprenticeships, and it is organized by the Fishmongers' Company – but the man who founded it was neither a Waterman nor a Fishmonger.

Thomas Doggett was an Irish comedian, a sort of eighteenth-century George Robey, younger brother Henry, who succeeded him, as chief suspect. Certainly Henry lost no time taking over. William was shot at seven in the evening, and Henry had him brought to Winchester next morning and buried in the cathedral by midday – though not without protests from the locals who reckoned Rufus was far too wicked to be buried in such a holy place. When the steeple was struck by lightning, Rufus got the blame, even though it happened seven years later.

He was in fact a thoroughly unpopular fellow and almost anyone would have happily killed him, not least the New Forest peasantry, who suffered under his harsh penalties for poaching. Anyone attempting to poach the royal deer was maimed or hanged; just for disturbing them you could have your eyes put out. One way or another, it was hardly surprising he came out of the forest feet-first.

3rd
AUGUST

A Foreign Field, Honey for Tea – and a Jolly at the Pink and Lily

Being born on this day in 1887 meant that Rupert Brooke, son of a Rugby housemaster, became eligible for service in the First World War, and his best-known lines refer to it: "If I should die, think only this of me; that there is some corner of a foreign field that is for ever England."

Brooke did die, on his way to the Dardanelles with the Royal Naval Division, but not through enemy action. A mild attack of sunstroke led to something more serious and his corner of a foreign field is on the island of Skyros, where his body still lies.

The other lines most remembered are:

"Stands the church clock at ten to three? And is there honey still for tea?" These two poems were so often requested on the Radio 4 programme *With Great Pleasure*, in which celebrities choose their favourite prose and poetry, that the producer had to ration them to one programme every other series.

But one of his poems remains virtually unknown outside the little Buckinghamshire village of Lacey Green. Brooke and a companion used to frequent the village pub, the quaintly named Pink and Lily – Mr Pink was butler at Hampden House and married the parlourmaid, Miss Lily. After one particularly convivial evening Rupert Brooke dashed off an uncharacteristically jolly little verse, which is still framed in the bar:

> *Never came there to the Pink*
> *Two such men as we, I think.*
> *Never came here to the Lily,*
> *Two men quite so richly silly.*

AUGUST 3RD
Yes, the church clock does stand at ten to three – or it did when this was taken

4th
AUGUST

Today, Liverpool and Caernarfon; Tomorrow the World!

The man who put "Cook's Tours" into the English language organized his first holiday excursion on this day in 1845; three days in Liverpool at recommended hotels with a sea trip to Caernarfon and a climb up Snowdon as optional extras. The package holiday was born.

Thomas Cook was a Leicester printer who published Temperance tracts, and he got into the travel business by running cheap-day rail excursions to Temperance galas. When he announced his Liverpool and Caernarfon package, the demand for the three hundred and fifty places was so great that tickets were re-sold at inflated prices. It seems that by inventing the package holiday he also invented the ticket tout.

The excursion left Leicester station at

Excursion Ticket.
LEICESTER TO FRANCE.
SECOND CLASS.
This Ticket to be given up at the Camden Station.

Excursion Ticket.
LEICESTER TO FRANCE.
SECOND CLASS.
This Ticket must be given up either at Dover or Folkestone, and exchanged for a Steam Packet Ticket.

Excursion Return Ticket.
FRANCE TO LEICESTER.
SECOND CLASS.
This Ticket to be given up at the Bricklayers' Arms Station.

Excursion Return Ticket.
FRANCE TO LEICESTER.
SECOND CLASS.
This Ticket must be given up on arrival at Leicester.

5 a.m., and nobody dared to be late. "Parties will have to be wide awake at an early hour, or they will be disappointed," the brochure announced sternly. "Promptitude on the part of the Railway Company calls for the same from passengers." One can visualize them saluting the guard as they marched down the platform.

Cook went along too, escorting the Wales-bound party on to the chartered packetboat, and leading the climb up Snowdon. At the summit he looked towards Scotland – much as Marco Polo may have looked towards China – and put it on his itinerary for the following year. Cook's Tours were on their way; in due course they even caught up with Marco Polo.

5th
A U G U S T

A Rush Job at Grasmere; even St Oswald Lends a Hand

Until as recently as 1841 the floor of St Oswald's Church, Grasmere, in Cumbria, was plain earth, and the rushbearing which takes place on this day, St Oswald's Day, or the nearest Saturday to it, still had a practical significance. The rushes not only provided a dry, soft carpeting which helped to keep the congregation's feet warm, they also kept the church fragrant with their aromatic smell.

There are rushbearings in other villages, but Grasmere claims to have the best. An elaborate procession has developed over the years, with six "Rush Maidens", in green and white dresses with chaplets of wild flowers on their heads, carrying the Rush Sheet between them, as if anticipating a descending body. The linen sheet with rushes and reeds sewn on to it was only introduced in the 1890s, long after rushes

AUGUST 4TH
One of Thomas Cook's early excursions, from Leicester to "France". Presumably they found out whereabouts in France when they got there

AUGUST 5TH
"Rush maidens" carrying the Rush Sheet at Grasmere's rushbearing ceremony. But so far as they are concerned, it doesn't seem a rush job

were actually needed, but it provides a photogenic centrepiece for the other children carrying the traditional "bearings", permanent frames which are re-decorated with flowers each year.

One of these recalls the death of St Oswald in AD642, killed and dismembered by the pagan King Penda. Another is Oswald's hand, symbolic of his generosity. According to legend it never withered with age, and remained a holy relic until the Reformation. Nothing to do with rushbearing, but on St Oswald's Day it is appropriate that Oswald should lend a hand . . .

6th
AUGUST

One Saved on Burial-space, the other on Eating-time

Two economically minded men who left their marks on history in very different ways are associated with this day: Ben Jonson and the fourth Earl of Sandwich. The first left us plays such as *Volpone* and *The Alchemist*, plus a charming little song called "To Celia" with a very familiar opening line: "Drink to me only with thine eyes". The latter gave us an early form of fast food, which still bears his name.

Jonson was not economical in monetary terms, indeed, he was constantly broke even when he was Poet Laureate. It was ground-space that he saved on, when he was buried. The story goes that he asked King Charles for a gift of land – not unusual, one gathers, among Charles's courtiers – but all he wanted was three square feet. When he died, on this day in 1637, he was buried in that small square, standing up. It happened to be in Westminster Abbey.

Lord Sandwich, on the other hand, was economical in his eating habits, to devote

more time to his gambling. On this day in 1762, instead of breaking for lunch, he ordered a manservant to bring him a slice of ham between two slices of bread, and ate it without rising from the gaming table or pausing in the game. And thus the sandwich was born.

7th
AUGUST

Spring Forward, Fall Backward, in the Good Old (British) Summer Time

An Act of Parliament on this day in 1924 introduced British Summer Time, nearly ten years after the death of the man who spent the last years of his life campaigning for it. William Willett was a Chelsea builder who started his crusade in 1907, perhaps with the idea of gaining more daylight hours for his men to work in. The idea did not catch on until the First World War, and then it was the Germans who adopted it first. Britain soon followed suit, but by that time Mr Willett was no longer around to say, "I told you so."

However, it was considered only a temporary wartime measure, and the 1924 Act made it permanent. There was a complicated formula to work out the date it should start every spring: the day following the third Saturday in April unless that was Easter Day, in which case it was the day following the second Saturday.

Over the years British Summer Time has been extended more than once, with one period of Double Summer Time to complicate things further. When the clocks do have to be altered, it always comes as a surprise.

*AUGUST 6TH
The Earl of Sandwich called for a slice of ham between two slices of bread. The idea caught on; so did the name*

As for remembering which way the clock should be altered, try: "Spring forward, Fall (autumn) backward." Or is it the other way round?

AUGUST 7TH
The memorial at Petts Wood in Kent to William Willett, who campaigned for "daylight saving". Needless to say, the sundial is set to British Summer Time

8th
A U G U S T

A £2.5-million Robbery – and I was there! (Later . . .)

The Great Train Robbery, which took place on this day in 1963, still holds the record for the largest sum ever stolen from a train. A GPO mail train from Glasgow to London was ambushed in the early hours of the morning near Mentmore in Buckinghamshire, close to a bridge over a quiet country lane, where the getaway truck was waiting. The engine driver later died.

I happened to become involved as a fairly green BBC news reporter, as my home was closest to the scene, and I gained a little reflected glory by filming a piece to camera on the bridge for Television News. None of us appreciated at the time just how much had been taken. At the initial news conference at Cheddington station a police spokesman quoted a figure of a quarter of a million pounds, but even that was enough to

be greeted with disbelief by the assembled Press. It later transpired that the gang got away with £2,631,784 in usable banknotes.

Seven months later, ten of the Great Train Robbers were sentenced to a total of 307 years in prison. Since then the activities of most of them have been well documented, but what remains a mystery is what happened to the money. Less than £350,000 was ever recovered.

9th
A U G U S T

Once more unto the Beach, dear Gymnosophists

Britain's first nudist beach was opened on this day in 1979 at Brighton. It caused quite a stir at the time, but in fact nudist camps had already been around for over half a century. The Germans started the ball rolling, but England was only three years behind. Wickford Nudist Camp in Essex was opened in 1923 by the grandly named English Gymnosophist Society.

The word was coined from the Gymnosophists, a sect of Indian ascetics who believed that food or clothing were detrimental to purity of thought. They had to eat a little food, but clothes were completely discarded.

Somehow the name never caught on in England, but naturism did – to a certain degree. At Brighton the nudist beach attracted jokers as well as would-be Peeping Toms, and in its early days a hardy quartet made use of it to gain a little personal publicity. On New Year's Day, 1981, they went swimming from the nudist

AUGUST 8TH
Police on the bridge where the Great Train Robbers made their getaway. It was my turn next . . .

beach, appropriately unclad. One of them was in fact a serious naturist, but the others said they had been playing in a football match and found this a good way of cooling down.

AUGUST 9TH
Celebrating the opening of Britain's first nudist beach in 1979 – was this how the page 3 picture was born?

The *Brighton Evening Argus* ran a discreetly posed photograph of them, under the inevitable headline: "Happy Nude Year." Surprisingly, nobody said they had a swinging time . . .

10th
AUGUST

They Sang to St Lawrence on the Hilltop – not any more

For many years on this Feast Day of St Lawrence, or the nearest Sunday to it, the parishioners of St Lawrence's Church, Whitwell, in Derbyshire, climbed the hill above the village to the ancient quarry from which the stones for the church originally came, and there they held an open-air service of thanksgiving. It became firmly established in 1874 when the rector, Canon George Mason, noticed that a number of older inhabitants used to climb the hill individually on this day to give thanks, and decided to encourage others to do the same.

The Feast Sunday Service developed into a full week of festivities, and by the turn of the century there was a sports day for the children, a cricket match, a fruit and vegetable show and a fancy-dress ball. It was the high spot of the Whitwell calendar.

The service is still held, but no longer on the hilltop. The clergy used to stand in the natural amphitheatre of the quarry while the congregation were on the crag above, but apparently the authorities decided this contravened modern insurance regulations, and the service is now held in the church precincts. However, the "Ballad of Deacon Lawrence", which Canon Mason wrote for the original service, is still sung, and the parish still honours St Lawrence. He was roasted on a gridiron, and it may sound slightly bizarre that he is patron saint of curriers – but curriers do not make hot curry, they groom horses.

11th
AUGUST

PLUTO was way ahead of the Chunnel – in its own Small Way

An early Channel Tunnel linking England and France was completed on this day in 1944. There were in fact two of them, one from Sandown to Cherbourg and the other from Dungeness to Boulogne. But nobody actually passed through them, they were

Morwenna is still a Winner, but Railways beat the Canal

Marhamchurch, near Bude in Cornwall, has two historical claims to fame, one mostly forgotten, the other remembered each year on the Monday nearest this day. The Marhamchurch Revel is held in honour of St Morwenna, who founded a monastic settlement here and gave the village its name.

A Queen of the Revel, one of the village schoolchildren, is crowned by Father Time, whose identity is secret – or as secret as anything can be in a small village. The crowning takes place in front of the church on the site of Morwenna's cell. Then the Queen rides in procession to the Revel Ground, and the revelling begins.

There was a time when the Revel was attended, not only by locals and holidaymakers, but by canalmen working on the Bude canal – first the navvies who built it, then the boatmen who used it. The canal passes through Marhamchurch to link Bude

AUGUST 11TH
PLUTO goes to sea. The oil pipeline to supply the D-Day invasion force is laid across the Channel

only two or three feet in diameter. Just a few pieces survive; one length lies abandoned in Shanklin Chine on the Isle of Wight, a forlorn reminder of one of the more unusual engineering achievements of the Second World War.

It had the codename PLUTO, not in memory of a mythological god or a cartoon dog, but because it was an acronym for Pipe Line Under the Ocean. It was actually a pipe line under the Channel, but PLUTC was unpronounceable.

Pluto was built to supply oil to the Allied Forces on the Normandy beaches and it proved rather more successful than Operation Mulberry, the other device for getting supplies to the troops. Submersible sections of concrete were taken across the Channel to create instant harbours where supply ships could dock. Unfortunately the one serving the American-held beaches was soon wrecked in a storm, but a second one on the British beaches was used until the port of Antwerp was open.

Mulberry was not an acronym. It just happened to be next on the Admiralty's list of names available for warships.

AUGUST 12TH
The Queen of the Marhamchurch Revel rides in the footsteps of St Morwenna

with Launceston, and for seventy years it carried beach-sand for fertilizer one way, and grain and slate the other. It had no locks except the one at the sea entrance. Cargoes were hauled from level to level in tub-boats, so they finished at Launceston 350 feet higher than when they started at Bude – and vice-versa.

Then the railways took over and the canal closed. Bude was left with a disused sea-lock – and Marhamchurch with its memories.

13th
AUGUST

The Soldiers Kissed her Shadow – but nobody dared Kiss Florence

Florence Nightingale died on this day in 1910 at the age of ninety, more than half a century after she became the "Lady of the Lamp" in the Crimea, but her fame remained undimmed. Even in her eighties she was still earning a place in the record books, as the first woman ever to be awarded the Order of Merit.

She went to the Crimea after an impassioned appeal in *The Times*: "Are there no devoted women among us, able and willing to go forth and minister to the sick and suffering soldiers?" There were in fact quite a number, including a black nurse called Mary Seacole who set up her own unofficial military hospital, and whose work has since been regarded as just as important as Florence Nightingale's, but it was Florence who became the legendary figure. "Her shadow, cast across the beds by her lamp as she walked through the

wards, was kissed in gratitude by the soldiers as it passed."

She came home a national heroine, and the public collected £50,000 to put at her disposal. With it she made history again, by founding the first-ever training school and home for nurses, at St Thomas's Hospital in London.

Longfellow waxed lyrical about her; well, fairly lyrical.

A lady with a lamp shall stand
In the great history of the land.
A noble type of good,
Heroic womanhood . . .

But Florence stood no nonsense about epitaphs, just as she stood no nonsense in the Crimea. Her tombstone says simply: "F.N. Born 1820. Died 1910."

FLORENCE NIGHTINGALE.
1820 - 1910

AUGUST 13TH
"A lady with a lamp shall stand, in the great history of the land . . ." The phrase has lived on too

14th
AUGUST

Not exactly a Miss World Contest – but the Fisher Girls had fun

On this day in 1908, more than forty years before Mr Eric Morley appeared on the scene, Britain experienced its first international beauty contest. The venue was

AUGUST 14TH
Early bathing belles were a lot more demure than they are today. Or were they?

the Pier Hippodrome at Folkestone, and the competitors represented England, Ireland, Austria, France and America. There were also "a number of fisher girls from Boulogne", who apparently crossed the Channel independently of the official French party and entered just for the hell of it.

Instead of a panel of judges, each member of the audience was allowed three votes. Since the audience was predominantly English, it was perhaps predictable that an English entrant won, a Miss Nellie Jarman from East Molesey in Surrey.

Eric Morley, publicity officer for Mecca Dance Halls, developed the idea into a Miss World competition in 1951, as part of the Festival of Britain celebrations. The odds again seemed in favour of an English win, since only five of the thirty contestants came from abroad, but this time there was a more impartial panel, and the first Miss World was a Swede from Stockholm, Miss Kiki Haakonson.

On this occasion bikinis were worn for the first time. Nellie Jarman of East Molesey might have been reluctant to appear in one – but those fisher girls would surely have loved it . . .

AUGUST 15TH
The Assumption of the Virgin Mary, depicted in a window at Walsingham's Slipper Chapel

15th

Even Henry VIII gave our Lady a Necklace – but only on Temporary Loan

This is the Feast of the Assumption, commemorating the death of the Virgin Mary and the assumption of her body into Heaven – a very special day in the Church's calendar, particularly in the Norfolk village of Little Walsingham, where Mary reappeared in a vision in the days of Edward the Confessor. She told the lady of the manor that she should build a replica of her home in Nazareth on the spot where a new spring would appear. The spring duly appeared, the shrine was built, and Walsingham became known as England's Nazareth, the most famous place of pilgrimage in the country.

Every king of England from Richard I to Henry VIII came here, and Henry seemed the most devout. He walked the last two miles barefoot, and placed a valuable necklace on Mary's wooden statue – but it turned out to be only a temporary loan. At the Dissolution, Walsingham was dissolved with all the rest. Henry took its treasures including no doubt the necklace, and had the statue taken to London and burnt – leaving the locals wondering where they went wrong.

These days the pilgrimages have been resumed and the shrines have multiplied – Greek and Russian Orthodox as well as Anglican and Roman Catholic. Even the old railway station is now occupied by the Brotherhood of St Seraphim of Sarov.

16th

"I left my Heart in West Wycombe Mausoleum"

On this day in 1775 a bizarre procession made its way up Wycombe Hill in Buckinghamshire to the mausoleum beside West Wycombe Church. It was headed by ten grenadiers, four German-flute players, two French-horn players, two bassoonists, six fife players, four muffled drums, eleven choirmen and two choristers. Eight militia officers, four fifes and drums and twenty soldiers brought up the rear. And in the middle, escorted by Lord le Despencer, six soldiers bore a bier on which was a lead urn containing the heart of Paul Whitehead, one-time secretary of the mock Order of St Francis, better known as the Hellfire Club.

Lord le Despencer was formerly Sir Francis Dashwood, prominent statesman and landowner, but better known in history as the founder of the Hellfire Club, which used to hold its unorthodox meetings at Medmenham Abbey or in the caves beneath Wycombe Hill – or on special occasions, in the great golden ball on top of the church tower.

Whitehead was a woollen-draper's apprentice who married an heiress, went into Parliament and was befriended by Dashwood. When he died he bequeathed his heart "to my noble friend and patron, Lord le Despencer, to be deposited in his mausoleum at West Wycombe".

In spite of the urn's inscription, "Unhallowed hands, this urn forbear", it disappeared in 1829, but the mausoleum, the church, and Dashwood's golden ball still dominate the Wycombe Valley.

17th
A U G U S T

The First Motoring Fatality – at Four Miles an Hour

Mrs Bridget Driscoll of Croydon achieved the dubious distinction on this day in 1896 of being the first pedestrian to be knocked down and killed by a motor-car. It seems an unlikely accident, because the car was only travelling at four miles an hour at the time, along the terrace at the Crystal Palace, but the driver was unsighted by two cars in front and failed to see her until it was too late – and she was so panic-stricken that she just stood motionless in the car's path. A wheel fractured her skull.

Curiously, there seems to be some competition for the honour of hosting the first car accident involving the death of the driver. In 1969 the Mayor of Harrow established a claim for the title by unveiling a plaque on Grove Hill which proclaimed it was the scene of the first such fatality. The driver was giving a demonstration to a prospective purchaser when the car crashed, and both of them died. To be fair, the plaque was primarily erected as a road safety warning; its main message is "Take Heed!" However, there is also a record of a driver being killed a year earlier, when a car went out of control on a hill at Purley in Surrey, crashed into an iron post and turned over against a tree.

A U G U S T 17TH
An early victim of the motor car, in the days when even 4mph could be lethal

A U G U S T 16TH
Sir Francis Dashwood's mausoleum at West Wycombe, where his friends were inclined to leave their hearts

On that occasion the passenger survived, so Harrow could claim to have had the first double fatality. Either way, the rest of the country soon caught up.

AUGUST 18TH
St Helena looks down on Colchester, named after her father – but was he really Old King Cole?

18th
AUGUST

If King Coel was Old King Cole, why was he so Merry?

This is the Patronal Day of St Helen, mother of the Roman Emperor Constantine, finder of the True Cross, and according to legend the daughter of Coel of Colchester, the original Old King Cole. If the legend is true, King Coel had little reason to be a merry old soul. He was besieged in Colchester for three years by Constantius, and the siege was only lifted when he handed over his daughter in marriage.

Alternatively, he agreed to pay tribute to Constantius, and a month afterwards he died, so the Roman took over the kingdom and his daughter. Either way, Helen – or Helena, again there are two versions – features on Colchester's civic charter, and her statue surmounts the City Hall.

Less romantic historians, however, say she had no connection with Colchester, and indeed was probably never in England at all. She was born in Turkey, and although she did marry Constantius he divorced her before he came to England, and their son Constantine was born in what became Yugoslavia. The Colchester story

was dreamed up later, they say, after Constantine had taken over from his father in England, because he would be more politically correct as the son of a British princess.

That may be more accurate historically, but I know which version I prefer – and I suspect in Colchester they feel the same way.

19th
AUGUST

If you want to go on the Waggon, you have to Keep Drinking

Saddleworth was moved from Yorkshire into Greater Manchester in the local government re-organization of 1974, thus causing considerable irritation and distress to its inhabitants. Perhaps to establish their Yorkshire-ness, it was in the same year that they decided to revive the ancient custom of rushcarting, on the first weekend after this day. It had died out some sixty years before, largely because of excess drunkenness and bad language, culminating in a fatal accident. The revived festivities are rather less riotous, but the tradition continues for

AUGUST 19TH
Rushcarting at Saddleworth, where "going on the waggon" means exactly the opposite

the "jockey" – the man who rides on the summit of the rushcart – to down a quantity of ale at every pub it passes. In this case "on the waggon" must mean, not foregoing alcohol, but being able to drink a substantial amount of it without falling off the cart.

Rushcarting originated in the days when rushes were taken to church to cover the earth floor. Great skill was needed to pack the maximum volume of rushes on to the cart. The finished load looks a cross between a bell-tent and a large half-lemon.

These days it is essentially an occasion for Morrismen, who haul the cart and dance around it. There is clog-stepping, gurning (pulling ugly faces) and a contest for telling tall tales, some of which will no doubt enter the folklore of the future – and books like this.

spaniel, his pet pig, and his devoted maidservant Prue. He was much too jolly for the Puritans, who dismissed him from his living at Dean Prior in Devon, but when the Restoration came, Herrick was restored too.

He was a great friend and fan of Ben Jonson, and wrote a mock prayer to "Saint Ben" in which he managed to find a rhyme for "Herrick":

Make the way smooth for me
When I, thy Herrick,
Honoring thee on my knee
Offer my lyric. . .

Maybe he should have stuck to "Gather ye rosebuds . . ."

AUGUST 20TH
Robert Herrick, the jolly parson who followed his own advice: "Gather ye rosebuds while ye may"

20th
AUGUST

He wrote "Gather ye Rosebuds while ye May" – and he did

"The greatest songwriter – as surely as Shakespeare is the greatest dramatist – ever born of human race" was born on this day in 1591. The man who wrote that was the poet Swinburne, who is rather better remembered today than the man he wrote it about, but Robert Herrick did write a song that still survives, "Cherry Ripe", and a poem of which at least the first line is familiar: "Gather ye rosebuds while ye may". And just in case you are trying to remember what comes next:

Old Time is still a-flying,
And this same flower that smiles today
Tomorrow will be dying.

The poem summed up Herrick's own philosophy. He was a jolly country parson, enjoying a comfortable bachelor life with his

21st
AUGUST

"Where his Spur strikes Today, his Head will strike Tomorrow"

As Richard III was riding across Bow Bridge in Leicester on this day in 1485, on his way to meet the forces of Henry Tudor, it is said that one of his spurs struck the side of the parapet. Inevitably an aged crone was on the spot to make a gloomy forecast. "Where his spur strikes today," she vouchsafed, "his head will strike tomorrow."

Richard was out of earshot and failed to take the warning. He made camp outside the city, and next morning he took Communion at the Church of St James at Sutton Cheney, where each year the Richard III Society holds a service on the Sunday nearest the anniversary. Then he rejoined his army and rode to Bosworth Field.

He fought valiantly, and in theory, with

AUGUST 21ST
The plaque at Leicester commemorating Richard III's last journey

an army twice the size of his opponent's, he should have won, but as he led a charge against the enemy lines he was unhorsed. Everyone knows what happens next: "A horse, a horse, my kingdom for a horse!" But he never got the horse until it was too late, and lost his kingdom anyway; he was killed by a blow on the head.

His crown was rescued from a hawthorn bush and put on the head of his successor, while the dead king's body was stripped of its armour and flung across the back of the belated horse. And as it carried him across Bow Bridge, his head struck the side of the parapet . . .

22nd
AUGUST

∽

Instead of a Hearty Breakfast, he Enjoyed a Kemble Pipe

In parts of Herefordshire they still talk about a "Kemble Pipe" when they are having a final, comforting smoke before going to bed. The expression stems from this day in 1678, though the circumstances were rather more unpleasant. Father John Kemble smoked his last pipe, not before going to bed, but before being hanged, drawn and quartered.

Father Kemble was an eighty-year-old Roman Catholic priest, who was arrested while saying Mass in Pembridge Castle. He was taken to London to face a trumped-up charge of plotting against Charles II, and although he resolutely refused to confess, he was sentenced anyway.

On the morning the sentence was due to be carried out, instead of the hearty breakfast which some prisoners in this situation are said to enjoy, he asked for a pipe of tobacco – and the "Kemble Pipe" went into folklore.

The calmness he displayed before his death was maintained as he went to the gallows, and the hangman was so impressed that he mercifully made sure he was dead before the gruesome drawing and quartering began. The body was brought back to John Kemble's native county, and a simple tombstone in the churchyard at Welsh Newton, near Monmouth, is inscribed: "Dyed the 22 of August, Anno D. 1678". It would be nice to think that his pipe was buried with him.

23rd
AUGUST

∽

He may have been a Rebel – but what a way to Go

The first celebrity to be hanged, drawn and quartered died on this day in 1305. William Wallace was a national hero to his fellow Scots, but a murderous rebel so far as the English were concerned, and they reckoned no death was too unpleasant for him.

This death was about as unpleasant as you could get. The victim was only partially hanged, so that he was still alive when the internal organs were removed and burnt, and the limbs were quartered. Parts of Wallace's body were put on show in various Scottish towns as a warning to others.

The English felt justice had been done. Wallace had beaten Edward I decisively at the Battle of Stirling, ravaged the North of England and showed no mercy to prisoners. But as one historian commented: "If the English put themselves into the position of robbers and oppressors in a country which did not belong to them, they were scarcely entitled to much mercy."

Wallace was finally defeated at Falkirk and was on the run for years until he was betrayed – alas, by a fellow Scot – and taken to London for trial and execution. A plaque near Smithfield Market records where he

died. But that did not end England's problems with the Scots, because a year later, along came Robert the Bruce.

24th
AUGUST

St Bartholomew and the Bartle – linked by a Pig?

"Burning the Bartle" takes place at West Witton in North Yorkshire on the Saturday nearest this day, St Bartholomew's Day – but

the connection with the saint is pretty obscure, apart from its name. The Bartle is a straw-filled effigy with lit-up eyes which is carried in procession through the village, calling at all the pubs, before being taken up a nearby hill and burnt on a bonfire.

It is carried by two men while a third chants a verse which starts: "In Penshill Crags he tore his rags, At Hunter's Thorn he blew his horn," and ends, "At Wadham's End he couldn't fend, At Briskill End he made his end. Shout, boys, shout!" And they do.

But what is the connection with St Bartholomew? He did not die by burning, he was said to have been flayed alive – hence his emblem, a knife. He is also patron saint

AUGUST 24TH
The Bartle in a stuffed shirt, who may represent a pig-thief who came to a bad end

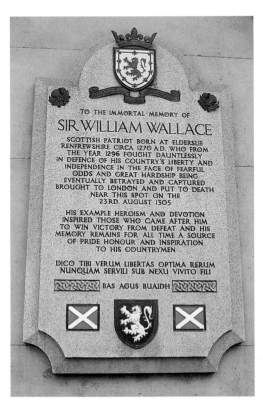

TO THE IMMORTAL MEMORY OF
SIR WILLIAM WALLACE
SCOTTISH PATRIOT BORN AT ELDERSLIE
RENFREWSHIRE CIRCA 1270 A.D. WHO FROM
THE YEAR 1296 FOUGHT DAUNTLESSLY
IN DEFENCE OF HIS COUNTRY'S LIBERTY AND
INDEPENDENCE IN THE FACE OF FEARFUL
ODDS AND GREAT HARDSHIP BEING
EVENTUALLY BETRAYED AND CAPTURED
BROUGHT TO LONDON AND PUT TO DEATH
NEAR THIS SPOT ON THE
23RD. AUGUST 1305

HIS EXAMPLE HEROISM AND DEVOTION
INSPIRED THOSE WHO CAME AFTER HIM
TO WIN VICTORY FROM DEFEAT AND HIS
MEMORY REMAINS FOR ALL TIME A SOURCE
OF PRIDE HONOUR AND INSPIRATION
TO HIS COUNTRYMEN

DICO TIBI VERUM LIBERTAS OPTIMA RERUM
NUNQUAM SERVILI SUB NEXU VIVITO FILI

BAS AGUS BUAIDH

of beekeepers, but that hardly helps. However, he is principally associated with Bartholomew Fairs, which often featured a Bartholomew Pig, roasted whole and served hot. One of the many stories attached to the Bartle is that it represents an eighteenth-century pig-thief who was chased over the fells – from Penshill Crags to Briskill End – and then killed.

Could he have stolen a Bartholomew pig? It's a swine of a theory – but can you think of a better one?

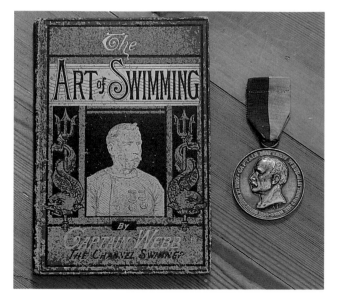

AUGUST 25TH Captain Webb's medal and instruction book on how to swim the Channel – but did Jean-Marie Saletti do it first?

25th
AUGUST

The First Man to Swim the Channel Unaided – or was he?

On the cliffs of Dover there are memorials to three men who made history in their own fields by crossing the Channel. A granite silhouette of an aeroplane set in the ground recalls M. Blériot's first flight across it; there is a memorial to C.S. Rolls, who flew the Channel both ways a year later; and the third, on the East Cliff promenade, commemorates the much more exhausting crossing by Captain Matthew Webb, the first man to complete a swim across the Channel without a lifebelt on this day in 1875.

Webb was a 27-year-old Merchant Navy captain who swam breast-stroke from Dover to Calais. It took him nearly twenty-two hours, which may seem a rather long time for a direct distance of twenty-one miles, but because of currents and the tide it is estimated that he actually swam thirty-eight

miles. It may have taken too much out of him; he died before he was forty.

There is evidence to suggest, however, that a French soldier was ahead of him by sixty years. Jean-Marie Saletti escaped from a prison hulk off Dover in July or August 1815, and is said to have swum across the Channel to freedom, landing at Boulogne. But he is not officially credited with the record – not in the English record books anyway.

26th
AUGUST

"War, Plunder and Massacre were his Life" – the Hero of Crécy

The Battle of Crécy, which was fought on this day in 1346, founded the legendary reputation of Prince Edward, eldest son of Edward III, better known to posterity as the Black Prince. He was only sixteen when he led the English army to victory and established himself as a folk hero. But his triumph at Crécy was partly stage-managed

AUGUST 26TH King Edward III, wearing an early version of the balaclava, briefs his son, the Black Prince, before the Battle of Crécy

– his father deliberately left him to command the vanguard and get all the credit – and partly handed to him on a plate by his opponent, King Philip of France. Philip saw that some of his men were retreating, and was so furious he ordered those who were still standing firm to fight their comrades as well as the English. Fifteen hundred French noblemen died, at the hands of the English and each other; the English fatalities totalled fifty.

With this victory under his belt, young Edward went on rampaging around France and Spain for most of his fairly short life – he died at 46. One historian summed him up: "War, plunder and massacre were his life, but his undoubted bravery and distinctive black armour enshrined him in the popular imagination."

He was well aware of his popular image and made sure it was preserved after his death. He left instructions that his effigy in Canterbury Cathedral should be "all armed in steel for battle" – and it still is.

27th
AUGUST

Rescued by the Angels of Mons – but only Metaphorically

One of the great legends of the First World War was created on this day in 1914, soon after it began. It was the second day of the British retreat from Mons, and the third and fourth divisions of the Expeditionary Force, "the Old Contemptibles", were being heavily pressed; it seemed impossible for them to survive. Then, according to a Fleet Street reporter, Arthur Machen, St George and the angels appeared, "clad in white with flaming swords", and held back the advancing Germans. The British lived to fight – and probably to die – another day.

AUGUST 27TH
"The Angel of Mons" in the First World War even inspired a Valse – but it was just dreamed up by a Fleet Street reporter

The report was written so graphically that some readers took it literally and the legend of the Angels of Mons was born. But Machen was in Fleet Street when he wrote it, and it was only intended as a piece of metaphorical imagery. Such is the power of the Press.

As for the origin of "the Old Contemptibles", that story may also have an element of myth. It stemmed from an army order – "almost certainly apocryphal", according to one authority – issued by the Kaiser, which commanded his men to "walk over General French's contemptible little Army". The order may have read "contemptibly little army",

which is not quite so bad, but the BEF relished the insult and adopted the name. The surviving "Old Contemptibles" held their final parade at Aldershot exactly sixty years later – and took tea with the Queen.

28th
AUGUST

The Farmworker Riots that went with a Swing

The Luddites, the factory workers in the Midlands and North who smashed up textile machinery in the early nineteenth century because they feared for their jobs, had a less-publicized equivalent in the South, where farmworkers had the same fears about

AUGUST 28TH
Rioting farmworkers just added to the troubles at Trouble House – but they made a change from drowning and hanging

threshing and haymaking machines. The Luddites took their name from their legendary leader, General Ned Ludd, and

their southern counterparts claimed to be led by a Captain Swing – which would make them, presumably, Swingers, though this seems to have been missed by the historians.

The first major incident in their campaign was on this day in 1830, when a steam threshing-machine was smashed near Canterbury. During the next two years many more machines were attacked, hayricks set on fire and threatening letters sent, signed by the mythical Captain Swing.

The inn sign of Trouble House, at Tetbury in Gloucestershire, features a typical incident. Among the many troubles it portrays is a blazing hay waggon, with farmworkers and soldiers fighting around it. Apparently as the waggon passed the inn a haymaking machine was spotted, concealed under the hay, and an angry mob attacked it. The troops were summoned and culprits were dealt with harshly. Ringleaders were executed or transported, while the farmers and their new machines – made hay.

29th
AUGUST

The Races with six Entrants, two Winners – and no Racing

The Kirkby Hill Races, as anyone in Kirkby (Yorkshire) can tell you, do not involve any racing. This is the local nickname for the curious procedure which is still followed on or near this day every other year, to appoint trustees of Dakyn's Charity.

The Rev. John Dakyn was a sixteenth-century rector who left funds for an almshouse "to redeem and expiate . . . my most grievous sins." He may have had in mind the part he played as one of Henry VIII's Commissioners in sending at least one martyr to the stake.

AUGUST 29TH
*The memorial to
John Dakyn, who
inaugurated the
Kirkby Hill Races –
which have nothing
to do with racing*

paper of the like form, and being enclosed and wrapped in round wax after the manner of balls of the same bulk, shall be put all together in a pitcher or pot, covered or shut – and the Rector shall take out of the pitcher two balls, as chance shall offer them . . . and those two men shall be wardens for the two years following."

You can't get much fairer than that.

The almshouse has been replaced by flats which are let rent-free to deserving pensioners, but the method he set out for appointing the trustees has remained unchanged over the centuries. It is carried out behind closed doors by the rector and churchwardens, in the presence of six potential trustees – "six of the gravest and honestest men of the parish".

"The names and surnames of the said six men shall be written upon several scrolls of

30th
AUGUST

The Church Roof got Calico – and the Queen got Balmoral

John Camden Neild, "The Queen's Miser", died on this day in 1852, leaving his entire fortune, worth some twenty million pounds in today's money, to Queen Victoria, "begging Her Majesty's most gracious acceptance of the same, for her sole use and benefit, and her heirs." She did graciously accept, and spent most of it, so it is believed, on buying the Balmoral estate.

AUGUST 30TH
*Balmoral might not
have been bought by
Queen Victoria
without her little
windfall from the
Queen's Miser*

Neild owned extensive property but spent very little on it, and doubled the inheritance his father left him by being excessively mean. He refused to have his clothes brushed in case it wore them out, and his nightshirt was so tattered that, when he left it behind after staying at a tenant's home, the tenant threw it on the fire.

Some of his property was at North Marston in Buckinghamshire, where he was in effect the squire, but when the rector asked him for help in repairing the church roof, it is said Neild gave him a sheet of calico to put over the hole and said, "That'll see me out."

Happily the Queen was a little more generous. She donated a reredos and stained-glass east window to the church in his memory, increased the few bequests he had made, and provided for Neild's old housekeeper, who was left nothing in his will.

It was nearly one hundred and fifty years, however, before the final repairs were done to the roof – courtesy of English Heritage, not John Camden Neild.

31st
AUGUST

A Master of Gamesmanship: the Great W.G.

On this day in 1908, to the grief of his fans, the relief of opposing teams, and the concealed delight of the many players, umpires and groundsmen who had suffered under his scathing tongue, Dr William Gilbert Grace finally retired from first-class cricket at the age of sixty. In forty-three years he had scored 54,896 runs including 126 centuries, taken 2,879 wickets and held 871 catches. He had also unnerved countless opponents with his blatant and unashamed gamesmanship.

The great hero of English cricket, whose almost sacred memory was honoured by Lord's in 1923 with the installation of the majestic Grace Gates, was singularly graceless on the field. In one Test match he ran out a young Australian by knocking down his wicket while he had innocently wandered up the pitch for the ritual patting-down between balls. If a batsman stood his ground against him after being given out, he would roar, "Pavilion, you!" – but his own reluctance to leave the crease in the same situation was legendary. And if he hit the ball skywards and a fielder looked like catching it, he would bellow "Miss it!" – and the poor chap frequently did.

Although an "amateur" he made an estimated million in today's money – but others profited too. Club grounds could double their entrance prices to see the irascible, flamboyant, ruthless – and utterly brilliant – W.G.

AUGUST 31ST W.G. Grace, renowned master of batting, bowling, fielding – and the art of gamesmanship

September

iars
ster

1st

Mr Higginbottom's Puddings might have Stopped the Wars of the Roses

Black-pudding lobbing may sound like a product of the Ministry for Silly Walks, but it was devised by a nineteenth-century landlord of the Corner Pin pub at Stubbins, near Ramsbottom, as a harmless way of allowing Yorkshire visitors and Lancashire locals to work off their natural antipathy. Apparently whenever Yorkshire trippers stopped at the pub on their way to the Lancashire coast, fighting broke out. Then the landlord, a Mr Higginbottom, had his brainwave – and now they lob Lancashire black puddings at roast Yorkshire puddings instead. The contest is repeated every year on this day if a Sunday, or the first Sunday afterwards.

The way Mr Higginbottom got the idea is almost as bizarre as the idea itself. He saw children apparently throwing stones at windows, but discovered the stones were Yorkshire puddings, left by their mothers to cool on the windowsills. So he built a platform outside his pub, about a foot square

on top of a twenty-foot stand. Twenty-one Yorkshire puddings are piled on top, and each contestant lobs three black puddings at them to knock them off.

Nearly two hundred people usually take part, and the prize is just as improbable – £100 plus as many cans of bitter as would equal, when balanced on top of each other, the height of the winner. I am not sure who finishes up with the puddings . . .

2nd

The Fire in a Bakehouse that Burned down a City

At one o'clock in the morning on this day in 1664, Thomas Farriner was asleep over his bakehouse in Pudding Lane, in the City of London, when a servant rushed in to rouse him. The bedroom was full of smoke and the staircase was already in flames. He and his wife and daughter, with the servant, escaped through a garret window and watched the blaze spread to the adjoining timber houses. The Great Fire of London had begun.

By the time it was over, four days later, nearly four hundred acres of closely packed shops and houses had been reduced to charred rubble; a hundred thousand people lost their homes. Remarkably, there were only eight fatalities.

On the personal instructions of Charles II, who took charge of the fire-fighting operation, entire streets were blown up to create firebreaks, which effectively stopped it spreading further. The King himself got so close to the blaze that his clothes were blackened by the smoke; the diarist John Evelyn described his efforts admiringly – "even labouring in person, and being present to command, order and encourage

*SEPTEMBER 2ND
The Monument in the City marks the bakehouse where the Fire of London began – but only if you lie it on its side*

*SEPTEMBER 1ST
The Corner Pin at Stubbins, where a peacemaking publican devised a novel way of allowing his customers to let off steam; black-pudding lobbing*

Workemen, by which he shewed his affection to his people and gained theirs." He gained even more when he distributed a hundred guineas among the firefighters.

The Fire is commemorated by Wren's Monument in the City. If it were laid down towards Pudding Lane, its tip would mark the location of Thomas Farriner's bakehouse, where it all began.

3rd
SEPTEMBER

Charles hid in the Oak Tree – and Arthur got away too

This was a day of mixed fortunes for the Royalists in 1651. The bad news was they lost the Battle of Worcester; the good news was that many of them escaped, most notably Charles II himself, who hid in the boughs of the famous Boscobel Oak while the pursuing Roundheads passed underneath. And then there was Arthur Jones . . .

It may not be the most romantic of names, but Arthur Jones was a dashing Cavalier just like the rest. His family built and owned the magnificent Chastleton House in the Cotswolds, after making a fortune from wool. This was where Arthur headed after the battle, and Cromwell's men, being no fools, headed there too. But Walter Jones, who designed the house, may have foreseen this kind of situation, because he provided a secret room, in which Arthur took refuge.

His pursuers searched the house, but found nothing. They demanded some refreshment, and Mrs Jones shrewdly laced their wine with a sleeping potion. They passed out in the bedroom next to the secret chamber, and Arthur passed out of the house

and into obscurity for the next couple of years.

Chastleton House stayed in the Jones family for centuries. It is due to be re-opened by the National Trust – complete with its secret chamber – in 1997.

SEPTEMBER 3RD Chastleton House in the Cotswolds, where Cromwell's men failed to keep up with the Joneses

4th
SEPTEMBER

Show me the way to Duirholm

St Cuthbert was one of our most-travelled English saints – and all his travelling was done posthumously. When he died at Lindisfarne in AD688 he left instructions that if there was a threat to the island from the Danes, the monks should leave for the mainland, taking his body with them.

In due course the Danes turned up, and the monks set off on their wanderings with the body of St Cuthbert, which was still miraculously preserved. They settled for some years in Chester-le-Street, then the Danes headed their way again and they moved on to Ripon.

SEPTEMBER 4TH The legend of the Duirholm milkmaids and St Cuthbert, portrayed on the tower of Durham Cathedral

When the Danes eventually moved out, the monks headed back for Chester-le-Street. On the way, however, they were "miraculously arrested"; they found they could not lift the saint's body. Equally miraculously, they were told they must establish St Cuthbert's permanent shrine at Duirholm, "home of the deer". They had never heard of such a place, but happily a couple of Duirholm milkmaids came by with their cow.

With the saint's body suddenly portable again, the monks followed the maids and the cow to what we call Durham, and the cathedral now stands on the saint's final resting place.

"The Translation of St Cuthbert" was celebrated for many centuries on this day. A carved cow on the tower of Durham Cathedral indicates it may not be entirely a myth.

5th
SEPTEMBER

Leefe Robinson VC –
Hero and Pub

Captain William Leefe Robinson, who was awarded the Victoria Cross on this day in 1916, was not only the first British pilot to shoot down a Zeppelin, but also one of the few VCs to have a pub named after him. First a tin shack, now a Beefeater Inn, the "Leefe Robinson VC" stands opposite All Saints' Church, Harrow Weald, in London, where he was buried soon after the First World War, victim of an influenza epidemic. He was still only twenty-three years old.

Leefe Robinson went to Sandhurst as soon as the war started, and had already been wounded in France when he gained his pilot's certificate and was put in charge of a

unit testing anti-Zeppelin machine guns. In September 1916 he had the chance to try one out on the real thing.

He was on night patrol when Zeppelins were spotted crossing the coast. He engaged one of them over London, and while thousands watched them from below in the light of searchlights he emptied two of his ammunition drums into it, without effect. With his final drum he fired at a different part of the hull; the airship burst into flames and nose-dived into a field. Leefe Robinson landed at Harrow Weald with just half a gallon of fuel in his tanks.

His flying career ended when he was shot down and taken prisoner. The camp commander knew the captain of the Zeppelin he had brought down, and Leefe Robinson did not have a comfortable time. He returned home in poor health, and when the 'flu epidemic broke out, he stood no chance. His VC was sold at Christies in 1988 for £99,000.

S E P T E M B E R 5 T H
The Leefe Robinson at Harrow Weald, commemorating the first British pilot to shoot down a Zeppelin and win the VC

6th
SEPTEMBER

Off went the Pilgrim Fathers –
but some had tried before

When the *Mayflower* sailed from Plymouth for the New World on this day in 1620, some of the Pilgrim Fathers on board had tried to do it all before. Beside an obscure creek at Fishtoft in Lincolnshire there is a stone memorial with the inscription:

"Near this place, in September 1607, those later known as the Pilgrim Fathers set

7th

SEPTEMBER 6TH
The Pilgrim Fathers
make it at last – after
two false starts

She was only a Lighthouse-keeper's Daughter . . .

Grace Darling, daughter of the keeper of Longstone lighthouse on the Farne Islands, became the darling of the public for the part she played on this day in 1838 in rescuing shipwrecked mariners, by rowing a tiny boat with her father through mountainous seas at the height of the storm. It was the sort of story the Victorians loved – and it was true.

Grace was twenty-two at the time, small and slightly built. From the lighthouse she saw nine people marooned on a rock about a mile offshore, the only survivors of the steamship *Forfarshire*, which had run aground and broken up. She urged her father to rescue them.

"If only I had another man to help me," said Mr Darling. "I can handle a boat," cried Grace. "Let me come with you!" You can almost hear the piano-player providing the background.

They set off for the rock, knowing they could not row back against the wind unless the survivors were fit enough to help.

sail on their first attempt to find religious freedom across the seas."

Unfortunately they tried to do it without the King's permission, and the treacherous captain of their hired craft gave them away. The leaders spent some time in the cells at Boston Guildhall and the rest returned home – but only temporarily. They raised enough money to hire another ship, and this time chose a remote stretch of coast north of Grimsby.

The men walked there, the women and children travelled more slowly by barge. So only the menfolk were on board when soldiers were seen and the captain insisted on setting sail, leaving the families behind. The ship dropped them off in Holland, where eventually they were all reunited. They settled there for some years until they heard about the *Mayflower* and managed to join the party – becoming, as it were, the Pilgrim Grandfathers.

SEPTEMBER 7TH
Grace to the rescue;
how a lighthouse
keeper's daughter
became the Darling
of the nation

165

Fortunately they were, and in two trips all nine were rescued.

The Government was impressed and gave her £50. The public was impressed even more, and raised over a thousand pounds. But like so many Victorian stories, it all ended in tears; Grace Darling died of consumption five years later.

8th
S E P T E M B E R

Do Perambulate with the Sheriff – but Stick to the Rules

When Queen Mary granted a charter in 1553 making Lichfield a separate county from Staffordshire, with the right to appoint its own Sheriff, she stipulated that the holder of the office should "perambulate the new county and city annually on the Feast of the Nativity of the Blessed Virgin Mary". The custom has continued ever since, on the Saturday nearest this day.

The Sheriff and retinue assemble at the Guildhall and set off on the twenty-mile circuit of the city boundary. Over the years the Ride has become so popular, with upwards of a hundred and fifty riders taking part, that detailed rules have been drawn up to keep everyone in order. They have to be over twelve, and those under sixteen have to be attended by an adult. Nobody is allowed to smoke, everyone has to wear hunting or show dress. "Boots with laces are not permitted."

In the afternoon races are held, culminating in the Sheriff's Plate. Only horses taking part in the Ride can compete, and there is another list of rules to comply with. Registrations forms are issued beforehand, and buffet or packed lunches can be booked.

It is all very highly and efficiently organized; Queen Mary would be much impressed. But one element of the Ride might bewilder her: a number of Land Rovers now take part.

SEPTEMBER 8TH "Perambulating" with the Sheriff through Lichfield; only the properly dressed can take part

9th
S E P T E M B E R

Air Mail had its Problems – but what a pretty Pillar Box

A sky-blue pillar box marked "Air Mail" at one end of Windsor High Street is a reminder of the first air-mail service in Britain, which started on this day in 1911. It was an historic occasion, but it had its problems. It was supposed to commemorate the Coronation of George V, but the coronation had taken place three months before. It covered only nineteen miles between Hendon and Windsor Great Park, but even so, one of the three planes that took off failed to make it. And the first-day cover envelope depicted a biplane flying over Windsor Castle; it was actually a Blériot monoplane.

In any case, the service was officially beaten into the record books by India. The

SEPTEMBER 9TH
Sky blue is an appropriate colour for a pillar box meant for air-mail letters

first air mail was flown from an exhibition in Allahabad to the railway station at Naini, five miles away. And when the Hendon–Windsor service did get going, it operated for only three weeks.

Later efforts to inaugurate British cross-Channel and transatlantic air-mail services had their problems too. The first regular service from London to Paris was so expensive it only carried forty-five letters a day, and the first service from Southampton to Montreal and New York was launched just four weeks before the Second World War.

But never mind. That's a jolly nice sky-blue pillar box.

10th
SEPTEMBER

The Bishops who share their Home with Ambrose's Skull

Wardley Hall at Worsley is the official residence of the Roman Catholic Bishop of Manchester, but for more than two centuries it has been known as the House of the Skull. In a niche beside the main staircase is a skull, assumed to be that of Father Ambrose Barlow, a Benedictine monk who was hanged, drawn and quartered for his beliefs at Lancaster on this day in 1641. In earlier

SEPTEMBER 10TH
Father Ambrose was martyred over 350 years ago, but he still sees the Bishop safely to bed

times all manner of unpleasant things happened if anyone attempted to move it, and although this has been the home of bishops for over sixty years, they seem quite happy to share it with the skull.

After Ambrose died his head was displayed in Manchester as a warning to others, but one of his Catholic relations, Francis Downes, managed to rescue it one night and hid it at Wardley Hall. During restoration work in 1745 a casket was found in the wall of the old chapel at the hall. It contained a skull "furnished with a goodly set of teeth and having on it a good deal of auburn hair".

Its identity has not been conclusively proved, but forensic tests show it belonged to a man of Ambrose's age and stature, it dates from that period, and it was severed violently from the body and impaled on something sharp. And Ambrose was reputed to have auburn hair.

11th
SEPTEMBER

Where his Tower was concerned, Sir Thomas was no Square

Sir Thomas Tresham of Rushton Hall in Northamptonshire, a Roman Catholic convert who spent many years in prison for his beliefs, died on this day in 1605, leaving behind one of the most unusual little buildings in the country. It still survives as a symbol of his devotion to the Holy Trinity – the Rushton Tower.

Everything about the Tower is in threes. It has three sides, each with three gables rising to three pinnacles. Each of its three storeys has three windows on each of its three sides. Each wall is thirty-three feet long, and the Latin inscriptions which run

SEPTEMBER *11TH*
Thomas Tresham's
triangular tribute to
the Trinity. Even the
chimney is three-
sided

round them have thirty-three letters on each wall. The windows have three or nine panes – triangular, of course – and the walls are decorated with trefoils in threes.

Among the assorted animals climbing the gables – each one symbolic of something – there are nine chickens, representing Sir Thomas's nine sons and daughters; he even had his children in multiples of three. And guess how many sides to the chimney . . .

The triangular chimney does actually work, and the Tower was not just a folly or even an obsession, it was built to be used. In the family accounts it is called the Warreners Lodge, and it was occupied by the keeper in charge of the rabbits. No doubt he had to wear a three-cornered hat.

12th
SEPTEMBER

Praise Percy Pilcher – but Remember the Gliding Coachman

Percy Pilcher may not sound a name to conjure with, but Percy played an important role in British aviation history. On this day in 1895 he made the first controlled glider

flight in Britain. He built a glider weighing forty-five pounds with a wing surface-area of a hundred and fifty square feet, and managed to keep it off the ground at a height of twelve feet for all of twenty seconds.

The statistics of this controlled flight are very precise and well-documented. Rather less precise – and a lot more fun – is the story of the first *un*-controlled glider flight, which was achieved more than forty years before by Sir George Cayley's coachman. Not even his name is known for certain; we have only an eye-witness account by Sir George's grand-daughter – and that was written seventy years later.

Sir George built a kite-shaped glider with a tricycle undercarriage, and persuaded his coachman to try it out across a small valley on his Brompton estate in Yorkshire. The reluctant aeronaut actually managed to fly across it, a distance estimated by the grand-daughter (who was only ten at the time) as about five hundred yards. He landed, however, "with a smash", and his words as he climbed out have fortunately been recorded for posterity: "Sir George, I wish to give notice. I was hired to drive, not to fly!"

But eventually Percy Pilcher picked up where he left off.

13th
SEPTEMBER

He took Quebec – and everyone wanted a Wolfe at their Door

General James Wolfe ended French power in Canada when he defeated Montcalm at the Battle of Quebec on this day in 1759, but he was mortally wounded during the fighting. He was only thirty-two, and became a posthumous national hero. As well as winning the battle, he was also credited with

SEPTEMBER 13TH
General Wolfe's statue is still ready to fight the French if they invade Westerham

two memorable pronouncements during the course of it.

As the British rowed down-river with muffled oars to the foot of the Heights of Abraham, Wolfe recited to himself Gray's *Elegy in a Country Churchyard*, then vouchsafed to a convenient biographer: "I would rather be the author of that poem than take Quebec." Having taken it, however, he modified that. As he lay dying he was told the good news and murmured: "Do they run already? Then I die content."

In the years that followed, places all over England tried to establish a link with Wolfe and Quebec. An escarpment at Matlock Bath in Derbyshire was christened the Heights of Abraham, a Wolfe Monument was erected at a place called Quebec near Ripon in Yorkshire, and in the grounds of Quebec Hall at Dereham in Norfolk the trees in the grounds were planted in the formation of the troops at the battle.

The genuine place of pilgrimage, however, is Westerham in Kent, where Wolfe was born. He spent his early years at the National Trust's Quebec House in the town, and his statue on the Green is entirely at home.

14th
S E P T E M B E R

Would it be Rude to the Holy Rood to find the Wells Undressed?

SEPTEMBER 14TH
From a pagan offering of a bunch of flowers to keep the water gods happy, well-dressing has become an artistic display which keeps the tourists happy

This is Holy Rood Day, one of the lesser-known Feasts which celebrates the Exaltation of the Cross – which again is a rather obscure way of describing the return of the True Cross to Calvary in AD629 after it had been stolen fifteen years before. Rather curiously, this is the day on which the well-dressing at Chesterfield is based, and when,

like so many Derbyshire towns and villages at this time of year, Chesterfield bedecks its wells and other water-associated objects with magnificent floral pictures.

Nobody is quite sure how well-dressing began. Certainly there seems little connection with the True Cross at Calvary. Far more likely it was originally a pagan way of appeasing the water gods, in the hope of attracting more rain – though in the Derbyshire dales during the holiday season there would be more enthusiasm for keeping it away.

The Church turned this pagan rite, like so many others, into a religious festival, and wells got blessed as well as dressed. Then it acquired another *raison d'être*, as a tourist attraction. The simple bunches of flowers which the gods were satisfied with in medieval times developed into elaborate pictures composed of petals, berries, seeds, moss and bark.

Many places like to prepare them in secret. Chesterfield prefers the public to watch – to see how the well-dressed well gets dressed.

15th

Not the Happiest Way of opening a Railway

The Liverpool and Manchester Railway opened on this day in 1830 – and managed to achieve the first-ever death of a railway passenger on its inaugural run. Eight locomotives had been built for the railway and all of them took part, with the *Northumbrian* in the lead, drawing the most elegant carriage with the Duke of Wellington and other dignitaries on board. The other seven followed behind, each pulling four carriages of a more plebeian design. The procession must have been quite a sight – or so the passengers in the first carriage must have thought, because the *Northumbrian* pulled up for them to watch the others pass.

"Several gentlemen alighted," says one account, "and Mr Huskisson, who was one of them, went up to shake hands with the Duke. While they were together, the *Rocket* passed rapidly on the other line. The unfortunate gentleman became flurried, and ran to and fro in doubt as to the best means of escaping danger. The engine-driver endeavoured to stop, but without success, and Mr Huskisson was knocked down by the *Rocket*, the wheels of which went over his leg and thigh."

The Rt. Hon. William Huskisson, Secretary of State for the Colonies, was rushed to hospital – the *Northumbrian* covered fifteen miles in a record-breaking twenty-five minutes – but he died the same night.

16th

Bless you! Bless you! Bless you!

This day brought enormous relief in 1983 to a fourteen-year-old schoolgirl in Pershore, Hereford & Worcester, called Donna Griffiths. Donna enjoyed her first sneeze-free day since January 13th, 1981, a total of 978 days. It is still the world sneezing record.

When it started, for no apparent reason, she was sneezing about every thirty seconds, and in the first year she must have sneezed a million times – though nobody counted. By that time she had passed the existing record of 194 days comfortably – or rather, very uncomfortably. "It's horrible," she said. "My friends at school used to tease me, but now they are used to it."

After two years, Donna had grown used to it too. "She doesn't even notice she is sneezing," said her mother. Gradually her rate of sneezing slowed to about twenty a day, and at long last it petered out.

SEPTEMBER 15TH
Cheers when the Liverpool and Manchester railway opened – but there were tears before bedtime

But it still remains a mystery. Donna had hospital treatment, tried homeopathic remedies, went on holiday in the clear air of the Welsh mountains, all to no avail. "It's not an allergy," said her mother, when it was at its height. "You can spray hair-spray or perfume near her and it doesn't affect her sneezes at all. Doctors say that her 'sneezing sensor' has jammed, and one day it will correct itself."

And one day – this day in 1981 – it did, and never returned. Now Donna lives by the sea at Brighton – and only sneezes when she catches a cold.

SEPTEMBER 17TH
Pouring wine needed a steady hand in the earliest days of photography

17th
SEPTEMBER

Three British Cheers for Fox Talbot – but Nice One, Nicéphore!

William Henry Fox Talbot, who died on this day in 1877, is generally regarded – in Britain at least – as the great pioneer of photography. He invented a way of fixing the camera's image by a negative–positive process which laid the foundations of modern photography, according to many experts. The National Trust, which now owns his magnificent family home in Wiltshire, Lacock Abbey, where his descendants still live, calls him simply "the inventor of photography".

But the French may take a slightly different view. Louis Daguerre was producing permanent photographs by his own method simultaneously with Talbot in the 1830s, and announced its success just before Talbot exhibited his photographs for the first time. And when the first action photograph was taken in Britain of a topical event, a mass meeting in 1848, it was a "daguerreotype" using the Frenchman's

process. One reputable encyclopaedia – a British one – dismisses Daguerre's efforts out of hand: "His invention proved a dead end, contributing nothing to later work." But at least it preserved his name; nobody ever talked about a "talbototype".

Actually another Frenchman, Nicéphore Niepce, is credited in the record books with the first true photograph, back in 1826. So three British cheers for Fox Talbot, *vive* Daguerre – and nice one, Nicéphore!

18th
SEPTEMBER

"The one Englishman who talked his Way into Immortality"

If there had been no James Boswell, would anyone remember Samuel Johnson? Not a question you would dare ask in Lichfield, Staffordshire, where Johnson was born on this day in 1709, and where the anniversary is celebrated each year with a civic procession involving pupils of his old school, and the laying of a laurel wreath

SEPTEMBER 18TH
Samuel Johnson's statue at Lichfield, thinking up another bon mot for his next meeting with Boswell

on his statue in the Market Place. But he was a great talker rather than a great writer – his only work of note was a dictionary – and if Boswell had not been around to record his utterances he could have sunk with little trace. As one reviewer wrote: "He remains the one Englishman who talked his way into immortality."

The first meeting between the two, when Johnson was in his fifties and already in full flow – sounds inauspicious. The conversation went: "You are from Scotland, Sir?" "I do indeed come from Scotland, but I cannot help it." That, Sir, I find is what a very great many of your countrymen cannot help."

But they were soon a double act, Boswell the straight man, Johnson with all the pay-off lines. One of the best-known, certainly one of the most typical, has endeared him to women for the last two hundred years. Boswell fed him the cue: he had been to a Quaker meeting where a woman preached.

"Sir," said Dr Johnson, "a woman's preaching is like a dog's walking on his hind legs. It is not done well, but you are surprised to find it done at all."

SEPTEMBER 19TH
Painswick lasses eating their special buns on Clypping Sunday

to them reaching three figures. So at Painswick there'll never be another yew . . .

The second tradition is the ancient Clypping Ceremony, which has been conveniently confused with clipping the yew trees. But although they are kept very neat and tidy, "clypping" is actually an Early English word for "enclosing" or "embracing", and on Clypping Sunday the villagers process through the yews and the children "embrace" the church by holding hands round it, singing the Clypping Hymn. Each receives a silver coin and a bun.

They also used to receive, it is said, a helping of puppy-dog pie. These days the puppy-dogs are china replicas, but they still tell how a local landlord ran out of meat to fill his pies, and rather than disappoint the revellers he stuffed them with strays instead.

19th
S E P T E M B E R

The Day the Children get a Clyp around the Yews

Painswick in Gloucestershire has three village traditions, all with different origins, which are mixed up into one annual celebration on this day, Old Mary Day, if it is a Sunday, or if not, on the Sunday following.

One tradition is connected with the yews in St Mary's churchyard. It is said that their number must never exceed ninety-nine, because the Devil would take great exception

20th
S E P T E M B E R

Extending the Gloved Hand of Friendship – but don't drop it

Barnstaple Fair is said to date back to the granting of a charter by the Saxon King Athelstan, but the charter is no longer around and the origin of the fair is lost, as the Town Guide admits, "in the mists of antiquity". There seems no particular reason, for instance, why it should always start on the Wednesday preceding this day – but it always does. And the opening ceremony has also remained unchanged, although King Athelstan might find the sight of a stuffed glove hanging out of a window at the Guildhall a little baffling. Did the Saxons wear gloves?

SEPTEMBER 20TH
The (stuffed) hand of friendship is extended from the Guildhall to launch Barnstaple Fair

It is, however, said to symbolize the hand of friendship being extended to all the visitors who come into town for the fair, and indeed the same symbol is used elsewhere, on similar occasions. One hopes the glove was never dropped as it was lowered out of the window, or it might have been confused with throwing down the gauntlet – which means precisely the opposite.

Inside the Guildhall the Town Council drinks toasts in a spiced ale made from a secret recipe and prepared in a magnificent loving cup. This fortifies them for the subsequent reading of the Proclamation, which happens three times in three different parts of the town. Then the Showmen's Guild takes over.

21st
SEPTEMBER

The Racing Coup that was won by a Horse Box

SEPTEMBER 21ST
Lord George Bentinck, who designed the first purpose-built horsebox and used it to fool the bookies

Lord George Bentinck, renowned racehorse owner, sportsman and gambler, pulled off one of the great racing coups of the last century on this day in 1836. He won the St Leger at Doncaster with a horse which all the bookmakers thought was a non-runner.

He achieved it with the first purpose-built horse box in history to be used for conveying a racehorse from one track to another.

Lord George designed the box himself. It had a padded interior with accommodation for two horses, and it was drawn by a team of six. He entered this three-year-old thoroughbred Elis both at Goodwood and at Doncaster. In those days it was the normal practice for owners to walk their horses to the races, in plenty of time for them to get over the journey. When the bookies saw Elis at Goodwood, therefore, with the St Leger only three days away, they assumed it would never get there in time. So they offered long odds to anyone who was daft enough to think it would – including, of course, acting anonymously through agents, the astute Lord George.

The horse box covered the 224 miles from Goodwood to Doncaster in time for Elis to step out of it, fresh as a transplanted daisy – and win the St Leger by a decisive two lengths. I just hope the horses that hauled it there had a bet on too.

22nd
S E P T E M B E R

Enter ITV – and Viewers got their First Flavour of Toothpaste

This day in 1955 marked the start of a radical change in the leisure habits of the nation. It was the day that Independent Television made its first transmission in the London area; regional independent stations soon followed.

SEPTEMBER 22ND
The first television commercial was for toothpaste – and ITV has been cleaning up ever since

Until then, television had been in the hands of the BBC, one channel geared mainly to the middle and upper classes – "elitist, patronizing, and perceived as the voice of the Establishment", as one reviewer put it. Independent Television, with commercial advertising space to sell in order to survive, went for the mass audience – and got it. In five years, half the British population was watching television at peak time every night – and two out of three were watching ITV.

The BBC did its best to discourage ITV viewers on this first opening night in 1955 – one way or another. It was just a coincidence, they maintained, that Grace Archer happened to be killed off in a fire in *The Archers*, their highly popular radio serial. And there were dire warnings about the catastrophic effect of interrupting programmes with commercials – which

probably guaranteed the first one a bigger audience than ever. It turned out to be an advertisement for Gibbs SR toothpaste – and the earth did not even quiver.

23rd
S E P T E M B E R

The Sea Battle that Ended in a Dance

The Battle of Flamborough Head between British and American ships during the War of Independence took place on this day in 1779. It holds only a minor place in the history books, but it produced a memorable riposte, worthy of a Nelson or a Churchill, from the Scottish-born American commander, John Paul Jones. It also helped to immortalize his name on the dance floor.

Jones's ship, the *Bon-Homme Richard*, took on two British men-o'-war, and became locked in close combat with one of them, the *Serapis* – literally so, because the bowsprit of

SEPTEMBER 24TH
*Horace Walpole had
a taste for the Gothic,
in his mansion at
Twickenham and in
his horror stories*

one ran up against the poop of the other, and Jones made them fast with his own hands. Captain Pearson, the English commander, blasted away at the underpart of Jones's ship, while Jones's men dropped grenades on the deck of the *Serapis*.

The British ship seemed to be getting the better of it, and Jones's master gunner, thinking all his superiors were dead, went to haul down the colours. Captain Pearson saw him and called on him to surrender – whereupon a bloodstained John Paul Jones emerged from the smoke and cried: "I have not yet begun to fight!" In the end it was Pearson who surrendered.

Jones continued to lead the Navy a merry dance – so much so that an American barn dance was named after him. The Paul Jones is not entirely forgotten on English dance floors too.

24th
SEPTEMBER

We'd remember Horace better if he'd had a Different Dad

Horace Walpole, who was born on this day in 1717, has been overshadowed in history by his famous father, Sir Robert, the first and longest-serving prime minister and arguably the most corrupt. But in literary and architectural circles, Horace takes precedence, as a pace-setter in both fields. He is credited with establishing the respectability and popularity of the horror story, fifty years ahead of Mary Shelley's *Frankenstein*, and his taste for the Gothic helped to start a vogue in architectural design as well.

While his father was governing the

SEPTEMBER 23RD
*John Paul Jones may
have seemed just a
pirate to the British
during the
American War of
Independence, but
he still led them a
merry dance*

country by his own devious means – he was the man who coined the phrase, "every man has his price" – Horace was keeping as far away from politics as possible, and after Sir Robert died he lost no time in moving out of the grandiose family home at Houghton Hall in Norfolk – where, typically, his forceful father had moved an entire village in order to improve the view.

Horace moved into a house at Strawberry Hill in Twickenham, which he rebuilt and extended in Gothic style, helping to launch the eighteenth-century Gothic Revival. It was there that he wrote *The Castle of Otranto*, described as "a fearsome supernatural tale", and helped to pave the way for all the horror stories that followed.

If he had been born this day into a different family, history might have taken more notice.

25th
SEPTEMBER

When you're on Stamford Bridge, don't be "Brogged from Below"

This is the anniversary of the Battle of Stamford Bridge – which I hasten to say has no connection with Chelsea Football Club. It was fought on this day in 1066 between King Harold and the combined forces of his brother Tostig, Earl of Northumbria, and the Viking King Harald Hardraada.

The opposing leaders met at the other Stamford Bridge, a few miles from York. Harold said his brother could keep the earldom if he behaved, but all he offered Hardraada was "seven feet of English earth, or perhaps a little more as he is somewhat tall". That didn't go down too well, and the battle began.

The key figure in the encounter was a giant Viking who held the bridge single-handed until a cunning Englishman paddled a boat under it, poked a spear through the slats and in the memorable words of the Anglo-Saxon chronicle, "brogged the giant from below". The battle was won.

The ancient tradition of eating "spear pie" was revived in 1966 for the 900th anniversary, but has faded again since. The original bridge has long since gone; the present one was built in 1727. As for the victorious Harold, he had just downed a celebratory drink in York when news arrived that William of Normandy had landed at Hastings. He headed south, and – well, you win a few, you lose a few.

26th

SEPTEMBER

Honoretta had her Wish, but alas, Poor Sir Thomas

The idea of cremation goes back many hundreds of years in other parts of the world, but it was frowned upon in this country until comparatively recently. The first recorded cremation, when it was still illegal, was on this day in 1769, when

Honoretta Pratt was cremated in an open grave at her own request. Since her father was a knight, her husband was Treasurer of Ireland, and the cremation took place in Hanover Square, no one argued.

Some eighty years earlier, however, the distinguished doctor and philosopher Sir Thomas Browne had expressed a similar view. "To be gnaw'd out of our graves, to have our skulls made drinking-bowls and our bones turned into pipes to delight and sport our enemies, are tragical abominations, escaped in burning burials."

He favoured the Roman practice of having one's ashes put in an urn, but instead of being burned and urned, Sir Thomas was buried at St Peter Mancroft Church in Norwich – and his fears were realized. Many years later his skull was "gnaw'd out of the grave" by workmen digging an adjoining one, and it spent a long period in a hospital museum before being re-interred.

The legality of cremation was not in fact established until 1894, when a Welsh judge ruled that "to burn a body decently and inoffensively is lawful". Cremations have been carried out decently and inoffensively – and legally – ever since.

SEPTEMBER 26TH Sir Thomas Browne advocated cremation long before it became legal, in case he was "gnaw'd out of the grave" – but he was buried, and his worst fears came true

27th

SEPTEMBER

They had a Yarn at Yarm – and the Railway Age was Born

The Stockton and Darlington Railway, the first public railway worked by steam locomotives, was opened on this day in 1825 – and the Age of the Railway was born.

George Stephenson's proudly named *Locomotive No. 1* hauled a splendid assortment of rolling-stock: the directors' coach at the front, six coaches for other passengers, six goods wagons, and right at the back, fourteen wagons full of workmen – perhaps in case something went wrong and they had to push.

The directors were enjoying the success of a gamble they took five years earlier, in the Commercial Room of the George and Dragon Hotel at Yarm, on Teesside. Under the chairmanship of a local enthusiast, Thomas Meynell, they resolved to promote the "S&DR" – described simply on a plaque at the hotel as "the first public railway in the world".

That was not entirely accurate. There had been public railways around before, but they all relied on horse-power. The Surrey Iron Railway, for instance, started carrying freight from Croydon to Wandsworth Basin in 1803. This too was born in a pub, the Spread Eagle at Wandsworth, but perhaps the beer was not so inspirational, or the horses flagged, and the railway folded after forty years. The S&DR, however, founded the chain of North-country railways which still exists today, and the half-mile railway viaduct over the Tees at Yarm is an ostentatious reminder of where it all began.

Penny Bazaar in Britain – and one of the most famous business partnerships in the world. Today fourteen million people shop at Marks & Spencer every week.

The man who made it all possible was a minor Leeds wholesaler whose name is less familiar. Isaac Dewhirst met Michael Marks in his early days in this country, lent him a fiver to set up as a trader – and introduced him to his cashier, Tom Spencer. When Marks decided to acquire his first permanent stall in Leeds's covered market, he invited Spencer to join him. They signed the agreement on this day, with Spencer investing £300 for his half-share of the business.

It was worth every penny – in pennies! Marks's slogan was "Don't ask the Price – it's a Penny" – and it worked. The first Penny Bazaar store in Manchester multiplied to twelve in the first six years. The range of stock widened – but everything still cost a penny. Again the unseen influence of Isaac

SEPTEMBER 27TH
A half-mile railway viaduct still looms over Yarm, where a group of businessmen met to promote the Stockton and Darlington railway

SEPTEMBER 28TH
How it all began: Michael Marks' first Penny Bazaar. Soon another name was added, and Marks and Spencer never looked back

28th
SEPTEMBER

"Don't ask the Price – it's a Penny" – Thanks to St Isaac?

On this day in 1894 an immigrant pedlar from Poland and a Yorkshireman with a head for figures teamed up to create the first

Dewhirst made it possible. It was he who is said to have suggested buying direct from manufacturers – a very generous suggestion from a wholesaler! – and that helped to keep down prices and found their fortunes.

Instead of St Michael, in fact, the M&S emblem might well be St Isaac.

∽

Landlords get Perks, Geese get Stubble Trouble

This is Michaelmas, traditionally the day to eat roast goose, though there is no evidence St Michael was particularly partial to it. More likely it just happens to be a prime time for stubble geese, those that are not necessarily unshaven but well fattened from eating the grain in the stubble. It was also the time for Hiring Fairs, sometimes called Mop Fairs because a maid looking for work would carry a mop. Shepherds carried their emblems too but who would go to a Crook Fair?

It was quarter-day for tenants too, and as well as paying their rent they often threw in a goose as a bonus. In fact, landlords did quite well out of these little extras: "At Christmas a capon, at Michaelmas a goose, And somewhat else at New Year's tide in case the lease flies loose."

There is also a "Queen Elizabeth and the Goose" story attached to this day, but any attempt to confirm it would be a wild goose chase. It is said she was dining off a Michaelmas goose in 1588 when news arrived that the Armada was defeated. "Henceforth shall a goose commemorate this great victory!" she cried. But the Armada was defeated in July, and she had already attended the thanksgiving service in St Paul's a month before.

∽

A Thorny Problem which has been Answered more than once

The story of Androcles and the Lion was adopted and recycled by George Bernard Shaw, and his has become the authorized version. It tells how a runaway slave called Androcles took a thorn out of a lion's paw, and when Androcles was captured and sentenced to the arena, he found himself facing the same lion – so instead of being eaten, he got his face licked.

But a similar story has been attached to other early martyrs and near-martyrs, not least St Jerome, whose day this is. In the Jerome version, the lion limped into a room where he was teaching, and he duly extracted the thorn and bound up the wound. The lion then insisted on remaining with him, which is why the saint is usually portrayed with a lion at his feet.

Much the same thing happened to a saint called Gerasimus, though in his case the encounter took place on the banks of the Jordan. And the story was brought up-to-date by the Kenya game warden George Adamson and the lioness Elsa; he and his wife looked after her as a cub, and after she returned to the jungle she often visited the couple who had cared for her.

So there have been many people who helped to point the moral that being kind to animals – particularly a lion with a thorny problem – is a Good Thing. But as this is St Jerome's Day, let's give him the lion's share of the credit.

SEPTEMBER 30TH "Excuse me sir, but I've got this thorn in my foot . . ." – and St Jerome joined the ranks of legendary lion-tamers

October

ABSTAINER'S DECLARATION.

"WATCH AND PRAY, THAT YE ENTER NOT INTO TEMPTATION."—MATT. XXVI. 16.

No. 16   June 27th 1882

I hereby agree to abstain from all Intoxicating Liquors, as beverages; and will endeavour to promote the objects of this Society.

Signed   Tom Mumby

Attestor.

"TO HIM THAT KNOWETH TO DO GOOD, AND DOETH IT NOT, TO HIM IT IS SIN."—James iv. 17.

1st

"Raise the Song of Harvest Home" – in Church, not the Pub

OCTOBER 1ST
The Rev. Robert Hawker of Morwenstow invented the harvest festival to convert an annual booze-up into a festival of thanksgiving

"Harvest Home" was the traditional way of ending the harvest. The last load of corn was brought in, with the harvesters singing a Harvest Home song, then the farmer entertained everyone to a harvest feast. This bucolic idyll, however, developed into an alcoholic booze-up, with the purpose of the celebration soon forgotten, and on this day in 1843 the Rev. Robert Hawker, Vicar of Morwenstow in North Cornwall, decided to adapt this basically pagan festivity into a Christian festival of thanksgiving. Harvest festival services are now held in virtually every church in the country, but it was Robert Hawker's idea.

And he had plenty. He revived the ancient practice of baking bread for the Eucharist on Lammas Day from the first fruits of the harvest. At weddings he would toss the ring in the air before handing it to the bridegroom, thus unnerving many a best man. And at baptisms, while drawing the line at doing the same thing with the baby, he would march up and down the aisle waving it aloft and crying: "We receive this child into the congregation of Christ's flock." It was regarded as distinctly eccentric in the first half of the nineteenth century, but like Hawker's harvest festival, it is a common enough practice now.

OCTOBER 2ND
At Braughing they still celebrate a "corpse's" survival on its way to an early grave

The Bearers dropped the Coffin and Woke up the "Corpse"

The first thing to note about Braughing in Hertfordshire is how to pronounce it. Forget "Brawing" and stick to "Braffing". The second notable feature is the excellence of the local sausage, commended in many a guidebook. And third, there is the Old Man of Braughing, whose remarkable escape from being buried alive is remembered every year on this day.

Matthew Wall was a rich sixteenth-century farmer, who was taken ill, pronounced dead, and taken to the church to be buried. As the bearers entered the churchyard one of them stumbled and they dropped the coffin. To their consternation, this provoked an angry banging from inside it.

This was not the spirit of Matthew Wall, complaining about their carelessness. It was Mr Wall himself, jolted out of his deep coma as the coffin hit the ground. When the bearers regained their nerve they took the lid off, and the Old Man of Braughing emerged to grow a little older.

He left a bequest to be divided between the vicar and churchwardens, twenty poor children and ten parishioners, to attend his thanksgiving service. What he left amounted

to a pound a year, which meant it had to be spread a bit thin, but the vicar still holds the service around the grave which Matthew Wall eventually occupied.

this day the process was repeated on a national scale.

Mrs George's efforts produced a letter of commendation from Queen Mary – and mixed feelings from the general public ever since.

3rd
OCTOBER

It started with Matchsticks and tiny bits of Ribbon

There are some who may feel that one good reason for emigrating to the United States is that they have only one flag day a year – and even then, they don't sell any flags. It merely celebrates the adoption of the Stars and Stripes as the national flag in 1777. In Britain it seems hardly a week passes without a flagseller appearing on the streets or the doorstep, and it started in earnest on this day in 1914, when the first national flag day was held.

The First World War had started a few weeks before, and the flag day was in aid of the Belgian Relief Fund. It is not recorded how much was raised, but it must have been substantial, because the idea soon caught on.

It originated, not from a politician or a professional moneyraiser, but from a Welsh housewife and her milkman. Mrs Harold George was cutting some ribbon into little pieces and attaching them to matchsticks for her young sons to play with, when the milkman called. He suggested she might sell the miniature flags in aid of a relief fund for servicemen's families that had just been set up. It proved such a success that word reached Whitehall, and on

4th
OCTOBER

The R101: "As Safe as a House – except for the Millionth Chance"

On this day in 1930 the R101 airship set off from its hangar at Cardington in Bedfordshire on its maiden flight to India. At Beauvais in Northern France it crashed and burst into flames, killing forty-eight of the fifty-four people on board. Among them was Lord Thomson, Secretary of State for Air, who announced before its departure that it was "as safe as a house except for the millionth chance". He is buried with the other victims at Cardington, and the giant airship's burnt and tattered ensign is inside the church.

OCTOBER 4TH The ill-fated R101, which crashed and burst into flames on its maiden flight. Its charred ensign is still in Cardington Church

But the crash was not entirely unforeseen. The airship was modified during trials, and the crew complained of its instability. And there were other warnings of a less tangible nature. The horoscope some years before of Sir Sefton Brancker, who also died in the crash, showed a blank after 1930, and more than one crew member dreamed of the flight ending in disaster. As one left home his son cried: "I haven't got a Daddy!"

As well as the loss of life, there was a loss of two million pounds to the taxpayer. The R100, sister airship to the R101, never flew. It was broken up, and the remnants sold for scrap. The giant hangars still stand at Cardington, as a memorial to them both.

5th
OCTOBER
〜

Once they Marched from Jarrow; now they can Take the Escalator
The name of Jarrow, to the older generation, will always be associated with the Jarrow Hunger March, which began on this day in 1936. It resulted from the closure of the Charles Palmer shipyards three years before. The yards were virtually the only industry the town had, and the widespread unemployment resulted in appalling poverty for thousands of people. Jarrow became known as "the town that was murdered".

The hunger march by unemployed shipyard workers was greeted by sympathetic crowds all the way to London, and focused the attention of the whole country on the dangers of an entire town becoming dependent on one industry.

But it would also be a pity to remember a town's entire history by one disaster. Jarrow's other claim to fame is its

association with the Venerable Bede, "the father of English history". The remains of his monastery still exist, flanked by the Bede Industrial Estate . . .

Jarrow has another distinction which is much more up-to-date. The escalators which

link the town with the foot-tunnel under the Tyne, like those on the other side of the river, are the longest in Britain – 192 feet. They are also the cleanest – or they were when I saw them. Long may the aerosol-sprayers leave them that way.

OCTOBER 5TH
A bleak episode during the Depression: Jarrow shipyard workers on their hunger march to London

6th
OCTOBER
〜

A Posthumous Award for Virgins: a Crown and White Gloves
St Faith, whose day this is, had two sisters called Hope and Charity, and with names like that in the days of the Emperor Hadrian they were pretty certain of an unpleasant end. All three were martyred, and so was their mother who had selected the names for them. All the sisters were unmarried, but

OCTOBER 6TH
A virgin's crant at
Abbots Ann, in
memory of a young
woman who died a
virgin; theories vary
about the white
gloves

Faith became particularly associated with virgins, and on this day it was the custom at Abbots Ann Church in Hampshire to bless the "Virgins' Crowns" which still hang there.

Since Elizabethan times it was the practice in some villages to mark the funeral of a virgin by hanging a paper crown in the church, decorated with a pair of white gloves which had been worn by one of the bearers or, if the bearers declined to part with them, were made of white paper. They were either a symbol of the deceased's purity, or a symbolic gauntlet thrown down to anyone who doubted it – again the versions can vary.

The earliest of the twenty-odd crowns on display at Abbots Ann is that of Mary Fennell, who was born in 1786 and died in 1811, but the original church was demolished and rebuilt some years before, and any earlier crowns may have been lost in the process. This is claimed to be the only church in England where Virgins' Crowns are still awarded, but the most recent one went up in 1978. Maybe these days fewer people qualify . . .

7th
OCTOBER

At Newark the Ringers Gopher it; at Twyford they Feast with it

"Lost in the Dark" bells used to be rung in many rural parishes to guide wayfarers home. Sometimes the bells were rung as a matter of routine, but in other cases imaginative tales are told of lost travellers hearing the bells, and leaving money to ensure they continued.

At Newark, for instance, a Flemish merchant called Gopher got lost in the autumnal mists on the Trent marshes, and left money for the bellringers to "Gopher it"

OCTOBER 7TH
The bells of Twyford
Church once guided a
lost traveller home.
He was so grateful,
the ringers still enjoy
a Feast at his expense

every evening for six weeks during the autumn. At Burgh-le-Marsh in Lincolnshire a sea-captain was saved by the bells from running aground, and bought a field called Bell String Acre to provide income for future bellringing.

Perhaps the best-documented instance is at Twyford in Hampshire, where a bequest was made, not only to pay for the bells to be rung on the morning and evening of this day, but also to provide the ringers with a "feast" when they finished. Mr William Davies of Twyford House was caught in a thick fog on Hazeley Downs and rode about aimlessly until the bells gave him a bearing. When the fog lifted he found he had been on the edge of a chalk pit.

Under his will dated April 22nd, 1754, a pound was paid from his Twyford estate

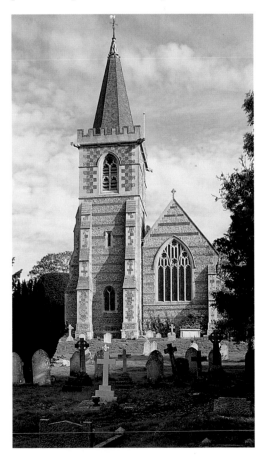

every year. Recently the estate was sold after the death of Mrs Marjorie Dykes, but she foresaw that the bequest might be affected and left a sum herself to maintain the tradition. The bells are still rung, and the ringers still enjoy their "feast" this evening.

8th
OCTOBER

"The First Great English Novel" – and not a bad Film too

Henry Fielding, author of what has been called "the first great English novel", died on this day while still in his forties. He wrote his rumbustious and at times near-the-knuckle *Tom Jones* while he was a justice of the peace for Westminster, after being called to the Bar seven years before, but his respectable middle-age had been preceded by a wild youth, when he "threw himself recklessly into the pleasures of London life". No doubt it

OCTOBER 8TH
This street of old houses at Cerne Abbas made a fitting film location for the exploits of Tom Jones and bedroom romps were filmed in the (ancient) New Inn

was during this period that he picked up a few ideas for his novel.

He supported himself in those earlier days by writing comedies for the stage, and even managed a theatre for a while, but it probably did not occur to him that *Tom Jones* would eventually be dramatized too, and become a highly successful film two and a half centuries later.

"It was the first novel in which all the characters are recognizable human beings," wrote one enthusiastic critic. "At the end we may ask ourselves what it has all been about, so little has really happened of any great importance. But that makes it all the more like real life; and how fortunate we are if we can say at the end of a day, as at the end of a novel, 'Well, nothing very important has happened, but I did enjoy it!'"

A few modern novelists might bear that in mind . . .

9th
OCTOBER

The "Names" at Lloyds ask not for Whom it Tolls

The ship which sailed out of Great Yarmouth, bound for Holland, on this day in 1799 was destined for disaster. She was wrecked on a sandbank off the Zuyder Zee the same night, with the loss of everyone on board. That might have been the last we heard of her, but her name is still a familiar one, and it has been connected with maritime disasters ever since. This was HMS *Lutine*, laden with bullion and specie to the value of half a million pounds – worth many times that amount today. For Lloyds of London it was one of the blackest days since it was founded in Edward Lloyd's coffee shop a hundred years before.

OCTOBER 9TH
The Lutine Bell at
Lloyds is rung at
times of disaster –
some of Lloyds'
"Names" would
rather not be
reminded

Eventually some fifty thousand pounds was salvaged, as a small consolation for Lloyds. They also acquired the *Lutine's* rudder – and the ship's bell. Making the best of it, they had the rudder made into an official chair for the chairman and used up the rest to make a secretary's desk. As for the Lutine Bell, it is still rung at times of disaster – once for a total wreck, twice if a ship is overdue.

It has also been rung to mark President Kennedy's assassination and Sir Winston Churchill's death. But these days the "Names" at Lloyds, some of whom have lost fortunes, ask not for whom the Lutine Bell tolls – it may toll for them.

10th
OCTOBER

It came upon the Midnight clear – Teddy Roe's Band

There are at least three theories about the name of Pack Monday Fair, which takes place at Sherborne in Dorset on the first Monday after this day. One is that it was originally Pact Monday, when the fair was an

occasion for hiring workers and making pacts, or agreements, with them. Alternatively it is a variation on Pack-Rag-Day which used to be celebrated in Lincolnshire, when servants packed their "rags" and went in search of fresh jobs – which in effect is much the same thing.

The third and most unlikely theory is that it marked the day when masons packed up their tools after restoration work on Sherborne Abbey, which had been damaged by fire. It is unlikely because the work was finished in 1490, by which time the fair had been running for about two hundred years.

But there is a link between the restoration work and the fair, because according to tradition the masons celebrated when they finished by launching themselves on the streets banging tins and blowing horns at midnight before the fair. They were led by their foreman, Teddy Roe, and "Teddy Roe's Band" has been keeping Sherborne awake before the fair ever since. In the 1960s it got so rowdy that the Band was banned. It has since been resumed, but with "Bobbies" as well as "Teddies" to keep order.

11th
OCTOBER

The Crash Landing that Started the Blackberry Ban

When the calendar was altered in the eighteenth century it meant, among other things, that saints' days were moved to new dates eleven days earlier – and this had a dramatic effect on the sell-by date of blackberries.

It goes back to when St Michael threw Satan out of Heaven and into Hell on Michaelmas Day. On the way Satan ricocheted off a blackberry bush, which even

OCTOBER 10TH
"Teddy Roe's Band"
embarks on another
midnight concert at
Sherborne

OCTOBER 11TH
*A jolly-looking Satan
who might be going
off to do some
blackberrying*

OCTOBER 11TH
*A jolly-looking Satan
who might be going
off to do some
blackberrying*

12th
OCTOBER

Nurse Edith Cavell: "I Realize that Patriotism is not Enough"

Nurse Edith Cavell was executed by a German firing squad on this day in 1915, after helping hundreds of British and French soldiers to escape from occupied Belgium. At her birthplace, Swardeston in Norfolk, a special service is held each year, and in London, largely unnoticed by the passing crowds, two nurses lay a wreath on her statue in St Martin's Place.

Edith Cavell first went to Brussels as a governess many years earlier. She returned home to train as a nurse at the Royal London Hospital, and became so proficient that in due course she was invited back to Brussels to found the nursing institute which still bears her name. When war broke out and the Germans invaded she treated German and Belgian casualties alike – but when the

a flameproof Devil found painful, and in his rage he spat on the blackberries, trampled on the bush, and cursed blackberries on that day for evermore. Consequently they are not fit to gather after Michaelmas Day. According to the old calendar that was October 10th, so today was when the blackberry ban came into force. But in 1752 blackberries must have deteriorated very suddenly towards the end of September, because they became unpickable on New Michaelmas Day, September 29th.

Wise old country folk, who know about these things, ignore the calendar change and continue to pick them. Nobody knows exactly what time of day Satan had his unpleasant experience, not even wise old country folk, but as he is the Prince of Darkness it was probably after nightfall, so it should be safe to pick them on Old Michaelmas Day itself. I confess I have often picked them after today's ban and they have been fine – but don't tell any wise old country folk.

OCTOBER 12TH
*Nurse Edith Cavell is
remembered in her
church at Swardeston*

Belgians recovered, instead of reporting for conscription into the German army, they somehow "got lost".

When French and British soldiers started arriving she set up an escape route across the Dutch border. As one biographer put it: "She was instrumental in sending back to the front line three or four rifle companies to fight German soldiers." But eventually she was caught and sentenced to death. She was fifty years old.

A German officer who saw her die said her poise and bearing was impossible to forget. Prime Minister Asquith told the Commons: "She has taught the bravest men among us the supreme lesson of courage." But her own words are the most memorable, perhaps as a message to Ulster, and Bosnia, and elsewhere: "I realize that patriotism is not enough. I must have no hatred or bitterness against anyone."

13th
OCTOBER

Is the Treasure under the Wash – or under Walpole St Andrew?

There is more than one date given for the loss of King John's treasure in the Wash, just as there is more than one theory about where it is now, but this day is as popular a choice as any. He had been feasting at King's Lynn (which perhaps is why the date is a blur), then set off for one of his favourite haunts, Newark Castle. The Wash in those days encroached much further inland, and John apparently followed the edge of it until he reached Walpole St Andrew, behind the safety of the old Roman Bank.

This is where the stories begin to differ. The popular version is that he headed from there towards Newark, taking a short cut

across the sands and marshes, was caught by the tide and had to abandon his heavily laden wagons to the incoming sea. There is a much more engaging theory, however, that the treasure was actually left at Walpole St Andrew – either abandoned as the sea

OCTOBER 13TH
Is this where King John's treasure really finished up, at Walpole St Andrew Church?

unexpectedly broke through, or intentionally buried. Certainly a professor from Nottingham University dug up some metal there in fairly recent times, and hopeful souls still turn up occasionally with mine detectors and spades.

As for King John himself, he reached Newark Castle safely, did some more feasting – and died of food poisoning a few days later.

14th
OCTOBER

If Harold Escaped, there's One in the Eye for the Historians!

This was the day that "all that" happened in 1066-and-all-that – but if the English had kept their heads, it might have happened quite differently. Harold held a commanding position on Senlac Hill, where the terrace of

Battle Abbey now stands. The Normans made a number of unsuccessful uphill charges against the wall of English shields, with their knights getting more and more weary in their heavy armour. Then the English threw away their caution – and their chances – and after repulsing them yet again, chased them down the hill.

The Normans rallied, faced them on level ground and turned the tables. Harold was wounded by that legendary arrow, and the Norman knights finished him off. William the Norman was now William the Conqueror – or William the Bastard, depending which side you were on.

He built an abbey on the battle site, setting the high altar on the spot where Harold fell. Nothing of this remains visible, but in 1903 "Harold's Stone" was erected where the altar once stood.

However, there is one niggling doubt about Harold's fate. One romantic theory is that his wounds were not fatal and he escaped from the battlefield to spend his declining years as a hermit in an anchorite's cell at St John's Church, Chester. If anyone could prove that, what a one-in-the-eye for the historians!

15th
OCTOBER

"Hey, what, Mr Gibbon! Scribble, scribble, scribble!"

It was on this day in 1764 that a young Englishman making the fashionable "grand tour" of Europe visited the ruins of the Capitol in Rome, and had an idea which led to a monumental work of several volumes, familiar to every history student since.

"As I sat musing among the ruins," wrote Edward Gibbon, "while the bare-footed friars were singing Vespers in the Temple of Jupiter, the idea of writing the decline and fall of the city first started to my mind."

The Decline and Fall of the Roman Empire covers sixteen centuries of Italian history. It took him ten years to research and fifteen years to write, with occasional breaks to fulfil his duties as a Member of Parliament. "Hey, what, Mr Gibbon," George III commented. "Scribble, scribble, scribble!" Indeed his sedentary life made him extremely plump, and it is said that when he knelt to propose marriage to a lady, he found it impossible to get up again. The lady never stopped laughing, and Gibbon never got married.

When he penned the final full stop, "a sober melancholy was spread over my mind, by the idea that I had taken an everlasting leave of an old and agreeable companion". His work had ended, but the work of thousands of students was just beginning.

OCTOBER 14TH
The anchorite cell at Chester to where some say King Harold fled after the Battle of Hastings

OCTOBER 15TH
Edward Gibbon was so chubby he could not get up again after kneeling to propose. The lady never stopped laughing, and Gibbon never got married

16th

O C T O B E R

OCTOBER 16TH
Sir John Gayer, the
Lord Mayor of
London whose happy
deliverance from a
lion is still recalled in
the Lion Sermon

The Lord Mayor and the Lion – it beats Dick Whittington and his Cat

In the City church of St Katharine Cree in Leadenhall Street, a special sermon is preached every year to mark this anniversary of the miraculous escape of a City merchant from a desert lion, many hundreds of miles away. It is not unusual for the text to be taken from the story of Daniel . . .

This is actually the story of Sir John Gayer, a West Countryman who followed in the footsteps of Dick Whittington and eventually became Lord Mayor of London in 1647. In the process of making his fortune, however, he established the Levant Company, and made several trading journeys to Turkey and the Near East. During one of these journeys he became separated from his companions in the desert, and as darkness fell on this night, he heard the roar of a lion. Alone and unarmed, he prayed for deliverance – then calmly went to sleep. When he woke next morning, the lion's footprints were all around him, but it had left him untouched.

Sir John returned home, became Lord Mayor, and – again rather different from the Whittington story – spent two years in the Tower for his loyalty to Charles I. But throughout his successes and tribulations he never forgot his encounter with the lion. On his death in 1649 – "he dyed in peace in his own house" – he left a handsome bequest to the poor of the parish

of St Katharine Cree, where he is buried, on condition that on each anniversary, the story of this night should be retold in the Lion Sermon.

17th

O C T O B E R

The Butchery at Butcher's Race – is the Ghost a Scot?

The Battle of Nevill's Cross, in which Robert the Bruce's son David led a Scottish army against the English, was fought near Durham on this day in 1346. Edward III was out of the country at the time, fighting the French, and David took the opportunity to cross the border and rampage around the English countryside. However, he was not a patch on his famous father, and when he met the English at Nevill's Cross, his forces were routed and he was taken prisoner.

One party of Scots was pursued by English cavalry and cornered near the village of Croxdale. Most of them were butchered on the spot, and the place has been called Butcher's Race ever since. They were buried in a mass grave at Kirk Newington.

An inn has stood for many centuries at the site of the slaughter, and sure enough, the Coach and Horses has a ghost, which is

OCTOBER 17TH
The Coach and
Horses at Butcher's
Race, said to be on
the site of a medieval
massacre

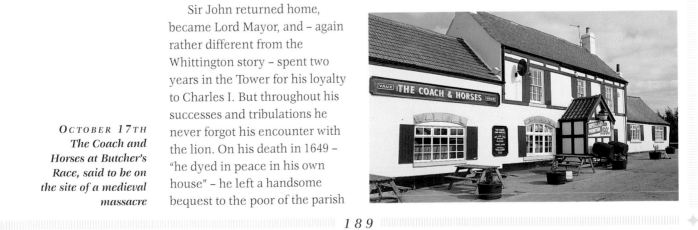

inclined to make heavy objects jump about on the bar. The landlord, an ex-policeman not given to flights of fancy, tells how he was talking to an equally sceptical friend about the ghost's alleged activities when his friend observed, "That's all a load of rubbish – I don't believe it" – and his beer glass exploded.

Unfortunately there is no evidence that the ghost is associated with Nevill's Cross; it is generally assumed to be a former ostler who hanged himself in the barn. But if someone could establish that the ghost has a Scottish accent . . .

18th
O C T O B E R

It's St Luke's Day – let's Whip a few Dogs

This is St Luke's Day, and also Whip-Dog Day, but there seems no connection between the two. Luke was a physician by profession and no mean artist in his spare time – he is said to have painted a portrait of the Virgin Mary – but neither of these activities normally involve beating dogs. In ancient paintings he is often portrayed with an ox, but this seems his only link with a four-footed friend.

The popular story is that on this day a priest was about to celebrate Mass – in York Minster, according to Yorkshire folk – when he accidentally dropped the pyx containing the consecrated wafers, and they were snatched up by a passing dog – which duly got whipped as a result. And the idea caught on.

This incident is not as unlikely as it sounds. Dogs used to attend church services with their masters, and were not always properly controlled. At places like Slaidburn in Lancashire, for example, the church still has the two dog-whips which were used by the sexton and his assistant to keep them in order.

On the other hand, there were a lot of strays and wild dogs roaming the streets in those days, and Whip-Dog Day was a jolly good opportunity to lay into them.

19th
O C T O B E R

Remember when Children were Encouraged to Fret?

Hobbies Weekly, which taught many generations of youngsters how to use fretwork sets and make wooden models, was launched on this day in 1895 – the forerunner of the countless home hobby magazines that now fill the newsagents' shelves. It stopped publishing exactly seventy years later, but 75,000 copies of the Hobbies handbook are still distributed, and the name lives on in Dereham, Norfolk, where Hobbies Ltd has always been based.

In spite of all the modern hi-tech toys and computers, there is still an interest in old-fashioned model-making, but while the original company employed up to two hundred people, there are now just ten.

The company was formed two years after *Hobbies Weekly* was launched, and soon had branches all over Britain. It suffered a major setback in 1917, when most of its plant and machinery was destroyed by fire, but the factory was rebuilt and "Hobbies" remained a household name between the wars. During the Second World War it switched to making specialized aircraft parts, and missed a generation of potential young customers. Business slackened, and when *Hobbies Weekly* ceased publication in

OCTOBER 19TH Memories of the days when a fretwork machine was hi-tech carpentry, and Hobbies was a household name

1965, the company was not far behind.

It was a former Hobbies employee, Ivan Stroulger, who revived the name, and the Hobbies premises now include a shop and museum, where elderly modelmakers are reminded of the days when children were actually encouraged to fret.

20th
OCTOBER

The Horse-racing Prince who backed his Jockey and gave up the Turf

On this day in 1791 the first of two races was run at Newmarket which led to the future King of England giving up the Turf, his greatest love, and never attending Newmarket again – and all in defence of his jockey, Sam Chifney, who was accused of throwing the race.

It was basically a feud between the Prince of Wales, later George IV, and the "perpetual president" of the Jockey Club, Sir Charles Bunbury. The Prince's horse Escape was entered for two races. Chifney maintained it had not had enough exercise to win the first race; the Prince's trainer and manager disagreed. Neither the Prince nor Chifney backed it (jockeys could bet in those days) and it came last.

Next day Chifney rode Escape in another race – with the odds understandably higher against it – and it came first, actually beating two horses which had finished ahead of it the previous day.

The Prince questioned Chifney closely and was convinced he was innocent. The two races were over different courses and distances, and Escape was renowned for inconsistency. The Jockey Club questioned him too but could prove nothing. However,

Sir Charles told the Prince that if Chifney continued to ride for him, "no gentleman would start against him".

It was a remarkable way to address a future king, and it got a swift response. Instead of sacking Chifney the Prince gave him 200 guineas a year for life, sold all his racehorses and, in spite of the Jockey Club's pleas, left the Turf. Many years later he did run racehorses again – but never at Newmarket.

21st
OCTOBER

And Remember, you heard it first in Madron!

The Royal Navy today celebrates one of its greatest victories and mourns the death of one of its greatest commanders. Lord Nelson's death at the Battle of Trafalgar in 1805 is commemorated by the laying of garlands on his ship, HMS *Victory*, in the

OCTOBER 20TH The Prince of Wales, with the sort of look he must have given the Jockey Club president when he accused his jockey of throwing a race

OCTOBER 21ST HMS Victory at Portsmouth. It is always garlanded on the anniversary of Trafalgar

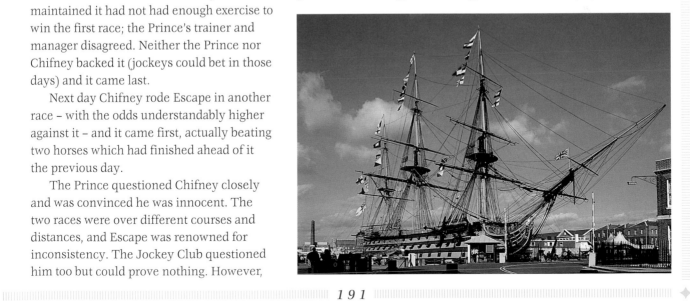

Royal Dockyards at Portsmouth, and there is a ceremony in his home village of Burnham Thorpe in Norfolk. One of the least-known and most significant of the other services is held at the far end of the country, in the village of Madron near Penzance.

It was here that news of the victory, and Nelson's death, first reached England. It was brought by a Penzance fishing boat which had made contact with one of the returning ships in the British fleet. Two services were held at St Maddern's church, one of thanksgiving and the other in Nelson's memory, and a banner was made for the occasion which is still on display in the church. A Trafalgar Service is always held there on the Sunday nearest this day.

Nelson's body was preserved in a barrel of the ship's brandy. It is said there was some confusion over which one he occupied, and when the *Victory* docked it was found that the crew had drunk every barrel dry.

In due course he was transferred to a more appropriate coffin, made of wood from the mainmast of the French ship *L'Orient*, which had been preserved since Nelson set it on fire off the Egyptian coast seven years before.

22nd
OCTOBER

The Great Western wasn't first across – but Brunel can breathe again

The 428-ton *Rising Star* set sail from Gravesend on this day in 1821, bound for Valparaiso and a modest niche in the corridors of British maritime history. She was built as a warship for use in the Chilean

OCTOBER 22ND
The Rising Star *was the first British steamship to cross the Atlantic – with a little help from her friends*

Revolution, but there was nothing record-breaking about that. She was also one of the earliest ships to be fitted with steam-powered engines, and she has gone down in the record books as the first British steamship to cross the Atlantic.

This would seem to nibble at the reputation of I.K. Brunel, whose *Great Western* is generally remembered as the pioneer steamship of transatlantic voyages; but there is a subtle difference in how they made the crossing. The *Great Western* used steam power all the way; the *Rising Star* undoubtedly made part of the voyage under sail. Nevertheless she was a steamship and she did get across seventeen years ahead of the *Great Western* – so let's grant her that little niche in the corridor.

As for the *Great Western*, she was still pipped to the title of the first British steamship crossing solely under steam. The much smaller *Sirius* set sail three days before her, and arrived in New York just a few hours ahead. But that still left the *Great Western* with another title: "The First Steamship In Regular Trans-Atlantic Passenger Service". So I. K. Brunel – breathe again.

OCTOBER 23RD
Members of the Sealed Knot at Edgehill. The Battle has been re-fought many times – even in the skies

23rd
OCTOBER

❦

The Battle with Several Encores – and the First Gallantry Medals

The Battle of Edgehill in Warwickshire was fought on this day in 1642, and the Sealed Knot occasionally re-enact it – but they are not the first to do so. On a number of occasions in the last three hundred years, ghostly armies have been reported fighting the battle over again, sometimes on the battlefield and sometimes – as in the first reported instance – in the skies.

It was at Christmas-time, and shepherds were indeed watching their flocks by night. When they looked up, however, it was not a star in the east they saw, but the opposing armies of Royalists and Parliamentarians locked in battle. It lasted for three hours, and there was an encore the following night, with repeat performances every Saturday. The run only ended, it is said, when some unburied bodies were found on the battlefield and were interred in consecrated ground.

The Castle Inn was built as an ornamental gatehouse on the centenary of the battle by the local squire and architect, Sanderson Miller. It stands on the spot where King Charles raised his standard and had a grandstand view of the battle. As a result of what he saw, the first-ever medals for gallantry were awarded under Royal Warrant to two of his officers, Sir Robert Welch and Captain John Smith.

Their gallantry, and the deaths of fifteen hundred soldiers, achieved little; the battle ended virtually in a draw.

24th
OCTOBER

❦

Could Lady Jane have had a Sideways Caesarian?

Lady Jane Seymour, perhaps the least-known of Henry VIII's six wives, died on this day in 1537, twelve days after giving birth to her son Edward. In her short period as Queen – only seventeen months – she notched up two notable achievements. She produced a son and heir for Henry, and she died in her bed of natural causes.

Well, fairly natural. It is reasonably certain that she died as a result of complications caused by a difficult labour, but a ballad of the day attributes her death to a request she made for a sort of sideways Caesarian. She insisted that the baby had to be born through her right side. The baby survived, but Jane did not – according to the ballad.

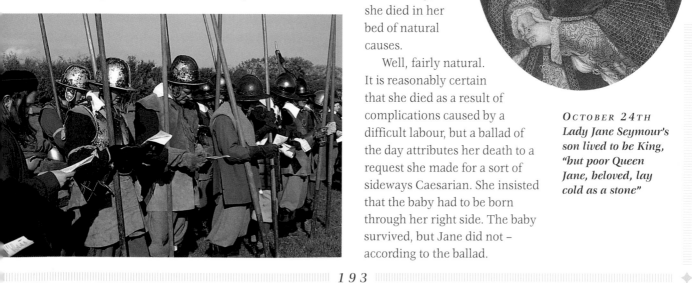

OCTOBER 24TH
Lady Jane Seymour's son lived to be King, "but poor Queen Jane, beloved, lay cold as a stone"

There was fiddling, aye, and dancing on the day the babe was born
But poor Queen Jane, beloved, lay cold as a stone.

Whichever way young Edward entered the world, he did not remain in it for very long. He died of pulmonary thrombosis at the age of fifteen, leaving behind a mixed legacy from his brief kingship. He founded Christ's Hospital, which was good news for the Bluecoat boys, and he named his cousin Lady Jane Grey as his successor – which was very bad news for Lady Jane. She was beheaded within the year.

25th
OCTOBER

The French got Stuck in the Mud – and Norwich got the Erpingham Gate

It is a little ironic that Henry's V's great victory over the French at Agincourt on this day in 1415 coincided with St Crispin's Day, because St Crispin was actually a Frenchman. He was martyred at Soissons with his brother, confusingly named Crispian – they must have constantly received each other's mail. Shakespeare treated them as one person: "And Crispin Crispian shall ne'er go by, but we in it shall be remembered."

That famous speech had other rousing lines as well, which budding Oliviers still relish. "We few, we happy few, we band of brothers"; "Gentlemen in England now abed should think themselves accursed they were not here" – and so on. But in fact this glorious victory of nine thousand over sixty thousand owed as much to French mud as English muscle. The French cavalry got bogged down before they could reach the

English lines, and Sir Thomas Erpingham's archers were able to pick them off at their leisure. The chivalrous King Henry himself ordered the slaughter of all French prisoners when he thought there might be a further attack, in case they escaped and joined in.

It was all very bloody, but at least something concrete came out of it – or rather, stone. Sir Thomas was so grateful for his survival he built the Erpingham Gate, which still stands at the entrance to the Cathedral Close in Norwich.

OCTOBER 25TH
The Erpingham Gate in Norwich was built by a survivor af Agincourt, in thanksgiving for victory

26th
OCTOBER

Merton College: "The Germ from which the rest were developed"

On this day in 1277 Walter de Merton, three times Lord Chancellor of England and later Bishop of Rochester, added a codicil to his will leaving the residue of his property to found Merton College, Oxford. In doing so, it is said he introduced the collegiate system which has existed at the university ever since. As one historian puts it: "Merton College must be considered the most interesting, if not the most beautiful, of Oxford colleges, because it was the germ from which the rest were developed."

When Merton was founded there were already halls of residence, but they consisted only of students' lodgings. Merton's bequest provided a chapel, a chaplain's residence, and accommodation for a warden to keep an eye on the students, all in the same premises.

There was plenty of money to play with. Merton owned property as far afield as Northumberland, acquired during the course of his duties. Quite a number of perks came the way of Lords Chancellors in those days, for which Oxford University has good cause to be thankful; three more of its colleges were later founded by holders of the same office.

27th
OCTOBER

Which side of the Atlantic did it start? It's a T-total T-toss Up

The man who coined the word "teetotal" – according to one story anyway – died on this day in 1846, and his etymological achievement was rated so highly at the time (presumably by his fellow teetotallers) that it was recorded on his tombstone.

Dick Turner, of Preston in Lancashire, was a passionate abstainer, and became so

OCTOBER 26TH Merton College, Oxford, "the germ from which the rest were developed"

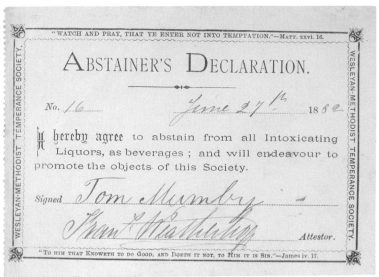

"WATCH AND PRAY, THAT YE ENTER NOT INTO TEMPTATION."—MATT. xxvi. 16.

ABSTAINER'S DECLARATION.

No. *16*   *June 27th*   18 *82*

I hereby agree to abstain from all Intoxicating Liquors, as beverages ; and will endeavour to promote the objects of this Society.

Signed *Tom Mumby*

Frant Weatherby   Attestor.

"TO HIM THAT KNOWETH TO DO GOOD, AND DOETH IT NOT, TO HIM IT IS SIN."—James iv. 17.

OCTOBER 27TH
An Abstainer's Declaration signed by a teetotaller like Dick Turner, who first coined the term teetotal – thanks to his stutter

worked up on the subject that it made him stutter. When someone at a Temperance meeting advocated partial abstinence, he hotly protested: "I'll have nowt to do wi' that. I'll be reet down t-total, or nowt."

When he died thirteen years later, his tombstone was inscribed: "Beneath this stone are deposited the remains of Richard Turner, author of the word 'Teetotal' as applied to abstinence from all intoxicating liquors."

Alas, American abstainers may have got in first. There is an equally plausible story that members of the New York Temperance Society, some years earlier, signed the pledge in two grades. The "Old Pledge" meant abstinence from spirits only, and their names were marked "O.P." If they opted for total abstinence, they were marked "T" – and referred to as "T-total".

So you can take your pick. Personally I prefer the Dick Turner version, because I like to think that "teetotum" was coined by a stuttering Red Indian who had just invented the spinning-top.

OCTOBER 28TH
Michael Faraday's workshop in the converted basement kitchen at the Royal Institution

28th
OCTOBER

Sir Humphry Davy's Greatest Discovery: "St Michael"

The dynamo, the device on which the electricity industry is based, was demonstrated for the first time at the Royal Institution on this day in 1831 by Michael Faraday. The converted servants' kitchen that was his laboratory, in the basement of the Royal Institution, and the primitive dynamo he built, are still on display there, and in the foyer is a statue of the man who is known affectionately within those walls as "St Michael".

Faraday left school at thirteen, became an errand boy for a London bookseller, and showed such enthusiasm he was apprenticed as a bookbinder. He not only bound books but read the scientific ones as well, and a customer who noticed his interest gave him tickets for a series of lectures by Sir Humphry Davy, at that time Britain's leading scientist. Faraday made copious

notes, wrote them up with his own additions, bound them himself and sent the book to Sir Humphry, who was so impressed he took him on as a laboratory assistant. The electro-magnet, the induction coil and the dynamo all followed – and Faraday himself became known as "Davy's greatest discovery".

He never patented anything, never commercialized his discoveries and never made much money; he just liked to "find out". But he did write a book called *Collected Researches in Electricity*, which an American called Edison found very useful.

29th
OCTOBER

His final One-liner: "What does thou Fear? Strike, man, strike"

Sir Walter Raleigh, seaman, courtier, writer, explorer and master of the ten-second sound-bite, was executed on this day in 1618 – and even in his final moments, his talent for the pithy one-liner did not fail him.

He asked to touch the executioner's axe and commented: "This is sharp medicine, but it is a physician for all diseases." Asked which way he preferred to lay his head on the block, he replied: "So as the heart be right, it matters not which way the head lies." It was only when the executioner hesitated, with axe upraised, that the nonchalance began to fray. "What does thou fear?" he asked impatiently. "Strike, man, strike."

It was a sad end to a sparkling career, ranging from defeating the Spanish fleet at Cadiz to discovering tobacco. Queen Elizabeth was impressed on both counts. "I have heard of many who have turned gold into smoke," she told him, "but you are the first to turn smoke into gold." She was quite good at the one-liners herself.

James I, though, was not impressed at all, and Raleigh spent thirteen years in the Tower. On his final morning, typically, he donned his best clothes and smoked his last pipe – perhaps remembering his first one, when a servant saw smoke rising from his armchair and doused him with water. His one-liner on that occasion is not recorded.

30th
OCTOBER

Meet the Quakers – Thanks to Gervase Bennet

The early members of what they prefer to call the Society of Friends were christened Quakers on this day in 1650 by a Derby magistrate, Gervase Bennet. Their founder, George Fox, appeared before him on one of the many occasions when he was arrested for his beliefs. Fox responded to the magistrate's questioning by exhorting him to "quake and tremble at the Word of the Lord" – and Bennet said he would call him and his followers "Quakers" thenceforth.

The Quakers, however, refused to quake in face of the persecution they suffered under Charles II. They were accused of subversion, treason, and sometimes even witchcraft. The most extreme case was at Long Stanton in Cambridgeshire, seven years after they were given their Quaker name, when they were accused of turning a woman into a horse and riding her around the countryside.

Surprisingly, John Bunyan supported the accusation, saying the woman's hands and feet were bruised, and her smock was torn

OCTOBER 29TH Sir Walter Raleigh having a final chat with the headsman about his axe. "This is sharp medicine, but it is a physician for all diseases..."

and bloody from the riders' spurs. The Quakers very reasonably enquired how anyone could ride a horse if it was wearing a smock.

Unusually for those days, common sense prevailed, and the Quakers were acquitted. It was not exactly John Bunyan's finest hour.

when the menfolk of the village were late home from Chiselborough Fair.

The story varies. The male-orientated version is that the men got lost in a fog on the way home, and very ingeniously made lanterns out of the mangolds in the fields to light their way home. Another version gives the womenfolk the credit for inventing these impromptu lanterns, or punkies, because they could not afford the real thing, and either they set off to help their husbands or they just got fed up waiting for them to come home. Alternatively, of course, it could go back to some Celtic festival of light, but don't suggest that in Hinton St George.

Punkie Night is well organized these days, and far preferable to the pernicious "trick or treat", which can be blamed on the States, not the Celts. A youthful Punkie Royal Family is drawn through the village on a decorated float, escorted by other children carrying their punkies and singing, "Gie us a candle, gie us a light, it's Punkie Night tonight."

And if you decline, nobody is going to empty your dustbin over the lawn.

31st

"Gie us a Candle on Punkie Night" – but it's not Compulsory

It coincides with the end of October and it involves hollowed-out mangolds or pumpkins with candles inside, but Punkie Night at Hinton St George in Somerset has nothing to do with Hallowe'en. It has been held on this night if a Thursday, or if not, the Thursday before, since the night

November

1st
NOVEMBER

NOVEMBER 1ST
*"Read all abaht it":
how W.H. Smith was
founded – by Mr and
Mrs H.W. Smith*

Yes, but who actually was W.H. Smith?

The first railway-station bookstall was opened at Euston by W.H. Smith on this day in 1848, and a new era in retailing began. By the turn of the century they had over a thousand, plus their High Street shops. They went into wholesaling, and diversified into do-it-yourself. Today W.H. Smith are the largest retail and distribution group in the country.

But who was W.H. Smith? The real founder of the Smith empire was Anna Smith. In 1792 her husband Henry died from influenza and left her to bring up the family and run the little shop named after him – not W.H. but H.W. Smith. She tried hard to sell it, but her advertisement for an "industrious person" to take over a business making all of £1 12s a week failed to produce a buyer. So she made the best of it, built up trade, and in 1816 left a going concern to her sons Henry Edward and William Henry.

William was the leading light. He had the brainwave of speeding up newspaper deliveries to the provinces by collecting the papers from the presses and rushing them to the early-morning stage-coaches; normally they had to wait for the evening coaches.

Soon he had customers in nine thousand towns and villages, happy to pay extra for their papers to arrive the same day.

So it was William Henry's initials that went on the shopfronts, and he shrewdly christened his son William Henry, to make sure they stayed there. It has been W.H. Smith ever since.

2nd
NOVEMBER

First Soulcakes, Now a Skull-horse on All Souls' Day

This is All Souls' Day, when it was traditional to hold services for the repose of the dead, and in one or two villages in Cheshire like Comberbach and Antrobus they still remember the associated tradition of soulcaking.

Poor people used to pray for the departed relatives of their richer neighbours in return for soulcakes, flat cakes made from flour, egg yolks, sugar, butter, currants and milk, and marked with a cross. Over the years the poor gave up bothering about the prayers and just asked for cakes, and in due course opted for hard cash instead.

"The roads are very dirty, my shoes are very thin, I've got a little pocket to put a penny in . . ."

NOVEMBER 2ND
*The Comberbach
skull-horse takes to
the road again on All
Souls' Day*

The Comberbach Soulcakers still collect money for charity, but they provide good value for it by performing an ancient mumming play starring the Comberbach skull-horse, a horse's skull on a hobby-horse body. The original skull is said to come from one of the offspring of Marbury Dun, a local thoroughbred buried in Marbury Park.

Some say the penny in the "little pocket" is the coin placed in the corpse's mouth to pay the ferrying charge to Hades, and the skull-horse derives from the dog-headed Mercury. But how about the other performers – King George, the Black Prince, a quack doctor and "little Dairy Dout with shirt-lap hanging out"? Best not to analyse the soulcaking play – just enjoy it.

perhaps Dr Richard Mead had a family connection with Hubert. Dr Mead was an eighteenth-century physician who is said to have paid for a drink at his local by giving the landlord, Mr Wells, his secret recipe for curing rabies.

Until quite recently the inn, at Little Odell in Bedfordshire, displayed the encouraging notice over the door: "George Wells has a recipe for the bite of a mad dog which has never failed!" – and it has been called the Mad Dog ever since.

3rd
NOVEMBER

How did the Saintly Ex-huntsman find a Cure for Rabies?

St Hubert, whose day this is, was an eighth-century French nobleman who spent so much time hunting that he neglected his spiritual duties. He changed his ways when a stag he was pursuing turned to confront him, bearing a crucifix and threatening him with eternal damnation. He became a monk and finished up as Bishop of Liège.

The moral of the story seems to be clear: don't waste your time hunting stags, particularly ones that carry crucifixes and talk. It therefore seems curious that Hubert is the patron saint of huntsmen; he seems more fitted to be patron of the League Against Cruel Sports.

Just as curiously, his descendants are credited with the power to cure rabies. Was this a common hazard in the hunting field? But if they do possess this power, then

4th
NOVEMBER

Never on Sundays – not if St Cleer is Around

There have been many miraculous punishments for either working or playing on the Sabbath – both seemed to be equally reprehensible. Offenders were swallowed up in pits, or suffered fatal illnesses, or just disappeared. The modus operandi favoured by St Cleer, the sixth-century Cornish hermit whose day this is, and who felt very strongly about this sort of thing, was literally petrifying. He just turned people into stone – and the three circles of standing stones near the village named after him are the prime example.

According to legend, Cleer found some villagers playing the ancient Celtic game of hurling on a Sunday, and took drastic action; the Hurlers have stood there motionless ever since. Archaeologists would say he must have taken the trouble to hand-shape some

NOVEMBER 4TH
*Symbolic stones (1):
The Hurlers at St
Cleer are a drastic
warning not to play
games on Sundays*

of the stones, and he also made sure the players forming the central circle were all the same height, because the tops of the stones are all level. In fact they would argue that the Hurlers were actually erected for some Celtic ritual – but they had better not let St Cleer hear them say so.

Another strange feature of the Hurlers was recorded in the seventeenth century: "a redoubled numbering never eveneth with the first". In other words, each time you count them you get a different total. But I find that applies to almost anything . . .

5th
N O V E M B E R

The Devil's Boulder – the Stone they dare not leave Unturned

Yes, of course it's Bonfire Night, but at Shebbear in Devon they have something more important to do. Each year on this day a procession carrying lanterns, torches and, more importantly, crowbars, makes its way to the huge stone on the green near the church, and they turn it completely over. If they fail to do so, some disaster will hit the village – nobody is quite sure what, because they've never missed a year.

The theories about this curious rite are so numerous that earlier chroniclers must have left no stone unturned to discover new ones. The most ingenious is that the boulder was the foundation stone of Henscott church across the river, but each night the Devil moved it across to Shebbear, until they gave up.

Alternatively it marks a holy spot associated with the church's patron saint, St Michael. Or it is one of the many stones the Devil dropped on his flight to Hell. Or he threw it at the church and it fell short. Or St Michael threw it at the Devil and buried him under it. My own theory is that the village children were playing with a big snowball on a Sunday and St Michael turned it to stone.

Now you have a go . . .

NOVEMBER 5TH
*Symbolic stones (2):
The Devil's Boulder
at Shebbear has to be
turned each year*

6th

NOVEMBER

7th

NOVEMBER

NOVEMBER 6TH
St Leonard's Forest in Sussex, where he was wounded while slaying a dragon and lilies-of-the-valley grew where his blood dripped

Maybe St Leonard should have Stuck to the Day Job

St Leonard, whose day this is, is the patron saint of prisoners, and it seems surprising he does not feature prominently in the emblems of organizations such as Amnesty International, because he is usually depicted holding symbolic broken fetters. Apparently he was regarded in such high esteem by Clovis, King of the Franks in the sixth century, that he was given permission to release any prisoners he visited. His postbag must have been enormous . . .

But this seems to have little connection with the legend of St Leonard's Forest, which lies between Horsham and Pease Pottage in Sussex, a couple of miles off the M25. St Leonard apparently took a break from his prison visits to slay a dragon here, but he was wounded in the process, and from the spots where drops of his blood fell, lilies-of-the-valley grew. The lilies can still be found there, though the woods were badly battered in the great gales of 1987.

It would seem, however, that the saint was better at freeing prisoners than wiping out dragons, because others have been reported roaming the same woods right up to the nineteenth century. Maybe he should have stuck to the day job, and left the dragons to St George . . .

The only Grave in the Abbey which no one walks over

On this night in 1921 an eerie little ceremony took place in the chapel of St Pol in France, quite close to where the front line had been until the Great War ended three years earlier. The bodies of four British soldiers were carried into the chapel. They had been brought from the four main battle areas of the war – the Aisne, the Somme, Arras and Ypres. No one knew their identities; they had been taken from unmarked graves.

A British Army officer, Brigadier-General Wyatt, selected one of the bodies at random, and the other three were taken away again to be reburied in a military cemetery. The selected one was placed inside a coffin, which in turn was placed in another. The outer coffin was made of oak with wrought-iron bands, and a Crusader's sword, brought from the Tower of London, was inserted under the bands.

The coffin was brought to England on the destroyer HMS *Verdun*, and four days later, on the anniversary of Armistice Day, it was taken in procession to Westminster Abbey. King George V stood at the head of the grave as it was laid to rest. Countless other heads of state from all over the world

NOVEMBER 7TH
The Tomb of the Unknown Warrior. Heads of state stand by it, no one ever walks over it

have stood there since – at the Tomb of the Unknown Warrior – to pay tribute to all the British casualties who have no known grave.

Little Lost Bear. By MARY TOURTEL

No. 1.—Mrs. Bear sends her little son Rupert to market.

NOVEMBER 8TH
Off goes Rupert Bear on his first adventure – and children have been following him ever since

NOVEMBER 9TH
A flypast has replaced the water pageant, but the Lord Mayor's coach is still the star of the the Show

8th
NOVEMBER

For Generations of Children, Rupert is a Bear Necessity

A new character appeared on the cartoon page of the *Daily Express*, under the heading "Little Lost Bear", on this day in 1920 – and it has been appearing ever since. This is the birthday of Rupert Bear, the most successful, unchanging and long-lasting of all children's comic-strip characters. Even during the wartime newsprint shortage, Lord Beaverbrook insisted he should still appear each day to preserve the nation's morale.

Beaverbrook had wanted a rival to the *Daily Mail's* Teddy Tail and the *Daily Mirror's* Pip, Squeak and Wilfred. The innately decent and terribly British little bear was conjured up by Mary Tourtel, a well-established illustrator, whose husband happened to be night editor of the *Daily Express* – and an amateur poet. She drew the

pictures, he wrote the verses – and Rupert Bear was born.

Today the Rupert Bear motif appears on more than two hundred products, early copies of the *Rupert Annual* fetch up to two thousand pounds, and he has his own fan club, the 900-strong Followers of Rupert. Throughout all this, successive artists have preserved him almost unchanged; only his jumper was altered in the 1930s from pale blue to red. Clothes are very important to Rupert; he must never, never appear undressed. And of course he must always be home in time for tea.

9th
NOVEMBER

The Lord Mayor's Show: Victorians thought it "out of place"

This was the traditional date of the Lord Mayor's Show, to celebrate the right granted to the citizens of London under Magna Carta to elect their Lord Mayor and celebrate the installation of each new incumbent. It has continued ever since, but not without its hiccups, notably in the middle of the last century.

Until then the procession had been a spectacular affair, involving floats, chariots, giants, triumphal arches, a water pageant – the lot; each new Lord Mayor wanted to outdo his predecessors. But under the Victorians the mood changed. In 1853, after an attempt to revive the old spectacle, a contemporary writer commented gloomily: "Good as was the intention of this pageant, it was felt to be out of place in this modern age of utilitarianism, and will probably never again be attempted."

And indeed the city barges were sold, the

water pageant abolished, and the procession was reduced to the other extreme – "shorn of all dignity or significance, and in the eyes of many, simply ludicrouse".

Happily the mood changed again, and the Lord Mayor's Show has regained much of its former spectacle, with little extras not available to the Victorians, like the flypast by the RAF. But for the convenience of trippers and traffic, it is now held on the nearest Saturday.

10th
NOVEMBER

Yes, it was Indeed Dr Livingstone

One of the most famous – and most parodied – greetings in history was spoken on this day in 1871, in a remote and feverstricken village called Ujiji on the shore of Lake Tanganyika:

"Dr Livingstone, I presume?"

Henry Morton Stanley had spent nine months searching for the explorer-missionary. Nothing had been heard of David Livingstone for five years, and an enterprising newspaper editor, James Gordon Bennett of the *New York Herald*, commissioned Stanley to find him. He was not actually lost, just unable to travel any further because of illness and lack of food.

Stanley was so overcome when they met that he could only raise his hat and murmur his polite greeting, more suited perhaps to an English garden party than such an historic moment. But in fairness one should also quote the words that followed, which fitted the occasion admirably: "I thank God, Doctor, that I have been permitted to see you."

But although they became firm friends, Livingstone refused to return home with him. Two years later, still searching for the source of the Nile, he fell ill again. "Build me a hut to die in," he told his bearers. And they found him next morning, kneeling at his bedside, dead.

11th
NOVEMBER

A Six-gun Salute on St Martin's Day – but they are only seven inches high

Every year on this day a six-gun salute is fired at Fenny Stratford in Buckinghamshire – but it has nothing to do with Remembrance Day. The guns are tiny "poppers", seven inches high and weighing less than twenty pounds apiece, and they need only four ounces of gunpowder. The Royal Horse Artillery was never like this.

This is also St Martin's Day, and in the early eighteenth century a local doctor at Fenny Stratford, Browne Willis, built St Martin's parish church on the site of an old chantry chapel. He built it in memory of his grandfather, who lived in St Martin's Lane in the London parish of St Martin-in-the-Fields, and who conveniently died on St Martin's Day in 1675. Pretty conclusively, this is a St Martin's Day custom.

The salute was first fired by Browne Willis at a dinner for the local gentry and clergy

NOVEMBER 10TH
Yes, he did say "Dr Livingstone, I presume" – but Stanley had another line too

NOVEMBER 11TH
Another six-gun salute by the Fenny Poppers to mark St Martin's day, but you have to look closely – they are only seven inches high

after the church was completed – one way of keeping guests awake after a good meal. When he died in 1760 he bequeathed the rent from his house to pay for the gunpowder as well as a memorial sermon each year, and the salute has been fired on St Martin's Day ever since, at noon, 2 p.m. and 4 p.m. precisely, in the local recreation ground.

There has been only one mishap, in 1859, when one of the poppers developed a crack and instead of just popping, burst. All six were then re-cast, and now they are periodically X-rayed to make sure they don't pop too violently again.

12th
N O V E M B E R

He helped another Prisoner through the Slough of Despond, 300 years later

"A tinker out of Bedford, a vagrant oft in quod, a private under Fairfax and a minister of God" was arrested on this day in 1660 for preaching without a licence.

Kipling's racy description of John Bunyan was not entirely fair. He was hardly a vagrant, just a travelling preacher who fell foul of the religious bigotry of his time. But certainly he was a tinker by trade, he served in Cromwell's army, and once the Baptists were allowed to have their own meeting houses he became a full-time minister. It was his time "oft in quod", however, which is best remembered, not least by another famous prisoner more than three hundred years later, Terry Waite.

NOVEEMBER 12TH The picture of John Bunyan which brought hope to Terry Waite three hundred years later

For most of his five years as a hostage Terry received no mail, until a picture postcard of the Bunyan memorial window got through to him from an unknown well-wisher. "Dear Terry, you are not forgotten. People everywhere are praying for your release."

Terry Waite's situation could not have been foreseen by Bunyan in *Pilgrim's Progress*, but somewhere between the Slough of Despond and the Valley of Humiliation, I am sure he could have worked it in.

13th
N O V E M B E R

The Stamford Bull-run – and a Bridge too Far

In the days of King John, according to legend, William Earl of Warren saw two bulls fighting in the meadow beneath his castle at Stamford in Lincolnshire. When butchers attempted to part them, one bull ran into the town and caused chaos in the streets. The earl followed on horseback, and was so entertained that he gave the meadow to the butchers of Stamford, on condition they provided a bull to be run through the town every year on this day.

The Stamford bull-run continued for centuries. The church bell was rung to get the roads cleared of the aged and infirm, then the bull was released into a street blocked at each end. There it was bombarded with missiles until it was thoroughly infuriated, then the barriers were removed and the main event began, the attempt to "bridge the bull". The townsfolk drove it to the bridge over the Welland, then closed in on it and by main force flung it over the parapet.

That was not the end. The bull would

NOVEMBER 13TH
*Where "running the
bull" became
"bridging the bull" –
it was tossed over the
parapet of Stamford
Bridge*

swim ashore, only to be chased again until everyone became exhausted, or bored, or hungry. Then it was killed and cooked.

Not surprisingly, the authorities in due course objected to all this. In 1839 animal-rights protestors joined forces with the police and army – perhaps for the first and last time – and the townsfolk reluctantly gave in. But the bridge is still there and the meadow beneath it is still the Bull Meadow.

14th
NOVEMBER

"Let Not Poor Nellie Starve" – but no Oranges please

The most successful orange-seller in the history of the fruit trade died on this day in 1687 aged 36. Many people assume that Nell Gwyn was selling her oranges at the Theatre Royal Drury Lane when King Charles took such a fancy to her that he bought up her entire stock, carried her off and made her his mistress. In fact she had already graduated to the stage when the King first saw her, thanks to an actor called John Lacey, a notable Falstaff of his day and no mean talent-spotter himself.

Mr Lacey observed the fifteen-year-old in the pit exchanging insults with the customers, gave her a few elocution lessons, persuaded her to cut down a bit on the swearing, and got her a small part in one of Dryden's plays. She was eighteen when Charles first saw her, orangeless but twice as succulent, and in the space of a couple of years she had borne two of his sons, acquired luxurious homes in Pall Mall and Windsor, and persuaded him to part with a fortune. He was still obsessed with her when he died: "Let not poor Nellie starve!"

She also managed to get a title for her elder son, by pointedly referring to him as a bastard in front of the King. When Charles remonstrated with her, she said there was no other way to describe him – so he made the lad an earl, who later became Duke of St Alban's. The title still exists today, but I am not sure whether oranges feature in the family crest.

NOVEMBER 14TH
*A change from selling
oranges and playing
bit parts in Dryden's
plays: Nell Gwyn
after meeting King
Charles*

15th
N O V E M B E R

❧

Married at 80, an Affair at 105 – it's Parr for the Course

A Shropshire farm labourer who left his home village only once, to visit London, was buried on this day in 1635 in Westminster Abbey, among the great and the good of the nation. None of them could match his remarkable achievement: Thomas Parr was 152 years old.

"Old Parr" was born at Winnington in 1483 and saw all the Tudors come and go. He remained a bachelor until he was eighty, then married and lived with his wife until she died thirty-two years later. When he was 105 he had an affair with a lady called Catherine Milton, and as a result did penance in a white sheet at the door of his parish church. After due consideration he married her – at the age of 120.

After he passed his century-and-a-half, Old Parr was visited by the local landowner, the Earl of Arundel, who was so impressed by his demeanour and intelligence – let alone his marital activities – that he persuaded him to travel to London to be presented to Charles I.

The long journey, the crowds who thronged to see him, and the unaccustomed life in London was all too much for Old Parr, and he died a few months later – but not before he had made quite an impact at court. The King asked him, rather loftily: "You have lived longer than other men, but what have you done more than other men?"

"Sire," said Old Parr, "I did penance for seducing a lady when I was over a hundred!"

He deserved that place in Westminster Abbey.

NOVEMBER 15TH Old Parr, still young at heart at a century-and-a-half. "I did penance for seducing a lady when I was over a hundred"

16th
N O V E M B E R

❧

He Survived the Toad and the Stench – but not the Red-hot Iron

Edward II, whose incompetence as a general led to defeat by the Scots at Bannockburn, and whose fondness for young men led to Queen Isabella disowning him at court, did not have much going for him as a medieval king. With his wife's connivance he was imprisoned in Berkeley Castle on this day in 1326, the prelude to a death far more unpleasant than anything he deserved.

The little room at the castle which served as his cell adjoined a deep pit in the thickness of the wall. Legend has it that a man-eating toad lived down it, which would indeed have been a nasty way to go, but that was not how Edward died. Nor did he die from the nauseating stench which rose from the pit, where the bodies of dead animals – and dead prisoners – were regularly dumped.

NOVEMBER 16TH The room in Berkeley Castle where Edward II met a singularly unpleasant end

He did in fact show remarkable stamina, and after ten months Isabella's patience ran out. He had already been officially deposed, but that was not enough. The order went out to speed up the process, and Lord Berkeley discreetly vacated his castle and left Edward with his two jailers, an unsavoury pair called Gurney and Maltravers. Exactly how they killed him has never been proved, but a red-hot iron played a significant part, and he died in such agony that his screams, so it is said, can be heard to this day.

But at least he didn't finish up in the pit. He was not allowed the standard burial in Westminster Abbey, but he does have a very decent memorial in Gloucester Cathedral.

17th
NOVEMBER

A Unisex Monastery, an Historic Synod and a Snake Clearance – Thanks to Hilda

St Hilda, whose day this is, founded England's first unisex monastery at Whitby in AD657, and in spite of possible distractions it became a famous centre of learning, but her main achievement was the Synod of Whitby seven years later, when she brought together the leading lights of the English church to decide whether it should follow the Celtic tradition or the rites of Rome. Rome won the day, which is why the Church came to be run by bishops answerable to the Pope, instead of having independent abbots doing their own thing. It also meant that the date of Easter was calculated on the Roman system, which has baffled laymen ever since.

Hilda's abbey was destroyed by the Danes and refounded by the Benedictines after the Normans came. Then Henry VIII

dissolved it, the elements battered it, and finally the German fleet shelled it during the First World War, so there is little to be seen of the Benedictine building, let alone Hilda's. But her memory is preserved at Whitby in a more bizarre way.

Legend has it that she ended a plague of snakes in Eskdale by driving them all to the cliff edge, then decapitating each one with a flick of her whip before they dropped over the edge, turning them to stone as they fell. The ammonites still found on the rocks below are not just fossilized shellfish but Hilda's headless horrors, petrified for posterity . . .

NOVEMBER 17TH
The site of the Synod of Whitby, which decided the Church should be answerable to the Pope. Henry VIII changed all that, and dissolved Whitby Abbey in the process

18th
NOVEMBER

An Old Score never Scored – but later, Patience triumphed

William Gilbert, writer of the comedy-dramas *An Old Score* and *Randall's Thumb*, was born on this day in 1836. *An Old Score*, alas, never scored, and *Randall's Thumb* got the thumbs-down too, but Mr Gilbert's later work became rather better known, when he teamed up with Mr Sullivan to create the

NOVEMBER 18TH
William Gilbert's
compositions never
caught on until he
met Mr Sullivan; then
his fortunes – like his
moustache – took an
up-turn

spectacularly successful *Savoy Operas*.

They might have been called the *Opéra Comique* Operas, because the earlier ones – *Pinafore, Pirates of Penzance*, and *Patience* – had their debuts at the Opéra Comique Theatre, but when the Savoy was built in 1881 it became the permanent home of Gilbert and Sullivan. The name sounded more prestigious anyway.

Experts still argue over which partner made the most important contribution, and the partners did plenty of arguing themselves – not always over opera. Their most famous quarrel was over the provision of a new carpet at the Savoy. But Gilbert did score over his colleague by having his name immortalized in the English language – "Gilbertian" is still used to describe anything comically topsy-turvy. "Sullivanesque", if the word ever existed, never caught on.

On the other hand, who knows what the "S" stands for in W.S. Gilbert? It turns out to be Schwenck – and even the ingenious Mr Gilbert would be hard put to immortalize that.

two years until his death in 1892, and towards the end of his life he became Alfred, Lord Tennyson, the first poet to be awarded a peerage. A cartoon appeared in *Punch* in 1883 showing him receiving his coronet from Mr Punch himself – the highest accolade of all.

Tennyson took his job seriously. Almost as soon as he was appointed he produced an "Ode on the Death of the Duke of Wellington". The Crimean War gave him plenty of scope – "Theirs not to reason why, Theirs but to do and die . . ." – and when the Danish Princess Alexandra married the future Edward VII in 1863 he came up with a multi-racial welcome:

Saxon and Norman and Dane are we,
But all of us Danes in our welcome to thee. . .

It was not as memorable as most of his poems. Tennyson may well have achieved a third record, as the poet producing the most phrases familiar to non-poets. "The old order changeth . . .", "In the spring a young man's fancy . . .", "'Tis better to have loved and lost . . ." He even foresaw the advent of the computer: "Our little systems have their day, they have their day and cease to be . . ." But my favourite, perhaps, is his epitaph for CAMRA members: "May there be no moaning at the bar, when I put out to sea . . ."

19th

"The Old Order Changeth" – but Tennyson kept going for 42 Years

NOVEMBER 19TH
Alfred Lord Tennyson
must have been so
busy wielding that
king-size pen that he
rarely had time for
a haircut

On this day in 1850 a new Poet Laureate was appointed to succeed William Wordsworth, and the new incumbent was to achieve two impressive records in the history of English poetry. Alfred Tennyson held the office longer than any other poet, for nearly forty-

20th
NOVEMBER

~~

Where was Edmund's Head? "Over here!" shouted the Head

St Edmund, whose day this is, was the Saxon king who, according to legend, was tied to a tree by the invading Danes, refused to renounce Christianity and was shot with arrows until he died. However, the story of where and how this happened is as full of holes as the unfortunate Edmund himself.

The location in East Anglia was named as Haegelisdun, which has been variously interpreted as Hellesdon, near Norwich, or Halgeston, which used to be near the Saxon kings' burial ground at Sutton Hoo, or Hoxne near Diss. Hoxne is the strongest claimant, and indeed a plaque on Goldbrook Bridge announces firmly that the King was hiding under it when the glint of his spurs was spotted by a courting couple and they gave him away to the Danes. The bridge is said to have been an unlucky venue for lovers ever since.

A fresco on nearby St Edmund's Hall depicts the story, and there used to be a tree in which arrowheads were found, but the actual evidence is pretty slim. The legend continues that Edmund's head was severed from his body, and was later found – having

helpfully shouted "Over here!" to the searchers – being guarded by a wolf. The evidence for that, not surprisingly, is slimmer still.

But the final chapter of the story is beyond dispute. Having gathered up the remains they went to bury St Edmund – at Bury St Edmund's.

21st
NOVEMBER

~~

Eoanthropus Dawsoni, *the Skull that Fooled them all – nearly*

What was thought to be one of the most significant archaeological discoveries of the century was proved on this day in 1953 to be a hoax. For over forty years the scientific world had accepted that the Piltdown Skull was evidence of a new genus of man. It turned out to be an ordinary human skull linked with the jawbone of an ape.

It all started in 1908, when Charles Dawson of Lewes claimed to have found part of a fossilized skull in a gravel bed near Piltdown Common in Sussex. Three years later – the hoaxer was very patient – he found another piece. Sir Arthur Smith Woodward was then drawn into the story. He examined Dawson's finds and pronounced them genuine. The Piltdown Skull was accorded official scientific status as *Eoanthropus Dawsoni*.

It was only when modern dating methods were used that the hoax was uncovered. The details were revealed in the *Bulletin of the British Museum* – perhaps the first time that this learned journal has raised a really good laugh.

Speculation about the hoaxer ended in May 1996, when a canvas travelling trunk was found at the Natural History Museum,

NOVEMBER 21ST
One of the great scientific hoaxes of the century is immortalised on a pub sign at Piltdown

NOVEMBER 20TH
The martyrdom of St Edmund, depicted in a window at Greensted Church, where his funeral procession rested

containing bones which had been stained and carved in the same way as the skull and other artefacts of the Piltdown Man. The trunk bore the initials of Martin A.C. Hinton, a curator at the museum in 1912. He was renowned for his practical jokes, and it is assumed he rigged up this one to deflate his rather pompous boss – Sir Arthur was Keeper of Geology at the Museum. But the revelation of the hoax came too late for them both.

22nd

Cecilia's Music charmed an Angel from Heaven; pity her Husband was around

St Cecilia, whose day this is, was one of those saints who had an interesting experience with an angel. She was a musical lady who some say invented the organ, and it was her musical skills that tempted an angel down from Heaven to visit her. They were in close conversation when her husband came upon them and, according to legend, "gave to both a crown of martyrdom which he brought from Paradise".

Was this good news or bad, Cecilia must

have wondered. It turned out to be bad, because she was indeed martyred, some say by semi-decapitation. The executioner struck one blow, then miraculously found his hand was stayed. It was still bad news: she was left to expire slowly.

She became the patroness of music, and it was once common for concerts to be performed in her honour on this day. Her memory is kept alive by the Worshipful Company of Musicians, a City of London Livery Company, which processes to a service at St Paul's on her day.

Incidentally, it was on St Cecilia's Day in 1859 that a Mr and Mrs Sharp had a baby boy and called him Cecil in her honour. It proved appropriate; Cecil Sharp became a composer and leading authority on folk music.

23rd

The Strip Farmers of Laxton; sounds Chilly, but it still Works

A Court Leet is held at Laxton in Nottinghamshire on or around this day each year to administer the only fields in England which are still farmed the medieval way, in long strips. While the rest of England was being enclosed by the big landowners in the eighteenth century, Mill Field, West Field and South Field somehow survived, although they have slimmed down over the years. Originally they covered nearly two thousand acres, whereas these days they are just under five hundred – but even five hundred is a lot of acres for three fields.

Each strip is allocated to a local farmer by the Leet, acting for the Lord of the Manor – currently the Crown Estates Commissioners. A jury appointed at the Leet inspects the fields each year, to make sure no farmer is

NOVEMBER 23RD
Many farmhouses at Laxton are still geared to medieval strip farming. In the main street they can be found side by side, end-on to the road

encroaching on his neighbour's strip or on the rights of way between them, and any transgressors can still be fined.

A little modern technology has been allowed to creep in. Some strips have been combined so that tractors and other farm machinery can operate on them. But the medieval cycle is still the basis of strip-farming after seven hundred years: one season of winter wheat, then a spring-sown crop, and the third year fallow. It may sound quaint – and the students at the Royal Agricultural College might have a quiet chuckle – but it works.

24th
NOVEMBER

First the Cut-off, then the Jump-off on St Catherine's Eve

St Catherine's Eve used to be a hectic day for lacemakers, on the eve of the traditional holiday on the morrow. This was "Cutting-off Day", when they had to sell the lace they had made. Lengths of lace were cut off from the long rolls they had been making. Individual lacemakers became expert in one particular pattern and reproduced it over and over again on their roll, so it was cut off and sold in lengths like patterned cotton or wallpaper. One traditional method of payment was to cover the length of lace with one-shilling pieces, but that must have been before market forces and cut prices took over – or did the dealers just leave bigger gaps between the shillings?

Having sold their stock, the lacemakers would celebrate in the evening with a Cathern Bowl, a powerful brew made from hot apple pulp, cinnamon and cider. Thus fortified, they faced the trickiest part of the celebrations.

Each girl had to jump over a lighted candle on the floor, swiftly enough not to singe her petticoats, but not so swiftly that the draught blew out the candle, or that would bring bad luck for the rest of her life.

"Kit be nimble, Kit be quick, Kit jump over the candlestick", the others chanted – but after a few glasses out of the Cathern Bowl, Kit didn't always make it. Hot pants may not have been a modern phenomenon . . .

25th
NOVEMBER

The White Ship went down – and the King never Smiled again

A shipwreck which altered the succession to the English throne and caused a civil war – a maritime disaster far more serious but much less publicized than the loss of King John's treasure in the Wash on October 13th – took place on this day in 1120.

Henry I and his family were sailing home from Normandy, Henry in the leading ship and his two sons and a daughter in the *White Ship*, the newest and fastest vessel in the Fleet. Knowing they could catch up, the captain of the *White Ship* and his passengers

NOVEMBER 25TH When the White Ship sank, Henry I's sons went down with it, leading to a change in the succession and a six-year civil war

decided to delay their departure – and the delay proved fatal. The crew, including the helmsman, spent the time drinking. When they eventually set off they hit a rock outside the harbour, and the ship immediately capsized.

Henry's elder son William, the eighteen-year-old heir to the throne, his brother Richard and their sister were drowned, with almost everyone else on board. Only one sailor survived to send the news to the King. "Immediately Henry fell to the ground overcome with anguish, and after being helped to his feet by friends and led into a private room, gave way to bitter laments." It is said that he never smiled again.

When he died his surviving daughter Matilda and his nephew Stephen battled it out for six years to take the throne, while England suffered a reign of terror from both sides. "God and his Angels slept," it was said – and all because a helmsman decided to drink and drive.

26th
N O V E M B E R

~⚬~

The Night the Eddystone Lighthouse blew down – with the Man who built it

The first Eddystone lighthouse, near Plymouth, was destroyed by a storm on this night in 1703, and the man who built it, Henry Winstanley, perished with it. He was no architect, just a larger-than-life entrepreneur with a talent for publicity. Nobody had attempted to build a lighthouse on such a limited area of rock before, and he saw the possibilities.

He volunteered to build it after one of his own ships had foundered on the Eddystone. In 1698, after two years' work, he personally

lit the tallow candles in the lantern, amid much acclamation. But his triumph was short-lived. That winter the sea regularly engulfed the lantern, and the tower shuddered dangerously. Winstanley responded by encasing it in a broader, higher tower strengthened with iron bands. It rose over a hundred feet above sea level, with an ornamental weathervane on top. The tower stood firm, and for five years not a ship was wrecked in its vicinity. Winstanley became a public hero.

In 1703, however, there were reports that the tower was unstable in gales. Winstanley, still with an eye to publicity, said he was prepared to brave out the fiercest gale on the lighthouse he had built. He was supervising repairs when the worst storm of the winter swept the country. It was the end of them both.

The current lighthouse is the fifth on Eddystone – half as high again as Winstanley's, and instead of a weathervane it has a helipad on top.

27th
N O V E M B E R

~⚬~

Mr Briggs's Bread is still supplied – pity about his Grave

The inscription on a brass plaque near the north door of Cartmel Priory in Cumbria reads: "Mr Rowland Briggs of Swallowmyr, who died ye 27th of Nove. 1703, gave the sum of £52 to the

NOVEMBER 26TH
Henry Winstanley's Eddystone lighthouse was highly decorative but slightly unstable; when it collapsed in a storm, it took him with it

NOVEMBER 27TH
The cupboard is never bare at Cartmel Priory, thanks to Rowland Briggs

Churchwardens of this Parish to be Secured upon Land; and the Interest thereof to be by them laid out in Bread and distributed to the most indigent Housekeepers of this Parish every Sunday for ever . . ."

Nearly three hundred years later, Mr Briggs's dying wish is still observed. Instead of buns, two fresh cottage loaves are placed each weekend in the "bread cupboard" – actually a pair of shelves – in the Priory, as requested on this day in 1703. The housekeepers who benefit are probably not so much indigent as forgetful; the bread was often taken on a Sunday by someone who had forgotten to buy any on the Saturday. Now there is Sunday opening in nearby Grange-over-Sands, the bread tends to stay on the shelves . . .

Mr Briggs made this bequest in memory of his wife Anne, who died twenty years before him. He made another on his own behalf, a payment of five shillings every Christmas Day "to ye sexton and his successors", provided they kept his grave "unbroken up". Alas, ye sexton or his successors slipped up. Although his grave is thought to be somewhere under the central crossing of the Priory, it is no longer marked.

Ireland, as a candidate for Sinn Féin – and she was unable to take her seat because she happened to be in Holloway prison at the time, detained for Republican activities.

It was another thirty-five years before a woman MP was elected in Ireland again, and this time it was an Ulster Unionist from the North.

Meanwhile Lady Astor was making quite an impact in the House. She used her maiden speech to oppose a motion to abolish the Liquor Control Board, and she pursued her liquor-control campaign until she achieved another distinction, as the first woman to have a Private Members' Bill become law – the Intoxicating Liquor (Sale to Persons under 18) Act. She continued to be a forceful and very active MP until 1945.

Coincidentally, on the same day Lady Astor began her political climb, seventy-one years later another forceful and very active lady ended hers. Lady Thatcher delivered her resignation to the Queen on this day in 1990.

NOVEMBER 28TH Nancy, Viscountess Astor, the first woman to sit in the House of Commons – and obviously delighted about it

28th
NOVEMBER

The day Lady Astor began – and Lady Thatcher left off

The first woman to sit in the House of Commons, the American-born Nancy, Viscountess Astor, was elected as Unionist MP for the Sutton division of Plymouth on this day in 1919 – but she was not the first woman MP. When women were allowed to vote in 1918, one of the Members they elected was Mme Constance Georgina Markiewicz. She was elected, however, in

29th
NOVEMBER

Goodbye Wolsey, Goodbye Ipswich College, Goodbye Bergholt Tower

Cardinal Thomas Wolsey, once the most powerful figure in England under Henry VII, died on this day in 1530 a broken man. After his failure to persuade the Pope to annul Henry VIII's first marriage, the King dismissed him, ordered him to his See of York, then had him arrested for high treason. He was

3 chy53353855555555555555555555

*NOVEMBER 29TH
The church bells at East Bergholt. Cardinal Wolsey never finished the tower, and the bells never got off the ground*

brought south again, riding on a mule, but only got as far as Leicester Abbey. "I am come to lay my bones among you," he told the abbot – and he did.

When he was not on duty, Wolsey liked to build places – Hampton Court was the most impressive. When he died he left two projects incomplete, both in his native Suffolk. In his home town, Ipswich, he started building a college to supply students for the College of Christ Church he had already built in Oxford. It was only half-completed, and all that survives is a brick archway near the docks known as Wolsey's Gateway.

His other local project was less ambitious. He undertook to build a tower for East Bergholt church, as compensation for the money he had levied towards his Oxford college. After he died the tower remained unfinished, and its bells are housed in a wooden cage in the churchyard.

The remnants of Wolsey's coat of arms on the tower and on his gateway are the only reminders that, if he had got Henry that annulment, Ipswich might have an historic college, and East Bergholt's bells might be in the tower where they belong.

30th
NOVEMBER

"We're from the Court Leet; he'll check the Chimneys, I'll test the Ale"

The Court Leet of Wareham in Dorset, one of the few in the country which still functions, meets on the nearest Friday to this day. It is presided over by the Lord of the Manor, currently Mr J.C.D. Ryder, whose father held the title for nearly sixty years. It no longer has any powers of enforcement, but it still ensures that its officers carry out an annual inspection of licensed premises in the town in the four days leading up to the Leet.

They include carnisters who test the quality of the meat, bread-weighers who use an ancient pair of scales, and perhaps the most popular job of all, the ale-tasters, who use pewter measures over two hundred years old. Among the other important officers in medieval times were Surveyors of Chimneys and Mantles; Wareham suffered a number of serious fires caused by blocked flues, and the surveyors had to ensure they were kept clean. They would have carried out their checks throughout the year, not just annually.

All these officers were the forerunners of our environmental health officers and trading standards inspectors. Until the 1880s the Court Leet met to hear their reports and impose fines on the offenders. These days, apart from a little formal business, it is a good opportunity to visit the local pubs.

*NOVEMBER 30TH
There are worse jobs: an official ale-tester wielding a 200-year-old mug on behalf of the Wareham Court Leet*

December

1st

D E C E M B E R

❧

A Cinque Port Deputy – out on a Limb at Brightlingsea

The original Cinque Ports were five ports in Kent and Sussex, granted special privileges in the twelfth century in return for providing ships and men to defend the English Channel. Confusingly, there were later thirty-two lesser Cinque Ports – the Trente-Deux Ports, perhaps? – known as Limbs, which were not necessarily near the Channel. In fact one of them, Brightlingsea, was north of the Thames in Essex.

Although the significance of the title has long since gone, Brightlingsea still maintains the tradition of electing a "Deputy of the Cinque Port Liberty of Brightlingsea, a Limb

DECEMBER 1ST
"Choosing Day" at Brightlingsea, when a Cinque Port Deputy is elected – and fined twenty pence for the privilege

of Sandwich", on this day if a Monday, or the first Monday after.

The "Choosing Day" ceremony takes place in All Saints' Church, with the local dignitaries in their traditional regalia, including a medal featuring the crossed sprats and oyster which symbolize the source of Brightlingsea's wealth. The Deputy is chosen from three reputable inhabitants who are Freemen of the town, and he pays a fine of twenty pence for the privilege. He

swears that "if any harm be pretended against the Mayor of Sandwich, I shall give present knowledge and warning thereof . . ."

The Deputy elects six Assistants, who are also fined twenty pence apiece. It is cheaper to be the Keeper of the Records, the Treasurer, the Historian or the Banner Bearer – they get their jobs for nothing.

2nd

D E C E M B E R

❧

The First Evening Classes – a Recipe for Revolution?

The first Mechanics' Institution in England, "for the instruction of mechanics at a cheap rate in the principles of the art they practise, as well as in all other branches of useful knowledge", was opened in London on this day in 1824.

There were those in high places who thought this was not a terribly good idea. They argued that "science and learning, if universally diffused, will speedily overturn the best-constituted government on earth". But the Institution prospered, and the government survived. There was a reading room, a school of design, a reference library and a museum, and when lectures were given, up to a thousand people filled the hall.

In the first six months, thirty more Mechanics' Institutions were set up in the major cities, and eventually there were four hundred of them all over the country. Then the early enthusiasm flagged. The "mechanics" were not allowed to run the institutions themselves so some were suspicious that it was all a cunning ploy by the bosses, while others could not afford the subscription – and a great many were not too bothered anyway.

But in the end control was handed over

to the members, who improved, as it were, the mechanics of the operation. Bodies like the Workers' Educational Association still carry on the tradition.

DECEMBER 3RD
The shrine of St Birinus in Dorchester Abbey, where the bells still protect the locals from snakebite

3rd
DECEMBER

Saved by the Bell – a Saintly Snake-repellent

St Birinus, whose day this is, can answer the question which must be constantly on the lips of the residents of Dorchester-on-Thames. Why are we so rarely killed by poisonous snakes?

Dorchester in Oxfordshire may not be as famous in history as its Dorset namesake, but it does have St Birinus and his snake-repulsing tenor bell. Birinus was the first Bishop of Dorchester in the seventh century, and his magnificent shrine, restored in the 1960s, can still be seen here. It was he who baptized Cynegils, the pagan king of the West Saxons, and established Christianity over a large area of the west and south of England.

His evangelical activities, however, may have taken his attention away from the snakes that were apparently rife in the Thames Valley. In 650 he was bitten by one and died, but on his deathbed he declared that the people of Dorchester would be saved from this fate if they stayed within sound of the church bells.

For seven hundred years, so far as we know, the bells kept

the snakes at bay. But in 1380 there may have been a danger of them falling silent, because one Ralph Retwold presented a new tenor bell and dedicated it to St Birinus. It came to be regarded as the saint's special snake-repellent – and it works. Nobody in Dorchester has died of snakebite for years and years.

4th
DECEMBER

His Opera had "Sparkling Vivacity" – and even his Epitaph was Gay

John Gay, who died on this day in 1732, is probably remembered by most of us only for *The Beggar's Opera*, which has survived through the centuries, helped by a re-write by Clifford Bax in the 1920s. As one condescending Victorian critic commented: "Though not a production evincing the highest order of genius it has, by its sparkling vivacity and humour, secured for itself transmission to posterity."

Certainly it was a great success when it opened at Drury Lane in 1728, and an even

DECEMBER 4TH
The Beggar's Opera *was John Gay's best-known work – but he wrote himself a good epitaph too*

greater one when it went on tour. The *Bristol News* reported: "We hear from Bath, that last Week all the Quality went to the Playhouse to hear the Rehearsal of the Beggar Opera . . . and that on Monday and Wednesday last, not withstanding the Pit and Boxes were laid together, they were so full that they turn'd as many away as went in."

Less is known about John Gay himself, but his friend Alexander Pope seemed to think he was a decent sort of chap. "Of manners gentle, of affection mild; In wit a man, simplicity, a child."

He may not have been in Pope's class as a poet, but *The Beggar's Opera* and a few good friends secured Gay a distinguished resting place in Westminster Abbey. Perhaps the best thing he wrote was his own epitaph:

Life is a jest, and all things show it.
I thought so once, and now I know it.

5th
DECEMBER

Britain's first Motorway – and no, it wasn't the M1

Britain entered the Age of the Motorway – rather belatedly – on this day in 1958. The southern section of the M1 is generally referred to as the first motorway in Britain – particularly in the South – and having reported its opening myself with due BBC solemnity, I may have encouraged that belief. But as so often happens, the South of England had ignored what was going on in the North, even though the Prime Minister had gone up there for the occasion. Harold Macmillan opened the Preston Bypass section of the M6, some eight miles of dual-carriageway, two-lane motorway, nearly a year before I helped to bang the publicity drum for the M1 in November 1959.

Needless to say, both North and South were way behind most of Europe and the United States, but Britain could have been first in the field. As far back as 1900, a Government minister was advocating highways "constructed for motor traffic and confined to motor traffic", and in 1920 Lord Montagu of Beaulieu designed a motorway which would link London and Birmingham – an idea which took nearly forty years to catch on.

As it was, Germany built its first autobahn in 1921, six miles of urban motorway that was deliberately intended to act as a race-track too, with loops at each end for the racers to swing round for the next lap. These days motorways don't have the loops, but little else seems to have changed . . .

6th
DECEMBER

Being a Boy Bishop is no Laughing Matter – or it could be Fatal

Boy bishops used to be appointed on this day in honour of St Nicholas of Bari, who was so amazingly pious in his youth that he earned the title for himself. It became the custom for cathedrals, churches and some public schools to appoint a choirboy to hold office from St Nicholas' Day to Holy Innocents' Day, three weeks later.

If a boy bishop died in office he was accorded full episcopal rites. There is a boy bishop buried in Salisbury Cathedral who died in a way which few adult prelates are likely to experience: it is said he was tickled so much by fellow choirboys during a

DECEMBER 6TH
The junior crook was made for the Boy Bishops of Berden to revive an old tradition

ceremony at which he was officiating that he actually died laughing.

Boy bishops were banned by Henry VIII, but his daughter Mary rather liked the idea and reinstated them. In 1555 it is recorded that a boy bishop officiated in her presence on this day. However, Elizabeth banned them again, and the only boy bishops in more recent times have been part of a charity stunt to raise money.

At Berden in Essex, for example, an enterprising vicar revived the practice in 1899. He made a special crook and cross for the boy bishop to carry as he led a procession collecting money for the church. Berden has not had a boy bishop since the 1960s, but the junior-size crook and cross are still on display.

7th
D E C E M B E R

The first Covent Garden: Snug for the Audience, Roomy for the Gods

The first theatre in London's Covent Garden – originally the garden and burial ground for Westminster Abbey – was opened on this day in 1732. There have been three others since, but the original auditorium was only fifty-one feet long, and space was so tight that each person was allowed just twenty-one inches. The ceiling, however, was magnificent, painted by an Italian artist to represent the gods banqueting in the clouds – where presumably they had a little more elbow room.

It was opened by John Rich, an actor-manager with two other notable distinctions. He helped to introduce pantomime into the English theatre – and he was nearly killed on stage by a member of the audience.

He built Covent Garden for serious plays, but his own most famous role was Harlequin, the traditional pantomime character, and it was his enormous success that established pantomime as Christmas entertainment. It was during *Macbeth*, however, in earlier days, that he had his near-fatal encounter. High-ranking patrons sat at the side of the stage, and one bad-mannered fellow strolled in front of the players during a performance to chat to a friend. Rich remonstrated and got hit in the face. He hit back, and the enraged patron attacked him with his sword; he had to be rescued by the other actors.

At Covent Garden he charged double for stage seats, ostensibly to stop overcrowding in the wings, but also, I imagine, to keep out belligerent boors with swords.

DECEMBER 7TH
The modern Opera House at Covent Garden is rather grander than the original, which had an auditorium just fifty-one feet long. A chair this size would have had to seat two

8th
DECEMBER

Rupert's Actress was first on Stage – Charles's Followed

Charles II may be renowned for his liaison with an actress, but he was only following a precedent set by his cousin Prince Rupert, whose mistress, Margaret Hughes, was the first woman to act on the English stage in public. She made her debut as Desdemona in *Othello* on this day in 1660. Until then all women's parts had been played by men, and, not surprisingly, the idea soon caught on. Within a month the ubiquitous Samuel Pepys was recording: "To the Theatre . . . and here the first time that ever I saw women come upon the stage."

It was a new experience for London audiences, but the Italians had seen it all before – and so had the English traveller Thomas Coryate, who visited Venice fifty years earlier. "I observed certain things that I never saw before, for I saw women act . . ."

King Charles lost no time in issuing a licence making it official in England. "Whereas women's parts in plays have hitherto been acted by men in the habits of

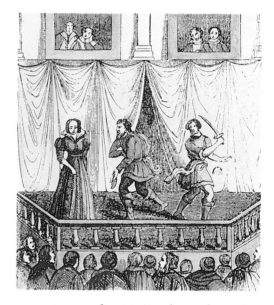

women . . . we do permit and grant leave for the time to come that all women's parts be acted by women."

His liberal attitude was soon rewarded. He met Nell Gwyn.

DECEMBER 8TH
"To the Theatre – and here the first time that ever I saw women come upon the stage" – a new experience for Samuel Pepys

9th
DECEMBER

We could have lost Paradise Lost without the Old Poets' Network

John Milton, who was blind for twenty-two of his sixty-six years but still wrote poetry rated as second only to Shakespeare's, died on this day in 1674. To avoid the Great Plague of London he retreated to "Milton's Cottage" at Chalfont St Giles in Buckinghamshire, and here he completed his best-known epic, *Paradise Lost* – but he might never have had the chance to start it.

Milton was political as well as poetical, and a great supporter of Oliver Cromwell. He spent ten years as his Latin Secretary, composing his despatches to foreign governments in Latin, and this did not make

DECEMBER 9TH
Milton's cottage at Chalfont St Giles, where he finished **Paradise Lost** *– with a little help from his friends*

him very popular with Charles II –
particularly as Milton had backed the
execution of his father. He was arrested and
some of his writings burned. He was
apparently saved from execution only
through the Old Poets' Network; it is said that
in Cromwell's time he rescued a Royalist
poet, Sir William D'Avenant, and D'Avenant
returned the favour.

Paradise Lost is evidence not only of
Milton's mental imagery but of the stamina of
his friends, who wrote it from his dictation. It
has 10,565 lines and contains seven thousand
different words – the average English speaker
rarely gets beyond three or four thousand,
and a good many of us manage with a few
hundred. If that makes it sound too daunting,
there is always his earliest poem, written
when he was fifteen. It is the hymn "Let us
with a gladsome mind" – and you must know
the chorus: "For his mercies ay endure, Ever
faithful, ever sure . . ."

10th
D E C E M B E R

Not Many Beasts at Boston Beast Mart – just the Mayor and Corporation

The tradition of proclaiming the Boston Beast
Mart, first authorized in 1576, has recently
been revived on this day – in the playground
of Boston Grammar School in Lincolnshire.
Before 1588 the Mart was held in another part
of the town, but local history says that in the
year of the Armada – though there seems no
connection – it was transferred to the School
Yard in South End, where shops were built.

Originally it was held on November 30th,
St Andrew's Day, but the date was probably
changed during the last century because of so
many counter-attractions on that day. It used

to attract beasts and buyers from a wide area
of Eastern England, but, even in those pre-
Ministry of Agriculture days, the movement
of cattle to market could be stopped because
of disease. In 1603 Lord Burghley and James
I, no less, sent letters to their "lovinge friends
the Maior and Aldermen of the town of
Boston", warning them to cancel the Mart for
this reason.

In due course the Mart dwindled in
importance, not through disease but
improved communications; traders went to
London instead. However, on this day "the
Maior and Aldermen of the town of Boston"
assemble in the playground for the
traditional proclamation, with the Chief
Constable helpfully acting as Town Crier.

11th
D E C E M B E R

To trace Eleanor's Funeral Route, join up the Crosses

King Edward I, Hammer of the
Scots, was on his way to give
them another hammering on
this day when news reached
him that his wife Eleanor, who
had accompanied him as far as
Nottinghamshire before being
taken ill, had just died. He
returned immediately, and
accompanied his wife's body
back to London.

His zig-zag route may seem a
little strange, but he planned it
to take in the various places
where they had spent happy
hours together, and at each one
he erected a monument in her
memory. There were twelve of

*DECEMBER 11TH
The Eleanor Cross at
Geddington, one of
the stopping places
for Queen Eleanor's
funeral cortege. She
and Edward I had a
hunting lodge there*

these "Eleanor Crosses", the final one at Charing Cross. That was destroyed by Cromwell's soldiers, and the present one is a copy, but three originals still survive, at Waltham, Hardingstone and Geddington.

Geddington's is perhaps the finest, with three statues of the Queen facing the three roads that run into the village square where it stands. The King had a hunting lodge behind the church, and there is still a north door into the church known as the King's Door, where he took a short cut from the lodge. But beware: the steps inside which led up to it have gone, and if you go in that way you face a four-foot drop.

Edward was devoted to his wife – "he bewailed the loss of her all the days of his life". Well, nearly all. He married again nine years later.

12th
DECEMBER

The Great Tin Can Band Rebellion: even the Police joined in

In Northamptonshire the annual concert of the Broughton Tin Can Band starts at midnight on the first Sunday after this day. Nobody is quite sure why, but nothing, it seems, is going to stop them. In 1930 the parish council did try – with remarkable results.

The "tin cans" include kettles, trays, saucepans – almost anything that makes a noise when you hit it, and the Band parades through the streets for about an hour. The council decided this "unholy clatter" was disturbing the peace, and announced they would bring in the police.

On Tin Can Night, instead of the usual handful, about a hundred and fifty people

turned out, including coachloads from nearby villages. One woman recalled, fifty years later: "The police were waiting, and we all stood silently watching them, a funny feeling for erstwhile law-abiding citizens. Then the church clock struck twelve and out came the buckets, baths and tins . . .

"The police surged forward but we outnumbered them anyway, and in the end they just walked with us, joining in the fun . . . Steadfastly, thoroughly, we traversed every street and lane, even more so than usual. More shouts and cheers, lights on in every window, people cheering at open doors – never been known before."

About fifty had their names taken and went to court, but a Tin Can Dance paid the fines. Broughton's Tin Can Band has played every year since; even during the war, one man went round banging a can to preserve the unbroken tradition.

13th
DECEMBER

The first Law to clean up the Beaches – a Bounty for Bodies

The plundering of wrecked ships was a popular, lucrative and almost respectable occupation for many centuries around our coasts. As one early historian put it: "The

DECEMBER 12TH
At midnight, the Tin Can Band disturbs the peace of Broughton with a bedlam of discordant sounds

DECEMBER 13TH
A boat-shaped headstone to shipwrecked mariners at St Mawgan also marks the enforcement of a new law

dwellers on the English coasts considered themselves the lawful heirs of all drowned men, and held that their first duty in the case of wreck was to secure, for their own behoof, the property which Providence had thus cast on their shores."

It did not occur to them to save any lives. Indeed, it was thought unlucky to rescue a drowning man – or so they claimed in their defence. A body being washed ashore was rarely given the dignity of a burial – just searched for valuables and abandoned.

But that changed in 1846, when a law was passed making it compulsory for such bodies to be buried at public expense – and the finders were rewarded. This may have resulted in some dying mariners having their deaths accelerated by impatient bounty-hunters, just when they thought they were safely ashore, but at least it kept the beaches clean.

The law was applied for the first time on this day in 1846, when ten men were found frozen to death in a boat washed ashore at St Mawgan in Cornwall. They were buried in a common grave, marked by a boat-shaped headstone. If anything of value was found in the boat, it was not recorded . . .

14th

DECEMBER

Albert cultivated the Christmas Tree Trade, but Charlotte planted hers first

Prince Albert of Saxe-Coburg, the Prince Consort, died on this day in 1861, just at the start of the Christmas tree season. It is popularly thought that he introduced the idea of Christmas trees into England from Europe, but in fact the first one enjoyed by the Royal Family was erected at the Royal Lodge, Windsor, by an earlier German consort, Queen Charlotte, wife of George III.

Judging by the description in her biography, her decorated tree probably looked much the same as the one that Albert erected at Windsor nearly fifty years later: "From the branches hung bunches of sweetmeats, almonds and raisins in papers, fruits and toys, most tastefully arranged, and the whole illuminated by small wax candles."

But while Charlotte's tree only got a mention in her biography, Albert's got a full-page picture in the *Illustrated London News* – and the idea caught on. Seeing he was on to a winner, Albert presented large numbers of trees each Christmas to schools and army barracks – and poor Charlotte never got a mention again.

DECEMBER 14TH Prince Albert and his family pictured round a Christmas tree – and the idea caught on

HERE LIE THE BODIES OF
JACOB WILLIAMS   DAVID ROBERTS
OWEN HUGHS   THOMAS COLLINS
CHARLES CAWLEY RICHARD CUTLER
WILLIAM LOYD   WILLIAM ELIOTT
THOMAS BROWN   JEMMY
who were drifted ashore in a Boat, frozen to death, at Tregurrian Beach in this Parish, on Sunday 13th December 1846

15th
DECEMBER

❧

After Six Years of War – let's have a Banana

The first bananas to arrive in England after the Second World War were landed at Bristol Docks on this day in 1945. The Lord Mayor was waiting to greet them, in morning suit

DECEMBER 15TH
Yes, we do have
bananas: the return
of an old favourite
after the Second
World War

figure in history was associated with its introduction. When bananas first appeared in a London shop window in 1633, nobody seems to have got too excited. Perhaps if Nell Gwyn had sold bananas instead of oranges, they might have had a bigger Press.

It was the Victorians who ate enough bananas to make it worthwhile importing them in quantity, but the big banana boom only came in the last decade. We now eat twice as many as we did in 1986 – six hundred thousand tons of them a year.

16th
DECEMBER

❧

The "Plague Village" was a "Mock Marriage Village" too

Eyam in Derbyshire is best known as the Plague Village. In 1665 the rector persuaded his flock to isolate themselves in the village when the Great Plague struck, thus preventing it from spreading, though much of the village succumbed. But Eyam had another remarkable rector in a very different way, the Rev. Joseph Hunt, who died on this day in 1710.

During a bibulous evening at the Miners Arms, he decided to marry the landlord's eighteen-year-old daughter – on the spot. He appointed a miner to officiate at a mock marriage, and Miss Anne Ferns became "Mrs Hunt". Everyone seemed to regard this as a rather jolly jape, except for the Bishop. He was appalled by "this ill-judged and disgraceful act" and ordered the rector to "do in earnest what was done in jest" and marry her properly.

and top hat, but he restrained himself from taking a bite until the twelve-year-old daughter of the Fyffes depot manager had sampled one. After six banana-less years she hardly remembered what they tasted like, but when she was traced fifty years later for the anniversary celebrations, she reported that she still enjoyed them – particularly mashed with cream and sugar.

There was no such welcoming ceremony when the first banana was brought into England, over three hundred years before. Unlike the potato or tobacco, no famous

Unfortunately Joseph Hunt was already engaged, and when he married Miss Ferns "in earnest", his fiancée sued for breach of promise. The lawsuit bankrupted him, and

DECEMBER 16TH
The Miners Arms at
Eyam, scene of a
mock marriage which
led to the Rector
being sued for breach
of promise

he spent the rest of his short life – he was only 27 when he died – locked in the church vestry, hiding from the bailiffs. His wife stayed with him and they had several children, who were brought up by the village; presumably there was no room for them all in the vestry . . .

17th
DECEMBER

Hatters should take off their Bowlers (and Billycocks) to Mr Coke

The bowler hat officially came into existence on this day in 1849, when the Norfolk landowner William Coke took delivery of a hard felt hat made to his own specifications by Thomas and William Bowler. Mr Coke

was fed up with having his tall riding hat knocked off by low branches, and he also wanted headgear which was safe as well as stable, so before accepting it he stamped on it twice to see if it would dent. The bowler survived, and a new fashion was born.

The origin of the bowler seems to be inextricably tied up with the origin of the rather similar billycock. It is said that Coke designed this as well, to wear at his shooting parties at Holkham Hall. It has a lower crown and a wider brim than the bowler, but it is just as hard. The main difference, it seems, is that the bowler was named after the makers, while the billycock was named after the designer – just an adaptation of Billy Coke.

Even hatters seem to get confused. Some of them referred to billycocks as "Coke hats", whereas Locks, the old-established hatters who ordered Mr Coke's bowler from the Bowlers, still call bowlers Cokes. Coke, incidentally, is pronounced "Cook", which can confuse things further.

One other question: if Coke wore a bowler for hunting and a billycock for shooting, what did he wear for fishing? He ought to have designed a third one – and made it a hat-trick.

DECEMBER 17TH
The hatters who
supplied the first
bowler and launched
a new fashion. This
customer has yet to
be persuaded

18th
DECEMBER

Over 100 years ago they were already complaining about the Northern Line

London Underground passengers have been known to complain bitterly about the decrepit condition of the Northern Line, but they may be consoled to know that they are travelling on an historic route. The City branch of the line, originally called the City and South London Railway, was the first section of the underground system to be successfully electrified. The first fare-paying passengers travelled on it – and probably complained about it – on this day in 1890.

The line was officially opened the month before, when the Prince of Wales travelled from King William Street to the Oval. It was not only the first but probably the last time that royalty has ever travelled on the Northern Line.

Present-day passengers would have no cause to complain about the fare, which was two old pence for any distance along the line. But they might not have been so happy about the time their journey took; the trains travelled at a gentle average speed of eleven and a half miles an hour.

The seating, however, compared very favourably with modern trains. The upholstered backs of the seats running the length of the carriage on each side were a comfortable five feet high, allowing plenty of scope to rest the head back and snooze. But the passengers still found something to complain about: they called the carriages "padded cells".

If you're in Richmond, watch out for the Poor Old Horse

"The Poor Old Horse" is liable to make an appearance on this day in Richmond, North Yorkshire, at any time between now and

DECEMBER 19TH
The Poor Old Horse looks a little gloomy, but its attendants are obviously enjoying their annual tour of Richmond's inns

Christmas. It is said to bring good luck to those who cross its path, but it has no definite itinerary or timetable. As one participant put it: "The horse's appearances during the festive period tend to be sparing, erratic and unpredictable, a closely kept secret between horse and guardian. Stories may circulate of a sighting, or rumours spread of its impending approach, but no one can be sure it will appear until several loud blasts on a hunting-horn and cries of 'Make way for t'owd hoss' signal its arrival."

"T'owd hoss" has a genuine horse's skull, which is covered in black astrakhan and mounted on a pole. It is held by a figure concealed in a cloak who can open and close its jaws – the loud snapping is an important part of the proceedings. For the past hundred years or more it has been looked after by the Peirse family, while its

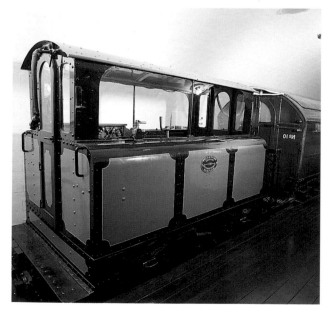

DECEMBER 18TH
One of the first underground trains is preserved in the Science Museum

attendants, who wear hunting pink with decorated hats, are mostly members of the Ward family.

They act the story of the Poor Old Horse, which was once young and fit but becomes old and useless – "My hide unto the huntsmen so freely I will give, My body to the hounds, sir, for I'd rather die than live… " Nobody is sure how old the old horse is or what it symbolizes, but it will still be around next year.

20th
DECEMBER

Joanna missed out on the New Messiah – but what about her Box?

Joanna Southcott, the Exeter domestic servant who claimed she would give birth to the new Messiah at the age of 64, died on this day in 1814; what seemed like a pregnancy was actually a tumour in the womb. But this did not shake the devotion of her followers, who still regarded her as "the woman clothed with the sun, and the moon under her feet, and upon her head a crown of twelve stars" – the description she took for herself from the Book of Revelations.

After her death the Southcottians put their faith in the locked wooden box which she left behind, with instructions that it should be opened only at a time of national emergency, in the presence of all the bishops in England. The bishops, however, seemed singularly unimpressed, and declined to attend its opening during the Crimean War or the Great War of 1914–18. The box stayed closed.

Eventually, in 1927, it was entrusted to the psychic investigator Harry Price, who x-rayed it, then invited the bishops to an opening ceremony. Only one turned up, and the others didn't miss much; the box contained a few books, a dicebox, some loose

DECEMBER 20TH
The cartoonist Thomas Rowlandson took a dim view of Joanna's prophecies

change, and – perhaps the only significant portent – a lottery ticket.

Fervent Southcottians, now known as the Panacea Society, remain unshaken. They just say it was the wrong box.

21st

❧

Give Money to the Mumpers and get a Palace in Paradise

This is St Thomas's Day, associated in past centuries with a-gooding, or a-corning, or mumping, which are just quaint olde-worlde words for begging. The a-gooders went in search of goodies, the a-corners carried a sack to collect grain, and the mumpers just took anything they could get. There are so many other occasions now for collecting from door to door that mumping has largely died out, except for the odd distribution of ceremonial shillings – which must be quite a relief for St Thomas, who was used as an excuse for all this, for no obvious reason.

The connection may go back to a legend involving a king called Gondoforus, who gave Thomas a large quantity of gold to build him a great palace. The saint had a reputation as an architect, and indeed he is often portrayed holding a builder's square.

Gondoforus then departed to a far country for a couple of years, and Thomas, instead of building the palace, gave all the gold to the poor – the original mumpers, perhaps. When the King returned he was understandably irritated, and threw Thomas into prison, pending execution. But his dead brother appeared and assured him that Thomas had indeed built him a great palace, not on earth but in Paradise.

The gratified Gondoforus released Thomas to build more celestial palaces

elsewhere, and gave away the rest of his gold – while the mumpers lived happily on his doorstep ever after.

22nd

❧

Was the Old Bricklayer the Last of the Plantagenets?

When King Henry I's daughter Matilda married the Count of Anjou, she found he had the odd habit of sticking a sprig of broom in his hat. He explained it was his family emblem – the Latin for a sprig of broom is *planta genista*, and he was Sir Geoffrey Plantagenet.

DECEMBER 22ND Eastwell Church, resting place of Richard Plantagenet – bricklayer, Latin student, and possibly Richard III's heir

Their son became Henry II, and various branches of the Plantagenets – who might equally be called the Brooms – ruled England for nearly three hundred and fifty years, until Richard III died on Bosworth Field in 1485.

Some sixty years later Sir Thomas Moyle was inspecting building work on his new mansion at Eastwell in Kent when he came across an elderly bricklayer reading a book in Latin – an unheard-of accomplishment for a lowly labourer. He questioned the erudite old brickie, and an amazing story emerged. As a boy he was boarded out, and a mysterious stranger paid the bills. Before the Battle of Bosworth he was taken to the King's tent, and the mysterious stranger turned out to be Richard III. The King publicly acknowledged him as his son. But the King was killed, the Plantagenets were out, the Tudors were in, and the lad ran away. He kept his head down, and learned how to lay bricks.

Sir Thomas looked after the old man until he died on this day in 1550. His name was entered in the church register as Richard Plantagenet; he just might have been Richard IV.

DECEMBER 23RD
Starry Gazie pie being served at Mousehole. The staring fish-heads are genuine, the beard is slightly suspect

23rd

DECEMBER

❧

Enjoy the Fish Pie on Tom Bocock's Eve – but don't catch the Fish's Eye

Starry gazie pie sounds delightful, but it is not the most attractive-looking dish. It is a fish pie with the fish-heads on top of the pastry, looking as if the fish are staring up through the crust. Nevertheless it is a special dish at Mousehole in Cornwall on this day, in memory of Tom Bocock, a local fisherman who is reputed to have saved the village from starvation. Apparently bad weather stopped all fishing for many days, until Tom Bocock, moved by the cries of the hungry children, set off alone into the storm and returned with seven kinds of fish, enough to feed the whole village for a week.

Nobody knows what year this happened, but this is Tom Bocock's Eve, and starry gazie pie is served at the Ship Inn. The pie seems

to have no connection with star-gazing – unless the fish-heads happen to be in a star-shaped pattern as they gaze up at the diners.

There is also a starry gazie song, with the chorus: "A merry place you may believe, was Mousehole on Tom Bocock's Eve. To be there then who wouldn't wish, and sup on seven kinds of fish." Ever since it was featured on radio and television in the 1970s rather too many visitors "to be there wish", and the main entertainment for the locals is watching their expressions when they get their first sight of the fish-heads.

24th

DECEMBER

❧

Ask not how often the Devil's Knell Tolls – it's counted electronically

The bellringers of Dewsbury Parish Church in West Yorkshire have been tolling the Devil's Knell on Christmas Eve since the Middle Ages. It is in memory of Sir Thomas de Scothill, who accidentally killed a servant, and to expiate his sin gave the tenor bell to the church. His idea of tolling it on this night

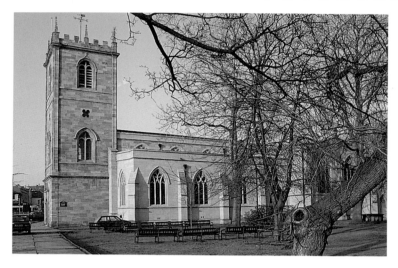

A Christmas Ride along the Bridle Path – and through the Local Pub

While most people are opening presents, or getting ready for church, or preparing for a family get-together on this Christmas Day, there is one person in West Sussex who is usually getting into riding gear. He is not heading for a morning canter or the hunting field, but for his local pub, the Fox at Bucks Green, to be the central figure in one of the more unlikely traditions attached to Christmas morning.

The Fox stands in the fork where two roads meet, and at one time a bridle path formed the third side of the triangle. For some reason not known to the present landlord, the pub was built right across this bridle path, creating for later, more rights-conscious generations an interesting problem. There was undoubtedly a right of way through the bar of the Fox, but it was obviously impractical to leave the doors permanently open – and it served no particular purpose anyway.

DECEMBER 24TH
The Dewsbury bells keep the Devil away – but finishing on time can be the devil of a job

was to keep the Devil away for another twelve months, but it is also a reminder that the Devil was vanquished by Christ's birth, death and resurrection.

The bell, "Black Tom of Scothill", is tolled once for every year in the Christian era – in 1996, for instance, it will be tolled 1,996 times. It is quite an exercise in precision bellringing, because the final stroke has to be exactly at midnight to herald Christmas Day. It takes about two hours altogether, and in the closing stages the speed may have to be adjusted. This is not too bad if it needs slowing, because a bell can be held briefly at the top of the swing, but speeding it up can be a bit trickier.

All this depends on the ancient skills of the ringers, but at least modern technology now helps with the counting. At one time the strokes were marked off on a piece of paper. Then a mechanical counter was used, operated by pressing a button for each stroke. These days the counter is triggered by an electronic device connected to the bell wheel. But try explaining that to Sir Thomas de Scothill.

DECEMBER 25TH
A horseman traditionally rides through the front door of the Fox at Bucks Green to maintain an ancient right of way through the bar

A very English compromise was reached. It was agreed that a horse and rider should pass through the pub every Christmas Day, using the doors at the front and rear and following the route of the original bridle path. The right of way would thus be preserved for another twelve months.

In 1995 the regular horseman was unable to make his traditional ride, and no alternative horse and rider could be found. Again there was a very English compromise. A volunteer rode through the pub on a bicycle.

DECEMBER 26TH
"We do not dance simply for the pleasure of it... We dance because this tradition matters to us." The long-sword dancers of Grenoside give their annual performance

26th
DECEMBER

The Sheffield Sword Dancers: "We belong to the Dance, rather than it to us"

The long-sword dancers of Handsworth and Grenoside, two communities on the outskirts of Sheffield, go into action on Boxing Day, preserving a tradition which once applied to many other Yorkshire villages. This was iron-mining country, and the original dancers were miners, but nobody is sure how and when it all began. Boxing Day was probably chosen because it was their only day off.

The uniforms are as impressive as the dances. In Handsworth they wear black velvet jackets with maroon waistbands and cuffs, brass buttons, and white braids across the chest. The maroon hats have two pom-poms at the front and a rosette and ribbons at the back. They have white trousers, black leather gaiters and heavy boots. Grenoside have scarlet jackets with green and red braid, and they wear iron-shod clogs.

There is a friendly rivalry between the two, but both dance for the same reason. One Grenoside dancer summed it up:

"We do not dance simply for the pleasure of it, for beer money or a good day out. We dance because this tradition matters to us. We often speak of 'our' dance, but in a sense we belong to it rather than it to us. It marks the season for all of us with a special sense that we have performed an important rite for ourselves and our witnesses."

Cecil Sharp of the English Folk Dance Society, the key figure in reviving sword-dancing in this century, would surely cry, "Hear hear!"

27th
DECEMBER

Darwin's Father opposed his Voyage on the Beagle – but the Nose had it

On this day in 1831, having hardly had time to digest his Christmas pudding, 22-year-old Charles Darwin set sail in the *Beagle* on a five-year voyage of scientific discovery which was to change the course of natural science. But he only managed to make the trip because of the shape of his nose.

Darwin's father, a botanist himself, had always been sceptical about his scientific ability. "You will never be good for anything but shooting and rat-catching", he encouragingly told the lad as he struggled through his schoolwork. At Cambridge Charles scraped through his BA degree, but he preferred bugs and beetles to books. When he heard the British government was organizing a round-the-world scientific voyage he decided that was for him – but his father disagreed. He would only consent, he said, if Charles could find one single person with any sense who would recommend he should go.

DECEMBER 27TH
"With such a nose as that, you ought to go far" – and he did. Charles Darwin spent five years on a voyage of discovery, and changed the course of natural science

Charles went to his Uncle Wedgwood, an old ally – and a student of noses. Charles had a rather distinctive one. "With such a nose as that," said Uncle Wedgwood, "you ought to go far." And he did – but only just. By an unlikely coincidence the captain of the *Beagle* was also a student of noses, and forecast that he would never achieve anything – but he accepted him anyway. The moral: when judging scientists, keep the nose out of it.

28th
DECEMBER

Unlucky Holy Innocents' Day – especially for the Whipped Children

In contrast to the festivities over Christmas, this is reckoned to be the unluckiest day of the year. Any venture launched on this day is said to be doomed to failure, and this has been taken seriously enough for many important events to be postponed instead of being held on Holy Innocents' Day.

King Edward IV, for instance, was due to be crowned on this day in 1461, and postponed it until the following day. As it turned out, his reign was not all that lucky. He spent two months as a prisoner of the Earl of Warwick in 1469, had to flee to the Netherlands the following year, remained in exile for five months, and died of pneumonia when he was forty. But at least he did better than his twelve-year-old son Edward V, who was king for only two months before being murdered in the Tower – a latter-day slaughter of the innocent.

It was King Herod's order on this day to kill all the small children of Bethlehem in order to destroy the infant "King of the Jews" which made it so unpopular. In past centuries children had a good reason for disliking it, because it was the custom to whip them soundly, "that the memory of Herod's slaughter of the innocents might stick the closer". Christmas must have seemed a long way away.

were flung to the floor again. "Soldiers and servants searched in vain underneath the solid table to find the cause of its convulsions, till one of the conscience-stricken knights suggested it was indignantly refusing to bear the sacrilegious burden of their arms."

In the Anne of Cleves House museum at Lewes there is a table carved from solid Petworth marble. On this day, some claim, the table whirls around, making a noise like a distant murmur: "Remember poor Thomas. Remember poor Thomas . . ."

DECEMBER 29TH
It looks like a spinning top, and indeed this table is said to whirl once a year

29th
DECEMBER

❧

Even the Table turned on the Knights who killed Becket

The story of the assassination of Thomas Becket, Archbishop of Canterbury, on this day in 1170 has been extensively chronicled. "Who will rid me of this turbulent priest?" is one of the best-known lines in Shakespeare, and even if Henry never said it, the result was much the same. Four knights took up the challenge and killed Becket in his cathedral.

What happened next is not so well known. According to *Historical Memorials of Canterbury*, published in 1855, the knights rode to South Malling Deanery, near Lewes. "On entering the house they threw off their arms and trappings, and placed them on the table which stood in the hall, and after supper gathered round the blazing hearth. Suddenly the table started back and threw its burden on the ground . . ."

The attendants replaced the arms, but soon a louder crash was heard, and they

30th
DECEMBER

❧

St Egwin foiled the Devil – and the Result was Meon Hill

St Egwin, whose day this is, was very active in Worcestershire in the seventh century. He is credited with saving Evesham Abbey from the Devil – and creating the sinister Meon Hill in the process. While the abbey was being built, the Devil is said to have hurled a hill-size lump of earth at it, which Egwin's

DECEMBER 30TH
Meon Hill, reputedly hurled by the Devil and still associated with sinister stories

prayers deflected. The massive clod ricocheted across the Vale of Evesham into Warwickshire, where it became the 600-foot Meon Hill. The hill has been associated with the Devil and other unpleasantries ever since. Even when it provided some good news in 1824 – a hoard of four hundred currency bars was dug up in the ancient earthwork fort on the summit – the treasure was still christened "Devil's Money".

Meon Hill has more than its share of strange tales. The appearance of a black dog is said to presage disaster, and this was given added weight when a black dog was found hanging near the body of a man found murdered on Meon Hill in 1945. Charles Walton had a pitchfork through his neck, pinning him to the ground, and his body was slashed with the sign of a cross – emblems of a ritual witch-slaying. The dog's involvement remained unexplained.

Watch out too for a pack of spectral hounds that ate their huntsman and now roam the neighbourhood with him on the night after St Egwin's Day. The huntsman was known to hunt on the Sabbath, and Egwin may have brought about his gruesome end as a punishment; anything is possible on Meon Hill.

31st
DECEMBER

❧

If they Spill the Blazing Tar Barrel – on their own Heads be it

The Old Year is seen off in many different ways on this night, but perhaps the most dramatic – and potentially the most hazardous – is at Allendale in Northumberland, where a fire festival takes place which may date back to pagan times, though no one can be sure.

The tradition is for forty-five men – again the reason for the number is obscure – to form a procession by the church, each carrying on his head the sawn-off base of a forty-gallon wooden cask filled with shavings, sticks and paraffin, known as the "tar kits". They are dressed, or "guised" (a local version of "disguised", perhaps?), in all manner of fancy costumes, preferably of

nonflammable material. They set fire to their tar kits and parade around the village boundaries, with the barrels blazing on their heads.

The procession ends up in the marketplace, where a pile of brushwood has been prepared, and each man hurls his tar kit on to the pile – no doubt with considerable relief. As one onlooker described it: "The flames shoot upwards as the old year dies, midnight strikes, and all hands join for the singing of Auld Lang Syne. New Year wishes are exchanged, there is a general confusion of noise, heat, smoke, dancing and singing, then the locals move off to 'first-foot' and the crowd melts away."

Not a bad way to round off a year – and to end a Book of Days.

DECEMBER 31ST Elegant young ladies used to balance books on their heads to improve their deportment. At Allendale on New Year's Eve, they do it the hard way...

Index

Abbots Ann, Hampshire   Oct 6
Abbotsbury, Dorset   May 13
Abingdon, Oxfordshire   Jun 20
air mail   Sep 9
Albemarle, Lord   Jun 9
Alice in Wonderland   Jan 14
All Souls' Day   Nov 2
Allendale, Northumberland   Dec 31
Anderson, Elizabeth Garrett   Jan 15
Androcles and the Lion   Sep 30
Angels of Mons   Aug 27
Appleton, Cheshire   Jul 5
Archers, The   Sep 22
archery   Jun 12
Askey, Arthur   Feb 5
Asscher, Isaac   Jan 25
Assumption, Feast of the   Aug 15
Astor, Viscountess Nancy   Nov 28

Bacon, Francis   Apr 9
Baden-Powell, Lieutenant General
   Sir Robert   Jan 24
bananas, return of after World
   War II   Dec 15
Bannister, Roger   May 6
Barlow, Father Ambrose   Sep 10
Barnstaple, Devon   Sep 20
baronets, first   May 22
battles
   Agincourt   Oct 25
   Bosworth Field   Aug 21
   Cape St Vincent   Feb 26
   Corunna   Jan 16
   Crecy   Aug 26
   Edgehill, Warwickshire   Oct 23
   Flamborough Head   Sep 23
   Hastings   Oct 14
   Marston Moor   Jul 2
   Nevill's Cross   Oct 17
   Sedgemoor   Jul 6
   Shrewsbury   Jul 21
   Sole Bay   May 28
   Somme   Jul 1
   Spion Kop   Jan 23
   Stamford Bridge   Sep 25
   Stirling   Aug 23
   Stoke, Nottinghamshire   Jun 16
   Towton   Mar 29
   Trafalgar   Oct 21
   Waterloo   Jun 18
   Worcester   Sep 3
   Quebec   Sep 13
Bawburgh, Norfolk   May 30
beauty contest   Aug 14
Beaverbrook, Lord   Nov 8
Becket, Thomas   Dec 29
Beecham, Sir Thomas   Apr 29
Beggar's Opera, The   Dec 4
Belisha beacon   Mar 13
bell-ringing   Oct 7, Dec 24
Belloc, Hilaire   Jul 27
Bentinck, Lord George   Sep 21
Berkeley Castle, Gloucestershire

Nov 16
Bible, King James' Authorized
   Version   May 2
Birkenhead   Jan 24
Black Prince   Aug 26
black pudding   Sep 1
blackberries   Oct 11
Blenheim Palace   Feb 6
Blidworth, Nottinghamshire   Feb 2
blood circulation   Jun 3
Blue Riband   May 27
Boat Race, University   Jun 10
Bocock, Tom   Dec 23
bombing, aerial   Jan 19
   first   May 10
bonfires   Jun 23
Bonnie Prince Charlie   Jan 31
Booth, General William   Jul 23
Booth, Hubert Cecil   Feb 25
Boothroyd, Betty   Apr 27
Borley Rectory, Essex   Feb 27
Borrow, George   Jul 26
Boston, Lincolnshire   Dec 10
Boswell, James   Sep 18
bowler hat   Dec 17
bowls   Jul 9
boxing   Apr 8
Boy bishops   Dec 6
Boy Scouts   Jan 24
Boys' Brigade   Jan 24
Boyton, Capt. Paul   Apr 11
Bradwell-on-Sea, Essex   Jun 22
Braughing, Hertfordshire   Oct 2
Bridgewater, Duke of   May 21
Briggs, Rowland   Nov 27
Brightlingsea, Essex   Dec 1
Brighton, East Sussex   Aug 9
British Expeditonary Force   Aug 27
British Summer Time   Aug 7
Brontë, Charlotte   Apr 21
Brooke, Rupert   Aug 3
Broughton, Northamptonshire
   Dec 12
Brown, Lancelot ("Capability")
   Feb 6
Brunel, Isambard Kingdom   Apr 30,
   Oct 22
Bucks Green, West Sussex   Dec 25
Bunbury, Sir Charles   Oct 20
Bunyan, John   Feb 18, Oct 30,
   Nov 12
Burford, Oxfordshire   May 15
Burton   Apr 24

Caernarvon, fifth Earl of   Jan 3
calendar reform   Jan 5, 13; Jul 4,
   Oct 11
canals
   Bridgewater   May 21
   Bude   Aug 12
   Portsmouth and Arun   May 26
Candlemas   Feb 2
car accident, first fatal   Aug 17

Cardington, Bedfordshire   Oct 4
Carew, Evelyn Lady Montefiore
   May 31
Carhampton, Somerset   Jan 17
Carlyle, Thomas   Feb 4
Carroll, Lewis   Jan 14
Cartmel Priory, Cumbria   Nov 27
Cass, Sir John   Feb 20
cat's-eyes   Apr 3
caul   Jun 19
Cavell, Edith   Oct 12
Caxton, William   Mar 1
Cerne Abbas, Dorset   Oct 8
Chalfont St Giles, Buckinghamshire
   Dec 9
Channel swimmer, first   Apr 11,
   Aug 25
Charlton St Peter, Wiltshire   Jun 2
Chartists   Apr 10
Chastleton House   Sep 3
Chatterton, George Edward   Mar 2
Chelsea, London   Feb 4
Chequers   Jan 8
Chesterfield, Derbyshire   Sep 14
Christmas Trees, introduction of
   Dec 14
churches and cathedrals   Jan 23,
   Mar 19, 28; Apr 5, 17; May 7, 17;
   Jun 13, 22; Jul 15, 31; Aug 5,
   Sep 4, 19; Oct 6, Nov 27
Churchill, Sir Winston   May 10
cinema, first purpose-built   Feb 22
Cinque Ports   Dec 1
Clare, John   Jul 13
Cleopatra's Needle   Jan 21
Cobbett, William   Mar 9
Cockerell, Sir Christopher   Jun 25
Coke, Sir Edward   Feb 1
Coke, William   Dec 17
Colchester, Essex   Aug 18
Coleshill, Warwickshire   Jun 30
Colne, Lancashire   Feb 22
Comberbach, Cheshire   Nov 2
Cook, Captain   Apr 28
Cook, Thomas   Aug 4
Corfe, Dorset   Mar 18
Coronation, first televising of
   May 12
Courts Leet   Nov 23, 30
Covent Garden   May 9, Dec 7
Coventry, West Midlands   Apr 15
Cowper, William   Apr 25
Cranmer, Thomas   Mar 21
Crediton, Devon   Jun 5
cremation   Sep 26
Crimea   Aug 13
Cromwell, Oliver   Jan 30, Mar 25,
   Jul 2
cuckoo   Apr 6
Curry Rivel, Somerset   Jan 5

D-Day   Aug 11
Daguerre, Louis   Sep 17

Daily Courant, The   Mar 11
Dakyn, Rev. John   Aug 29
Darling, Grace   Sep 7
Darlington, County Durham
   Jun 11
Dartmoor Prison   Mar 20
Darwin, Charles   Dec 27
Dashwood, Sir Francis   Aug 16
Davy miners' lamp   Jan 9
Davy, Sir Humphry   Jan 9, Oct 28
de la Mare, Sir Peter   Apr 27
de Mowbray, Lady   Jan 6
de Ruyter, Admiral   Jun 9
de Scothill, Sir Thomas   Dec 24
de Valois, Catherine   Feb 23
Dean Prior, Devon   Aug 20
decimal coinage   Feb 15
*Decline and Fall of the Roman
   Empire, The*   Oct 15
Defoe, Daniel   Jun 30
department store, first purpose-
   built   Mar 15
Derby, The   May 4
Dereham, Norfolk   Apr 25
Devil's Boulder   Nov 5
Devil   May 19, Oct 11, Dec 30
Dewsbury, West Yorkshire   Dec 24
Disraeli, Benjamin   Apr 19
doctor – first woman   Jan 15
dog-days   Jul 3
Doggett, Thomas   Aug 1
Dorchester-on-Thames,
   Oxfordshire   Dec 3
Dover   May 25
Drake, Sir Francis   Jul 9
driving test   Mar 13
Dryden, John   Apr 13
Dublin   Feb 28
Durham Cathedral   Sep 4
Dymoke, The Hon. John   Mar 6
dynamo   Oct 28

East Bergholt, Suffolk   Nov 29
Ebernoe, West Sussex   Jul 25
Eddystone Lighthouse   Nov 26
Egerton, Francis   May 21
Egremont, third Earl of   May 26
Elliot, George   Jun 21
Ely, Cambridgeshire   Jun 28
Epsom   May 4
Erpingham, Sir Thomas   Oct 25
Estur, Edward   Jun 13
Eton College   Jun 4
Eyam, Derbyshire   Dec 16

Faraday, Michael   Oct 28
Farmworker Riots   Aug 28
Farne Islands   Sep 7
Fawcett, Eric   Mar 24
Fenny Stratford, Buckinghamshire
   Nov 11
Ferrers, fourth Earl   May 5
Festival of Britain   May 3

Field of the Cloth of Gold   Jun 7
Fielding, Henry   Oct 8
fire festival   Dec 31
Fishtoft, Lincolnshire   Sep 6
Fitzgerald, Edward   Mar 31
flag day, first national   Oct 3
Fleming, Alexander   Feb 13
Floral Dance   May 8
Folkestone, Kent   Aug 14
Fotheringhay Castle   Feb 8
four-minute mile   May 6
Fox Talbot, William Henry   Sep 17
Fox, George   Oct 30
Furry Dance   May 8

Garrick, David   Feb 19
gas lamps   Jan 28
Gatcombe, Isle of Wight   Jun 13
Gay, John   Dec 4
Gayer, Sir John   Oct 16
Geddington, Northamptonshire   Dec 11
ghosts and hauntings   Jan 23, Feb 27, Apr 12, 24; May 31, Jun 11, Oct 17, 23
Gibbon, Edward   Oct 15
Gibson, Reginald   Mar 24
Gilbert and Sullivan   Nov 18
glider flight, first   Sep 12
Gondoforus   Dec 21
goose   Sep 29
Gordon, General   Jan 26
Gorleston, Norfolk   Feb 12
gout   Jun 3
Grace, Dr William Gilbert   Aug 31
Grasmere, Cumbria   Aug 5
Gray, Thomas   Jul 30
Great Fire of London   Sep 2
Great Train Robbery   Aug 8
Great Wishford, Wiltshire   May 29
Greensted-juxta-Ongar, Essex   Mar 19
Greenwich Time Signal   Feb 5
Grenoside, South Yorkshire   Dec 26
Griffiths, Donna   Sep 16
Guildford Cathedral   May 17
Gwyn, Nell   Nov 14

Hackney cab   Apr 1
Haig, General Douglas   Jul 1
Hampden, John   Jan 4
Handsworth, South Yorkshire   Dec 26
Hansard, Luke   Mar 9
Harriot, Sir Thomas   Jul 28
Harrow Weald, Greater London   Sep 5
Harrow, Greater London   Aug 17
Hartland Point, Devon   Jun 17
Harvest Home   Oct 1
Harvey, William   Jun 3
Hawker, Rev. Robert   Oct 1
Haxey   Jan 6
hearse, first motor-powered   Apr 15
Hellfire Club   Aug 16
Helpston, Cambridgeshire   Jul 13
Helston, Cornwall   May 8
Hereditary Grand Champion of

England   Mar 6
Herod   Dec 28
Herrick, Robert   Aug 20
Hilgay, Norfolk   Feb 12
Hill, Rowland   Jan 10
Hinckley, Leicestershire   Apr 12
Hinton St George, Somerset   Oct 31
Hiring Fairs   Sep 29
Hobbies Weekly   Oct 19
Hobson, Thomas   Jan 1
Holy Innocents' Day   Dec 28
Holy Rood Day   Sep 14
Holywell, Cambridgeshire   Mar 17
Hore-Belisha, Leslie   Mar 13
horse racing   May 4, Sep 21, Oct 20
horse-box, first purpose-built   Sep 21
Hotspur, Harry   Jul 21
House of Commons   Jan 4, Feb 24, May 10, 11
Houses of Parliament   Apr 10
hovercraft   Jun 25
Hoxne, Suffolk   Nov 20
Hubberholme, North Yorkshire   Jan 2
Hughes, Margaret   Dec 8
human cannonball, first   Apr 2
hunger march   Oct 5
Hunt, Rev. Joseph   Dec 16
Hurlers   Nov 4

Irving, Sir Henry   May 24
ITV   Sep 22

Jarrow, Tyne & Wear   Oct 5
Jenner, Edward   May 14
Jockey Club   Oct 20
Johnson, Dr Samuel   Sep 18
Jones, Arthur   Sep 3
Jones, John Paul   Sep 23
Jonson, Ben   Aug 6
Journey's End   Jun 6

Keats, John   Jan 20
Kemble, Father John   Aug 22
Khartoum, Siege of   Jan 26
Kidd, Captain William   May 23
Kilburn, North Yorkshire   Jul 8
King's Lynn, Norfolk   Feb 14
King's Shilling   Apr 12
Kings and Queens
   Charles I   Jan 4, 30
   Charles II   May 25, Sep 2, Nov 14
   Charlotte   Dec 14
   Coel   Aug 18
   Edward the Martyr   Mar 18
   Edward I   Dec 11
   Edward II   Nov 16
   Edward III   Jun 12
   Edward VI   Oct 24
   Edward VII   Feb 9
   Eleanor   Dec 11
   Eleanor of Aquitaine   May 18
   George III, birthday of   Jun 4
   George IV (as Prince of Wales)   Oct 20
   George VI   May 12
      coronation of   Jun 15

Harold   Sep 25, Oct 14
Henry I   Nov 25
Henry II   May 18, Dec 29
Henry VII   Jun 7, Nov 29
Henry VIII   May 20, Jul 20, Aug 15, Nov 29
James VI of Scotland and I of England   Jun 19
John   Oct 13
Mary Tudor   Jul 7
Mary, Queen of Scots   Feb 8, May 16
Richard III   Aug 21
Seymour, Lady Jane   Oct 24
Victoria   Jan 29, Aug 30
   coronation of   Jun 27
William II   Aug 2
William III   Mar 8
Kiplingcotes, North Yorkshire   May 4
Kirkby, Yorkshire   Aug 29

lacemaking   Nov 24
Lacey Green, Buckinghamshire   Aug 3
Landseer, Sir Edwin   Mar 7
Laxton, Nottinghamshire   Nov 23
Leefe Robinson, Capt. William   Sep 5
Levellers, the   May 15
Lewes, East Sussex   Dec 29
Lichfield, Staffordshire   Feb 19, Sep 8, 18
lifeline, self-propelled   Feb 12
lighthouses   May 20, Sep 7, Nov 26
Lindale, Cumbria   Jul 14
Lindisfarne   Feb 17
Lion Sermon   Oct 16
Little Odell, Bedfordshire   Nov 3
Little Walsingham, Norfolk   Aug 15
Littleport Martyrs   Jun 28
Livingston, Dr David   Nov 10
Lloyds of London   Oct 9
Logie Baird, John   Jan 27
London Bridge, sale of   Apr 18
long-sword dance   Dec 26
Lord Mayor's Show   Nov 9
lottery   Jan 11
Lovell, Viscount   Jun 16
Lusitania   May 7
Lutine Bell   Oct 9

Mace, Jem   Apr 8
Macklin, Charles   Jul 11
Manby, Aaron   Apr 30
Manby, George William   Feb 12
Marchesi, Louis   Mar 14
Marcle Hill, Herefordshire   Feb 7
Marconi, Guglielmo   Mar 27
Marhamchurch, Cornwass   Aug 12
Marks & Spencer   Sep 28
Martineau, Harriet   Jun 27
Mary Rose   Jul 19
Marylebone, London   May 5
Mayfield, Sussex   May 19
McAlpine, Sir Robert   Feb 16
McCulloch, Robert   Apr 18
Mechanics' Institutions   Dec 2

Mentmore, Buckinghamshire   Aug 8
Meon Hill, Warwickshire   Dec 30
Merton College, Oxford   Oct 26
Michaelmas   Sep 29
Middleham, Wensleydale   Mar 28
Midsummer's Eve, Old   Jul 4
Milton, John   Jan 1, Dec 9
Monmouth, Duke of   Jun 26, Jul 6
Moore, Sir John   Jan 16
Moore, Sir Thomas   Jul 20
Mother's Day/Mothering Sunday   Mar 10
motorway, first   Dec 5
Mousehole, Cornwall   Dec 23
Much Marcle, Herefordshire   Feb 7
mumping   Dec 21

National Anthem   Feb 9
National Gallery   Mar 22
Neild, John Camden   Aug 30
Nelson's Column   Mar 7
Nelson, Admiral Lord Horatio   Feb 26, Oct 21
Nelson, Henrietta   Apr 4
New Forest   Aug 2
newspaper, first daily   Mar 11
Nightingale, Florence   Aug 13
North Marston, Buckinghamshire   Aug 30
Norton St Philip, Somerset   Jun 26
Norwich, Norfolk   Feb 26, Jul 26, Oct 25
nudist beach   Aug 9

O'Connor, Feargus   Apr 10
Oak Apple Day   May 29
Old Mary Day   Sep 19
Olney, Buckinghamshire   Apr 25
Operation Mulberry   Aug 11
Order of St Patrick   Feb 28
Order of the Garter   Apr 23
Oxford   Mar 21

Pack Monday Fair   Oct 10
Padley Martyrs   Jul 12
Padstow, Cornwall   May 1
Paine, Thomas   Jun 8
Painswick, Gloucestershire   Sep 19
Panacea Society   Sep 20
Paradise Lost   Dec 9
parking meter   Jul 10
Parliamentary reporting   Mar 9
Parr, Thomas ("Old Parr")   Nov 15
Peasants' Revolt   Jun 14
penicillin   Feb 13
Penn, William   Mar 4
Pennsylvania   Mar 4
Penzance, Cornwall   Jun 24
Pepys, Samuel   Feb 23, Apr 22, May 9, 25; Jun 9, Dec 8
Perceval, Spencer   May 11
Percy, Henry   Jul 21
Perranporth, Cornwall   Mar 5
Peterhouse College, Cambridge   Jul 30
photography   Sep 17
Pilgrim Fathers   Sep 6

Pilgrim's Progress Feb 18, Nov 12
pillory Jun 30
Piltdown Man Nov 21
Pitman, Isaac Jan 12
Plantagenet, Sir Geoffrey Dec 22
Plimsoll, Samuel Feb 10
Poet Laureate Apr 13, Nov 19
polythene Mar 24
Pope, Alexander Jul 31
postage stamp Jan 10
potatoes Jul 28
Potter Heigham, Norfolk May 31
Priestley, J.B. Jan 2
Prime Minister, assassination of
   May 11
Primrose League Apr 19
Prince Albert Dec 14
Prince Rupert Dec 8
printing press Mar 1
Promenade Concerts Mar 3
public lavatory, first women's
   Feb 11
Pubs, Inns and Hotels Jan 2, 5, 17;
   Mar 17, Apr 7, Jun 1, 6; Sep 1, 5;
   Oct 17, Nov 3, Dec 25
Punch and Judy May 9
Punkie Night Oct 31

Quakers Oct 30
Queen Mary May 27

R101 airship Oct 4
radio Mar 27
railways
   City and South London Dec 18
   first death of a passenger Sep 15
   Liverpool and Manchester
      Sep 15
   London and North Eastern
      Jun 2
   narrow-gauge Mar 16
   Stockton and Darlington Sep 27
   underground Dec 18
   Wells & Walsingham Light
      Mar 16
Raleigh, Sir Walter Feb 1, Jul 28
   execution of Oct 29
Rich, John Dec 7
Richmond, North Yorkshire Dec 19
Ripley Castle Jul 2
Roget, Dr Peter Mark Jan 18
roller skates Apr 22
Roman Catholics, persecution of
   Jul 12
Round Table Mar 14
rowing Jun 4, 9; Aug 1
Royal Festival Hall May 3
Royal Observatory, Greenwich
   Feb 5
Rubáiyát of Omar Khayyám Mar 31
Rupert Bear Nov 8
rushbearing Aug 5
rushcarting Aug 19
Rushton Tower, Northamptonshire
   Sep 11
Ryde, Isle of Wight Jan 23

Saddleworth, Greater Manchester

Aug 19
Saint, Thomas Jul 17
St Agnes' Eve Jan 20
St Alkelda Mar 28
St Barnabas' Day Jun 11
St Bartholomew Aug 24
St Birinus Dec 3
St Boisil Jul 18
St Boniface Jun 5
St Catherine's Eve Nov 24
St Cecilia Nov 22
St Cedd's Cathedral Jun 22
St Chad Mar 2
St Cleer Nov 4
St Cuthbert Sep 4
St Distaff Jan 7
St Dunstan May 19
St Edmund Nov 20
St Egwin Dec 30
St Faith Oct 6
St Felix Jun 2
St Finan Feb 17
St George's Day Apr 23
St Gregory Mar 12
St Helen Aug 18
St Hilda Nov 17
St Hubert Nov 3
St Ives, Cornwall Feb 3
St James' Day Jul 25
St Jerome Sep 30
St John, Feast of Jun 24
St Katherine Cree, London Oct 16
St Lawrence, Feast Day of Aug 10
St Leonard Nov 6
St Luke Oct 18
St Mark's Eve Apr 24
St Martin's Day Nov 11
St Mawgan, Cornwall Dec 13
St Morwenna Aug 12
St Nectan Jun 17
St Nicholas of Bari Dec 6
St Osmund Jul 16
St Peter's Day Jun 29
St Piran Mar 5
St Swithun Jul 15
St Thomas Dec 21
St Vincent Jan 22
St Walstan May 30
Saletti, Jean-Marie Aug 25
Salisbury Giant Jul 16
Sandwich, fourth Earl of Aug 6
Salvation Army Jul 23
Sawston Hall, Cambridgeshire
   Jul 7
Scott, Capt. Robert Falcon Mar 23
Selfridge, Harry Gordon Mar 15
Sewell, Anna Mar 30
Sewell, Mary Mar 30
sewing machine Jul 17
Sharp, Cecil Nov 22
Shaw, Percy Apr 3
Shebbear, Devon Nov 5
Sherborne, Dorset Oct 10
Sheridan, Richard Brinsley Feb 24
Sherrif, Robert Cedric Jun 6
Shipley, West Sussex Jul 27
shipwrecks Dec 13
shorthand Jan 12

Shylock Jul 11
Sibson, Leicestershire Apr 7
Sidney Sussex College, Cambridge
   Mar 25
Slaidburn, Lancashire Oct 18
smallpox May 14
Smith, William Jan 24
Smithfield, London Aug 23
sneezing Mar 12, Sep 15
Soham, Cambridgeshire Jun 2
South Pole Mar 23
Southcott, Joanna Dec 20
Southwold, Suffolk May 28
Speaker of the House of Commons
   Apr 27
Spooner, Rev. William Archibald
   Jul 22
Stamford, Lincolnshire Nov 13
Stanley, Henry Morton Nov 10
Stanton Harcourt, Oxfordshire
   Jul 31
Star of Africa diamond Jan 25
Starry gazie pie Dec 23
steam locomotive Feb 21
steamship Oct 22
   first iron Apr 30
Stewart, Charles Edward Jan 31
Stow, John Apr 5
strip farming Nov 23
Stubbins, Greater Manchester
   Sep 1
Sunday, sporting competition on
   Apr 26
Sutton Cheney, Leicestershire
   Aug 21
Swaffham Prior, Cambridgeshire
   May 7
Swardeston, Norfolk Oct 12

taxi-rank, first Apr 1
teetotallers Oct 27
television Jan 27
Tennyson, Alfred Lord Nov 19
Tetbury, Gloucestershire Aug 28
thanksgiving Oct 1
Thatcher, Lady Margaret Nov 28
Theatre Royal, Drury Lane, London
   Feb 24
thesaurus Jan 18
Thetford, Norfolk Jun 8
Tichborne, Roger Charles Apr 20
tin mining Mar 5
Titanic, SS Apr 14
Tolpuddle Martyrs Mar 19
Tom Jones Oct 8
Tomb of the Unknown Warrior
   Nov 7
trade union, first Mar 19
Tresham, Sir Thomas Sep 11
Trevithick, Richard Feb 21
Trinity House May 20
trousers Jun 18
Trysull, Staffordshire Apr 17
Tunbridge Wells, Kent May 19
Turner, Dick Oct 27
Turpin, Dick Apr 7
Tussaud, Madame Marie Grosholtz
   Apr 16

Tutankhamun Jan 3
Tweedmouth, Northumberland
   Jul 18
Twyford, Hampshire Oct 7
Tybald, Simon Jun 14
Tyburn May 5
Tyers, Robert John Apr 22
Tyrwhitt, Sir Thomas Mar 20

Ulster May 22

vaccination May 14
vacuum cleaner Feb 25
Vanbrugh, Sir John Mar 26
Victoria Cross Jan 29, Feb 29, Sep 5

W.H. Smith Nov 1
Waite, Terry Nov 12
Wallace, Sir William Aug 23
Walpole St Andrew, Norfolk Oct 13
Walpole, Horace Sep 24
Wapping, East London May 23
Wardley Hall, Worsley Sep 10
Wareham, Dorset Nov 30
Warren, William, Earl of Nov 13
Wars of the Roses Mar 29
wassailing, Jan 5 Jan 17
waxworks Apr 16
Webb, Capt. Matthew Apr 11,
   Aug 25
well-dressing Sep 14
Wellingham, Norfolk Jan 19
Wembley Stadium Feb 16
West Witton, North Yorkshire
   Aug 24
West Wycombe, Buckinghamshire
   Aug 16
Westminster Abbey Nov 15
Whalton, Northumberland Jul 4
Whip-Dog Day Oct 18
Whitby Abbey Nov 17
Whitby, Synod of Feb 17, Nov 17
White Horse Jul 8
White Ship Nov 25
Whitehall, London Jan 30
Whittlesford, Cambridgeshire
   Apr 24
Whitwell, Derbyshire Aug 10
Wilberforce, William Jul 29
Wilkinson, John "Iron Mad" Jul 14
Willett, William Aug 7
Wilson, Admiral Sir Arthur Knyvet
   Feb 29
Winchester Cathedral Jul 15
Window Tax Jul 24
Winstanley, Henry Nov 26
Wolfe, General James Sep 13
Wolsey, Cardinal Thomas Nov 29
Wood, Sir Henry Mar 3
Woodbridge, Suffolk Mar 31
Woodroffe, Lieut.-Com. Thomas
   Jun 15
Workington Hall, Cumbria May 16

Yarnton, Oxfordshire Jun 29
Yaxley Hall, Suffolk Apr 4

Zeppelin Jan 19, Sep 5

Bibliography

The following is a select listing of reference material consulted in the preparation of this title.

The publishers wish to express their gratitude to the many individuals and organisations whose material and specialised knowledge, so generously shared, was invaluable in the preparation of this book.

Anon. Folklore, *Myths and Legends of Britain*, Reader's Digest, 1973
Anon. *W.H. Smith Through The Centuries*, W.H. Smith Group, 1992
Atkins, H. and A. Newman, *Beecham Stories*, Robson, 1978
Bell, D. *Seamen of Britain*, Nelson, 1943
Bord, J. and C. *Ancient Mysteries of Britain*, Paladin, 1987
Brentnall, M. *The Old Customs and Ceremonies of London*, Batsford, 1959
Brook, D. *The Romance of the English Theatre*, Rockliff, 1946
Brown, M. *Dorset Customs, Curiosities and Country Lore*, Ensign, 1990
Brown, R.L. *A Casebook of Military Mystery*, Stephens, 1974
Chambers, R. (ed.) *The Book of Days*, Chambers, 1866
Cooper, Q. and P. Sullivan, *Maypoles, Martyrs and Mayhem*, Bloomsbury, 1994
Creasey, J. *Round Table – The First 25 Years*, RTBI, 1953
Cull, E. *Portrait of the Chilterns*, Hale, 1982
Darwin, A. *Canals and Rivers of Britain*, Dent, 1976
Evans, I.H. (ed.) *Brewer's Dictionary of Phrase and Fable*, Cassell, 1981

Frost, D. *Book of the World's Worst Decisions*, Deutsch, 1982
Harrison, S. *The Channel*, Collins, 1986
James, E.O. *Seasonal Feasts and Festivals*, Barnes and Noble, 1961
Jones, J. and B. Deer, *Cattern Cakes and Lace*, Dorling-Kindersley, 1987
Kightly, C. *The Customs and Ceremonies of Britain*, Thames and Hudson, 1986
Little, B. *Portrait of Somerset*, Hale, 1969
May, J. *The Book of Curious Facts*, Collins & Brown, 1993
McWhirter, N. (ed.) *The Guinness Book of Records*, Guinness Superlatives, annually
McWhirter, N. (ed.) *The Guinness Book of Answers*, Guinness Superlatives, 1978
Meras, P. *Castles, Keeps and Leprechauns*, Congdon & Weed, 1988
Pepys, S. *The Diary of Samuel Pepys*, Collins, 1825
Robertson, P. *The New Shell Book of Firsts*, Headline, 1994
Russell, I.F. *Sir Robert McAlpine and Sons*, Parthenon, 1988
Skipper, K. *The Norfolk Connection*, Poppyland, 1991
Sutton-Jones, K. *Pharos*, Russell, 1985
Vine, P.A.L. *London's Lost Route to the Sea*, David & Charles, 1986
Walker, C. *Mysterious Britain*, Grange, 1989
Waring, P. *A Dictionary of Omens and Superstitions*, Souvenir, 1978
Welcome, J. *Infamous Occasions*, Joseph, 1980
Wightman, R. *Portrait of Dorset*, Hale, 1965

Acknowledgments

Andrew Perkins Apr 7; Jun 6; Dec 16
Brian Shuel Collections Feb 2, 14; Aug 5, 24; Dec 12, 26, 31
British Library Mar 11
Dean and Chapter of Durham Cathedral Sep 4
Don French, Sandown, Isle of Wight Jan 23, Jun 13
Eton College Jun 4
Express Newspapers Nov 8
Fishmongers Company Aug 1
Fox Talbot Museum, Lacock Abbey Sep 17
Guildhall Library Mar 25
Hulton Getty Feb 15, 16; Apr 18, 27; May 6, 12; Aug 8, 9; Dec 15
Imperial War Museum, London Jan 29; Jul 1; Aug 11
Ironbridge Gorge Museums Trust Aug 25
Jarrold Publishing Jan 2, 4, 5, 6, 9 (courtesy of Mr C and Mrs E Albrighton), 10, 12, 14, 17, 19, 30, 31; Feb 1, 3, 4, 5, 6, 7, 8, 18, 20, 22, 26 (courtesy of Norwich City Council), 28, 29; Mar 4, 5, 6, 7, 10, 14, 15, 16, 17, 18, 19, 20, 21, 22, 26, 28, 29, 30; Apr 3, 4, 5, 6, 9, 10, 12, 15 (courtesy of A. Pargetter & Son Ltd, Coventry), 20, 23, 24, 30; May 1, 2, 3, 7, 8, 9, 10, 13, 14, 15, 16, 17, 18, 19, 20, 22, 26, 28, 29, 30, 31; Jun 1, 5, 8, 10, 14, 16, 17, 20, 22, 24, 26, 28, 29, 30; Jul 2, 5, 6, 8, 9, 10, 11 (courtesy of the Tate Gallery), 12, 13, 14, 15, 16 (courtesy of Salisbury & South Wiltshire Museum), 18, 19 (courtesy of the Mary Rose Trust), 21, 23, 25, 26, 27, 30, 31; 2, 3, 7, 12, 15, 16, 18, 19, 20, 21, 22, 23, 28, 29, 30; Sep 1, 2, 3, 5, 7 (courtesy of the Grace Darling Museum), 8, 9, 10, 11, 13, 14, 18, 20, 21 (courtesy of King's Lynn & West Norfolk Borough Council), 22 (courtesy of Unilever), 24, 26, 27; Oct 1, 2, 4, 6, 7, 8, 10, 12, 13, 14, 16, 17, 19, 21, 25, 26; Nov 1 (courtesy of W.H. Smith), 2, 3, 4, 5, 6, 7, 9, 11, 12, 13, 16, 17, 20, 21, 23, 27, 29, 30; Dec 1, 3, 4, 6, 7, 9, 11, 13, 17, 22, 23, 24, 25, 29 (courtesy of Sussex Archaeological Society), 30
Leeds Museums and Galleries Jan 26
Madame Tussauds Apr 16
Marks and Spencer Sep 28
Mary Evans picture library Jan 1, 3, 15, 16, 24, 28; Feb 13, 21, 23, 27; Mar 1, 3, 8, 9, 23, 27, 31; Apr 1, 2, 8, 13, 14, 19, 21, 22; May 4, 5, 11, 21, 24, 25, 27; Jun 3, 7, 9, 12, 19, 21, 23, 25, 27; Jul 28, 29; Aug 4, 6, 13, 14, 17, 26, 27; Sep 6, 15, 23, 30; Oct 5, 11, 15, 20, 24, 27, 29, 30; Nov 10, 15, 18, 19, 25, 26, 28; Dec 4, 8, 14, 20, 27
Museum of London Jan 21, Feb 24
Norfolk Museums Service (Norwich Castle Museum) Feb 12
National Portrait Gallery Jan 18; Feb 10, 19; Apr 29; Jul 22; Aug 31; Nov 14
Paul Slattery Sep 19; Oct 23, 31
Rex Features Jan 8; Oct 9
Richard Tilbrook Jul 7
Ripley Castle Jul 2
Science and Society Picture Library, Science Museum Jan 27; Feb 25; Jul 17; Oct 22, 28; Dec 18